Cross-Border Bank Mergers: Who Gains and Why?

European University Studies

Europäische Hochschulschriften

Publications Universitaires Européennes

Series V

Economics and Management

Reihe V Série V

Volks- und Betriebswirtschaft

Sciences économiques, gestion d'entreprise

Vol./Bd. 3301

PETER LANG

Frankfurt am Main · Berlin · Bern · Bruxelles · New York · Oxford · Wien

Dirk Schmautzer

Cross-Border Bank Mergers: Who Gains and Why?

PETER LANG
Internationaler Verlag der Wissenschaften

Bibliographic Information published by the Deutsche Nationalbibliothek
The Deutsche Nationalbibliothek lists this publication in the Deutsche Nationalbibliografie; detailed bibliographic data is available in the internet at <http://www.d-nb.de>.

Zugl.: Münster (Westfalen), Univ., Diss., 2007

D 6
ISSN 0531-7339
ISBN 978-3-631-57923-7

www.peterlang.de

Acknowledgements

This study would not exist without the various people who supported me and whom I would like to thank for their help. First and foremost, is my thesis advisor, Prof. Christian Harm, Ph.D., who accepted me as his doctoral student and was a helpful mentor and a critical but constructive partner for discussion. I would also like to thank him for putting me in contact with his colleagues and friends at the New York University and the City University of New York for further insightful discussions. There, I am indebted to Prof. Yakov Amihud, Ph.D., Prof. Gayle DeLong, Ph.D., and Prof. Ingo Walter, Ph.D. for taking the time to discuss my approach and findings in detail and offering valuable advice. I would also like to thank Prof. Dr. Andreas Pfingsten for co-refereeing my thesis and Prof. Dr. Mark Trede, Prof. Dr. Bernd Wilfling, and all other members of the Institute for Econometrics and Business Statistics at the University of Münster for their feedback and support with regard to the empirical part of the study. Furthermore, I very much appreciated the support of my colleagues at the Department of International Business in Münster: Marie-Ann Betschinger and Stephan Schulte provided helpful comments – not to mention a great atmosphere – during our doctoral seminars and Doris Hohmeier valuable administrative support.

My colleagues at McKinsey & Company, Inc. provided me with access to various databases for the empirical part of this study and my friend and colleague Jens Wimschulte was an invaluable discussion partner for various corporate finance and banking topics. Finally, I am grateful for the moral support of my girlfriend Irina (who went so far to become my wife during the process), my parents, and my friends. Any remaining errors are mine alone.

Overview of Contents

Contents

List of Figures

List of Tables

List of Abbreviations

ABHAR	Average buy-and-hold abnormal return
AR	Abnormal return
BHAR	Buy-and-hold abnormal return
BIS	Bank for International Settlements
Bn	Billion
CAGR	Compounded annual growth rate
CAPM	Capital asset pricing model
CAR	Cumulative (average) abnormal return
CBBM&A	Cross-border bank mergers and acquisitions
CEO	Chief Executive Officer
CF	Corporate finance
CIR	Cost-income ratio
DE	Dynamic efficiency
DEA	Data Envelopment Analysis
DFA	Distribution Free Approach
Eds.	Editors
E.g.	For example (Latin: exempli gratia)
Et al.	And others (Latin: et alii)
FDHA	Free Disposal Hull Analysis
FDI	Foreign direct investment
FI	Financial intermediary
FSP	Financial services provider
GDP	Gross domestic product
I.e.	That is (Latin: id est)
I.i.d.	independently and identically distributed
IM	International management
IT	Information technology
KWG	Kreditwesengesetz
MBR	Market-to-book ratio
M&A	Mergers and acquisitions
OLI	Eclectic theory of foreign direct investment
OLS	Ordinary Least Squares
OP	Operating performance
P.	Page

R^2	Statistical coefficient of determination
ROA	Return on assets
ROE	Return on equity
SAPR	Standardized average portfolio returns
SFA	Stochastic Frontier Approach
SIC	Standard Industrial Classification
SME	Small and medium enterprises
TBTF	Too big to fail
TFA	Thick Frontier Approach
UK	United Kingdom
US	United States
USD	United States Dollar

1. Introduction and Overview of Study

In July 2004, Emilio Botín, CEO of Spain's largest bank Banco Santander Central Hispano, noted that "if mergers are already complicated within one country, imagine the situation when two are involved. [A cross-border bank merger] would not be good for clients, employees or shareholders."[1] Since Santander at that point already had a rich cross-border acquisition history, particularly in South America, some market participants might have had their doubts with regard to this statement. But probably few had expected what happened later the same month: Abbey National, the UK's second largest mortgage lender and sixth largest bank with 741 branches and more than 18 million customers, announced that it had received an approach by another bank that may lead to an acquisition. This was not a surprise, since after a disastrous foray into investment banking, Abbey had lost its once strong position in the British market and had been in takeover talks before. The surprise was the suitor, who was nobody else but Santander and the deal, with a total value of almost US dollar 16 bn, turned out to be the world's largest cross-border bank merger up to that point.

While Mr. Botín may have had his own tactical reasons to denounce the suitability of the transaction before it happened, his statement points to what seems to be the paradox of cross-border bank mergers and acquisitions (CBBM&A): whereas there are reasons and quite a few hints in earlier research that these deals are not in the best interests of shareholders, they do not only continue to happen, but even seem to be growing in frequency and size.

While domestic mergers and acquisitions (M&A) are already difficult to conduct, complex long-term investments, researchers and practitioners have long noted an impressive list of additional hurdles for CBBM&A.[2] First, the large distances involved make many traditional ways to realize benefits from mergers, such as trimming overlapping branch networks, impossible. Second, physical, cultural, and economic distance increase transaction costs and complicate the implementation of operational change. Third, acquirers are often reported to face stiff resistance from host country stakeholders such as politicians, unions or regulators, that all have the power to hold up deals or seriously impede the desired outcomes. Other research has shown foreign-owned banks to be generally

1 AFX News (2004).
2 E.g., Buch and DeLong (2004), Härle (2005).

less efficient than their domestic counterparts[3] and foreign ownership is often achieved via M&A. Hence, these hurdles seem to be serious, generally making bidders unable to overcome the competitive disadvantage of being foreign.

And yet a recent spate of multi-billion dollar deals suggests these transactions are increasingly in vogue. Besides the Santander/Abbey deal, 2004 also saw the acquisition of Charter One by Britain's Royal Bank of Scotland for more than USD 10 bn, which helped the British giant to expand significantly in the US. The market did not cool down in the following year. This cost the Santander/Abbey deal its status as the largest ever when Italy's UniCredit acquired Germany's Hypovereinsbank for more than USD 18 bn. Even markets previously considered more or less closed to foreign competition were contested when Italy's Banca Antonventa was acquired by the Netherland's ABN Amro (deal value: USD 6 bn) in 2004 and Banca Nazionale del Lavoro fell prey to France's BNP Paribas (deal value: 11 bn USD) in 2005. Later the same year China, even before it had fully opened its banking market to foreigners, experienced a bidding war between consortia led by American Citigroup and French Société Générale for a controlling stake worth more than USD 3 bn in the troubled Chinese Guangdong Development Bank. If this casual empiricism is indeed representative of the industry as a whole, one could well speak of a CBBM&A deal frenzy.

Increases in cross-border acquisitions of financial services firms have regularly been attributed to changes in banking regulation, advancements in information technology (IT) and globalization.[4] However, these reasons still do not seem sufficient to fully explain the rise in CBBM&A. Extensive research on the wealth implications of general M&A has frequently concluded that such transactions are mostly not wealth-creating and are, in fact, sometimes even wealth-destroying for the acquiring institutions.[5] Bank-specific research, mostly based on domestic US deals, has led to similar results.[6] But if domestic deals already fail to create value, how can cross-border deals, even if changes in banking regulation, advancements in IT and globalization have made them less costly, achieve a better result?

The goal of this study is to shed some light on the apparent paradox of CBBM&A by answering two interrelated questions. First, the study is interested in what the effects of CBBM&A on shareholder wealth are and if, in that sense, CBBM&A are on average successful. Exactly because these transactions differ in many respects from general and domestic banking M&A, their results might also differ. Findings would be of obvious interest to managers, shareholders, analysts,

3 See Berger et al. (2000).
4 E.g., Berger et al. (2000), Buch (2005).
5 See, e.g., Bruner (2002) for an overview of the results of the general M&A literature.
6 See section 4.1 for details.

and regulators. Second, this study is interested in the causes of wealth effects. If there were a relationship between deal outcomes and a set of factors that are publicly available before the deal occurs, knowledge of these factors and their effects could aid managers, shareholders, and analysts in deciding which deals to pursue, accept, or recommend and which not.

To analyze these questions, the study proceeds in seven chapters: (1) Introduction and Overview of Study, (2) The Market for Cross-Border Bank M&A, (3) Theoretical Foundations of Banking and M&A, (4) Previous Empirical Evidence on Wealth Effects of Cross-Border Bank M&A, (5) Design of Analysis, (6) New Empirical Evidence on Wealth Effects of Cross-Border Bank M&A, and (7) Conclusion and Outlook.

Chapter 1 introduces the study by confronting selected research with some casual empiricism on CBBM&A. Based on this, the two main research questions of the study are developed. These regard the average wealth effects of CBBM&A and the factors that determine them. Furthermore, an overview of the study structure and key findings is given.

Chapter 2 provides the backdrop for the further investigation of the two research questions. First, it shows that the casual empiricism used in the introduction is indeed representative of a long-term trend, namely the rise of CBBM&A in various dimensions. A recent strong upturn in deal frequency and volume suggests that the industry has recovered from a short dip in this growth trend, associated with the global economic slowdown during the turn of the century. Second, it sheds more light on the role of selected macroeconomic trends, namely deregulation, advances in IT, and globalization as drivers of CBBM&A. The discussion also identifies first indications of potential determinants of wealth effects, such as the regulatory environment in the host and home countries of the deal partners, physical bidder-target distance, or firm size, that are closely linked to the discussed macroeconomic trends.

Chapter 3, the first part of the literature review, discusses the characteristics of banks and of M&A that have relevance for the research questions at hand. In addition, since empirical results are rarely independent of the methodology used, an overview of the main methods to measure M&A wealth effects is given. The chapter leads to definitions of banks and CBBM&A for this study. Also, it finds that determinants of wealth effects are best identified by merging two strands of literature. This is firstly the corporate finance (CF) literature, that uses firm-specific motives for M&A to identify potentially relevant firm-specific determinants. Secondly, this is the international management (IM) literature, that also covers country- and industry-specific determinants. Finally, the discussion on the different methods of measuring wealth effects identifies event studies, which measure the impact of the information content of an event such as M&A on security price behavior, as the superior methodology to address the posed research questions.

Chapter 4, the second part of the literature review, focuses on prior empirical findings, both on the general direction, size, and benefactors of wealth effects and on the factors, that determine them. Here, the goal is to summarize findings and highlight gaps in the prior literature. With regard to general wealth effects, all evidence indicates that deals are beneficial for target shareholders. Bidders rather suffer losses or at best break even, which seemingly causes the two effects to offset each other. However, there seem to be other reasons for these results than deals being only wealth redistribution mechanisms. Notably, there is evidence of underlying efficiency gains which should, ceteris paribus, increase net wealth, i.e., the joint shareholder wealth of bidder and target. With regard to determinants of wealth effects, a joint review of the CF and IM literature reveals several factors, both on a firm- and a country and industry-level, that supposedly have some explanatory power.

Problematically, the review also identifies several gaps in the previous literature, that limit the applicability of these findings. With regard to general wealth effects, all previous studies are found to suffer from at least two and often multiple of the following problems: use of research methods, that do not allow for proper inferences on wealth effects, biased or small samples, and lack of a net wealth and long-term perspectives, respectively. With regard to determinants, the identified gaps again include the use of methodologies, that do not allow for proper inferences on wealth effects, a lack of joint tests on all identified determinants and conflicting findings in prior research without any efforts to reconcile them. Thus, the need for an empirical investigation of CBBM&A wealth effects and all their identified potential determinants using proper event study methodology and a large, global sample of deals is derived.

Chapter 5 first transforms the findings of the literature review into testable hypotheses. Then, an adequate event study methodology is selected. This firstly consists of a traditional short-term study, that measures the wealth effect of deal announcements on the announcement day and a short period surrounding it. Secondly, this consists of a long-term study, that also measures wealth effects in a three-year period after the deal has been concluded. Both methods include various methodological adjustments to account for identified potential pitfalls of using event studies.

With regard to testing the impact of potential determinants of wealth effects, a methodology is selected that incorporates dichotomization analysis, i.e., the comparison of the wealth effect from deals, that differ with regard to a single potential determinant and regression analysis, which analyzes the simultaneous impact of several potential determinants. A comparison of the selected array of methods with the identified potential pitfalls of using event studies suggests that the developed approach is relatively robust against these problems.

Chapter 6 provides empirical evidence on the two key questions posed above. First, the properties of the sample drawn to test wealth effects and their determinants are discussed. While the applied research methods and sample selection criteria only allow to analyze listed companies and thus significantly reduce the size of the sample, the latter is, nevertheless, shown to be the largest such sample in terms of jointly listed bidder-target entities and seems well representative of the overall CBBM&A market. With regard to general wealth effects, the chapter presents the first comprehensive evidence, that deals are wealth-creating in the short-term, albeit only on a net basis with target gains more than compensating for bidder losses. In the long-term, no abnormal bidder returns can be identified which supports the validity of inferences based on the short-term and is in line with the notion of efficient capital markets.

The inquiry into the determinants of abnormal returns reveals that bidders create most wealth when they take over targets that are already relatively cost-efficient ex-ante and do not acquire in "hot" deal phases, i.e., acquire when everybody else does. This is in line with the hypothesis that targets need to be sufficiently efficient in order for M&A to increase efficiency further. It also supports the notion of limited opportunities to cut costs in CBBM&A and acquisitions in "hot" phases being signals of bidder overvaluation and agency problems. Deals that feature cost-efficient targets and do not occur in "hot" phases are also the ones that create most net wealth.

Other evidence suggests that taking over targets with low standalone growth perspectives, that are not too different from a cultural perspective, reside in rather "unfree" markets and refraining from motivating the deal by a need to diversify geographically also create bidder wealth. With regard to target banks, wealth creation seems to increase with the opportunities that the host country offers to the bidder. Thus, there is evidence that targets in large markets, where the bidder encounters many of his home country clients, gain most. This is in line with the notion of a competitive market for M&A in which most benefits of deals accrue to targets. Targets are also found to benefit from being acquired in a "hot" deal phase and from culturally and functionally different acquirers, which indicates that targets benefit from agency issues in the bidder organization.

Overall, the chapter for the first time presents evidence that many determinants of wealth effects, that have been identified as relevant in domestic banking M&A, are also important in a cross-border context. However, the specifics of cross-border deals often modify the resulting effects. It also presents the first directly applicable evidence on the wealth effects of some determinants, such as the level of economic freedom in the host country, and shows that the use of a proper event study methodology can reconcile previously disputed findings in the literature on other determinants, such as the market size of the host country.

Chapter 7 summarizes the findings and highlights implications for future research. The latter is directed towards a more thorough analysis of agency effects as M&A deal drivers and potential corporate governance measures to address them. The applied method of identifying potential determinants of shareholder wealth from a joint review of the CF and IM literature is also recommened as a potentially fruitful approach for future research.

The chapter furthermore develops recommendations for managers, shareholders and policy makers. An implication for managers and shareholders in bidder organizations, that want to increase shareholder wealth, is to scrutinize deals with regard to the quality of the target organization, especially its cost efficiency and not to acquire during merger waves. Policy makers and their electorates are in turn advised to endorse CBBM&A more strongly in the future. This is because these transactions also seem to have socially desirable consequences in that they generally increase the welfare of all involved stakeholders. The study structure and key findings are summarized in figure 1.1.

Figure 1.1: Overview of Study Structure and Key Findings

Chapter	① Intro-duction and Overview	② The Market for CBBM&A	Literature Review: ③ Theoretical Foundations	Literature Review: ④ Previous Empirical Evidence	⑤ Design of Analysis	⑥ New Empirical Evidence	⑦ Conclusion
Key Content	• Casual empiricism on cross border M&A • Research questions • Study structure and key findings	• Historical development of CBBM&A in various dimensions • Macro-trends influencing CBBM&A	• Characteristics of banks • Characteristics of M&A • Methods for measuring wealth effects	• Empirical findings on wealth effects • Identification of potential determinants • Evidence on determinants • Identification of gaps in the literature and implications for future research	• Hypotheses on CBBM&A • Choice of short- and long-term event study methodology • Choice of methods to measure determinants and their impact	• Results from event studies, regression- and dichotomization analyses	• Summary of results • Implications for managers, shareholders, policy makers, and future research
Key Findings	• CBBM&A seemingly strongly on the rise despite assumed negative wealth effects • Need to understand wealth effects and determinants better	• Growth in importance of CBBM&A • CBBM&A influenced by deregulation, IT advancements and globalization • First indications of potential determinants of wealth effects	• Appropriate definitions of banks and CBBM&A • Determinants of wealth effects are best identified from a joint review of the CF and the IM literature • Event studies seem the most appropriate methodology to analyze wealth effects	• Positive wealth effects for targets and rather negative ones for bidders seem to cancel out • Availability of a set of potential determinants of wealth effects • Applicability of previous research limited due to methodological issues, sample size, etc. • Need for further event study research based on a large, global sample of deals	• Selected methods together with the included adjustments should well be able to address the identified issues in the analysis of abnormal returns	• Transactions create net wealth – target gains more than compensate for bidder losses • Target quality and "temperature" of the equity market as important determinants of bidder and net wealth • Host country characteristics determine target wealth	• Need for further research on agency effects as deal drivers • Potential benefits from integrating CF and IM study approaches also in future research • Need for bidder managers and shareholders to select quality targets • Because of potentially beneficial social consequences, policy makers should endorse deals more

2. The Market for Cross-Border Bank M&A

In the previous section, CBBM&A was portrayed as a phenomenon of high and growing importance to managers, shareholders, and policy makers. This conclusion, however, was only based on a few recent deals. Therefore, the goal of *section 2.1* is to validate it using a broader empirical perspective. An overview of the development of CBBM&A from the mid 1980s until today, including its importance relative to domestic banking M&A, to cross-border deals in other industries, and its geographical patterns is given. The introduction also hinted at a critical role of deregulation, technological progress and globalization for CBBM&A. Therefore, the goal of *section 2.2* is to describe the impact of these trends on CBBM&A in more detail. *Section 2.3* concludes with a summary.

2.1 The Market Development 1985 to 2005[7]

One of the most intuitive indicators of the importance of CBBM&A is the frequency with which these transactions occur. Focarelli and Pozzolo (2001) and the Group of Ten (2001) provide overviews of the development of this indicator over the 90s. Buch and DeLong (2004) even cover the total period between 1985 and 2001. This information is summarized in figure 2.1.

Obviously, the numbers diverge. Focarelli and Pozzolo (2001) and the Group of Ten (2001) show a roughly similar development from about 35 deals occurring per year at the beginning of the 90s to somewhere between 70 and 100 deals per year at the end of the decade.

---

7 CBBM&A or international banking in general are probably almost as old as the banking profession itself, see e.g., Jones (1990) for a short history of international banking. However, comprehensive global data is only available from the mid 1980s onwards and there are indications that deal levels before that point were generally low, mostly due to legal obstacles to cross-border banking. Brealy and Kaplanis (1996, p. 578) illustrate the increased relevance of international banking relative to earlier periods with the example of the historic Medici bank, which, despite its considerable influence during the middle ages, employed only a maximum of 57 people in 8 offices worldwide and contrast this with Citigroup that, in mid 1990, employed 81,000 people in 3500 offices located in 93 countries. For these reasons, this study restricts itself to a review of the period from 1985 onwards.

Figure 2.1: Development of Cross-Border Bank M&A Deal Frequency

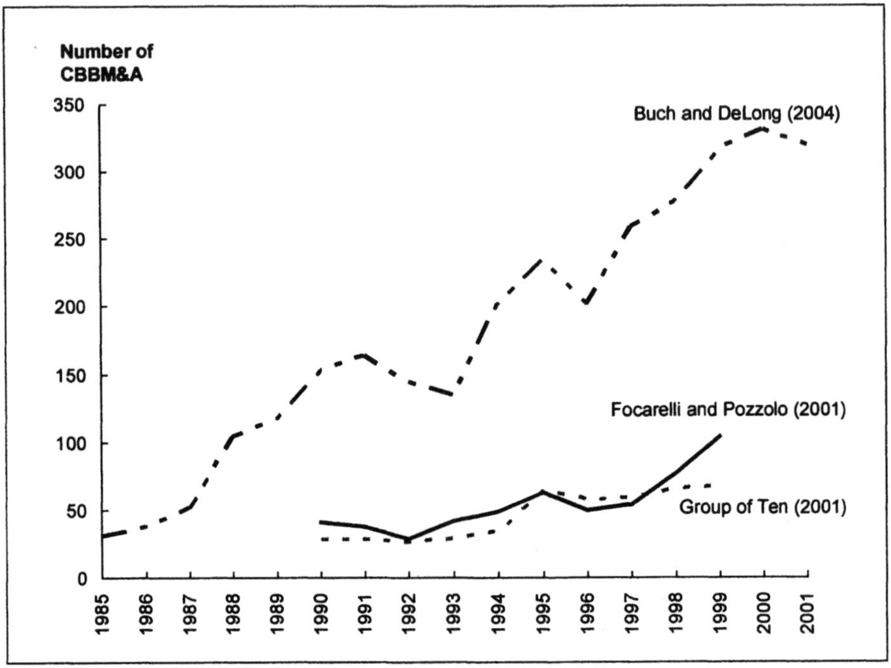

Source: Based on Focarelli and Pozzolo (2001), Group of Ten (2001), Buch and DeLong (2004)

Buch and DeLong (2004), however, find four to five times higher deal levels. Interestingly, this difference is despite reference to the same data source, Thompson SDC, and the use of bank-merger definitions that in all cases accounts for horizontal and vertical deals. There are, however, some differences in geographical scope and bank definitions between Focarelli and Pozzolo (2001) and the Group of Ten (2001) and even larger differences between the latter two and Buch and DeLong (2004) that most likely account for the diverging results.[8] Since the definitions used by Buch and DeLong (2004) are closer to those used in this

8 Focarelli and Pozzolo (2001) cover all OECD countries and define banks according to the standard industry classification (SIC) whereas the Group of Ten (2001) focuses on the Group of Ten (plus Spain and Australia) and uses the Thompson SDC bank definitions. Buch and DeLong (2004) are the only ones to allow for vertical deals in which banks are targets and also the only ones with a truly global geographical scope.

study,[9] their figures are probably more applicable as a reference. This also underlines the importance of a transparent and adequate CBBM&A definition.

In any case, despite different levels of deal frequency, all three studies report compounded annual growth rates (CAGRs) of the deal frequency between 8 and 10 percent, leading to a rough doubling of the frequency during the 1990s. Thus, there is indeed evidence that CBBM&A is a phenomenon of growing importance in terms of deal frequency. With regard to growth in deal volume and the size of the average transaction, figure 2.2 paints a similar picture.

Figure 2.2: Development of Cross-Border Bank M&A Deal Volume

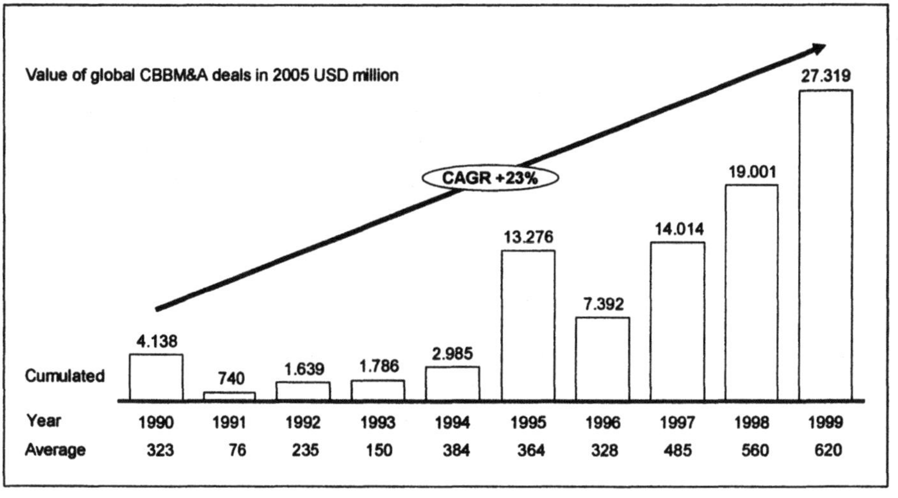

Source: Adapted from Group of Ten (2001)

The cumulated transaction value rose from USD 4 bn in 1990 to USD 27 bn in 1999,[10] equivalent to a CAGR of 23 percent. Since numbers are based on the Group of Ten (2001) which, as discussed above, uses a CBBM&A definition that is narrower than the one used in this study, these numbers should be looked upon as conservative estimates.[11] Parallel to increasing deal volume, the average deal

9 See sections 3.1.1 and 3.2.1 for the banking and CBBM&A definitions used in this study.

10 The original (purchase) values reported by the Group of Ten (2001) are restated in 2005 real terms using the US GDP deflator provided by Global Insight.

11 Author's estimates based on the figures presented in Berger et al. (2000) suggest a rise from USD 12 bn in 1990 to USD 46 bn in 1998, again in 2005 real US dollar terms.

size also increased from USD 300 to 600 million.[12] Thus, the importance of CBBM&A also grew in terms of deals volume and average transaction size.

Further interesting insights emerge if CBBM&A are compared to domestic banking M&A. Buch and DeLong (2004) provide evidence in terms of relative frequency whereas the Group of Ten (2001) again takes a deal value perspective. Results are summarized in figure 2.3.

Figure 2.3: Development of Cross-Border Bank M&A Relative to Domestic Bank M&A

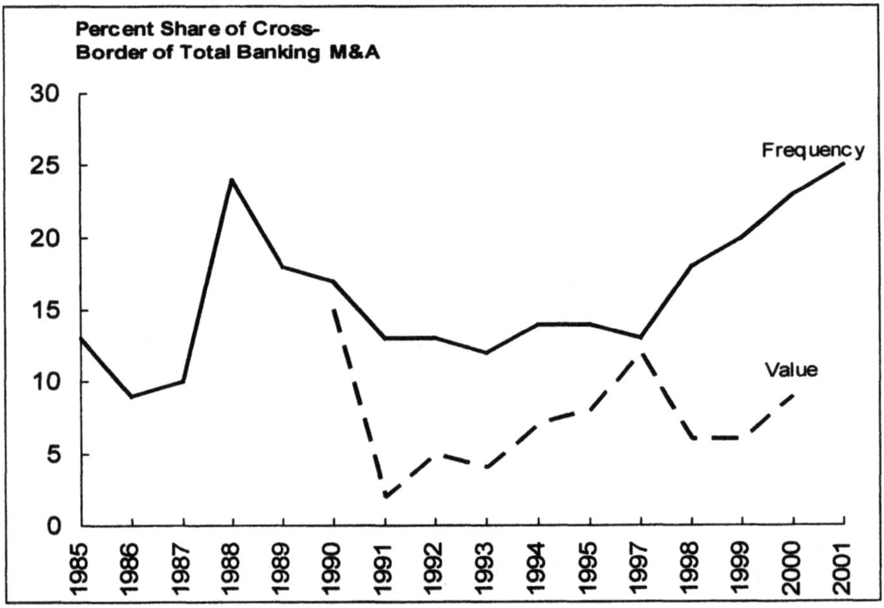

Source: Adapted from Group of Ten (2001), Buch and DeLong (2004)

Even though these figures are only based on Europe and the US, this should be more than offset by the fact that they also include deals between insurances or other non-bank financial intermediaries. Thus, these numbers can be looked upon as an upward estimate. The implied CAGR (19 percent) is comparable to the one implicit in the Group of Ten (2001) data.

12 Numbers are again in 2005 real terms. The average deal sizes reported by the Group of Ten (2001) are based on deals with a value attached to it in SDC while data on deal frequency is based on all deals, including a large number of deals without a reported value. This is the reason for inconsistencies between deal frequencies, cumulated deal values, and average deal values.

Obviously, the relative importance of CBBM&A also grew in importance, at least during the end 1990s. However, there are some caveats to this. First, the share of CBBM&A on total M&A, both in terms of deal frequency and value, seems to have dropped from relatively high levels during the end 1980s and early 1990s and only recovered at the end of the decade to these previous levels. The observed patterns are probably partly due to changes in the overall economic climate but might also be related to high expectations with regard to heavy deregulation, especially in Europe, that were not met.[13] Second, the lion's share of banking M&A obviously still occurs at the domestic level: during the 1990s, even using the high figures provided by Buch and DeLong (2004) roughly every 6th deal in the banking industry was cross-border. Moreover, only every 13th dollar spent was used for a cross-border acquisition. This is in line with additional hurdles in CBBM&A relative to domestic deals. Due to the special role that information asymmetries and regulators play in banking, one could assume that these hurdles are even higher for CBBM&A than for other cross-border deals.[14] However, the data does not permit such conclusions. This would require an industry comparison of the relative importance of cross-border deals to domestic deals. Focarelli and Pozzolo (2001) provide such a comparison, again based on deal frequency. Results are shown in figure 2.4.

Unsurprisingly, the higher relative importance of domestic deals seems to be a common phenomenon across industries. However, the average share of cross-border deals in banking is especially low, almost half of the industry average of 24 percent.[15] This is similar for other financial service providers (FSPs), such as investment funds.

However, it seems neither attributable to banks and FSPs being service industries (as other service industries have about as many cross-border mergers as the industry average) nor to being financial intermediaries (FIs), as there are even more cross-border mergers in insurance, another financial intermediation business, than in other industries.[16] Similar to the figures provided by Buch and DeLong (2004) above, Focarelli and Pozzolo (2001) in their study also show that only at the end of the 1990s CBBM&A gained in relative importance. This suggests that hurdles to cross-border M&A have indeed been higher in the bank-

13 See Buch and DeLong (2003) and the more detailed discussion in section 2.2.1.

14 See section 3.1 for a more detailed discussion on the characteristics of banks.

15 Differences between averaging the yearly figures for the 1990s provided by Buch and DeLong (2004) and the averages provided by Focarelli and Pozzolo (2001) probably stem from the above mentioned differences in CBBM&A definitions. Differences are, however, much smaller than those for absolute deal frequency.

16 See section 3.1.1 for a definition of financial intermediation.

Figure 2.4: Relative Importance of Cross-Border M&A Across Industries

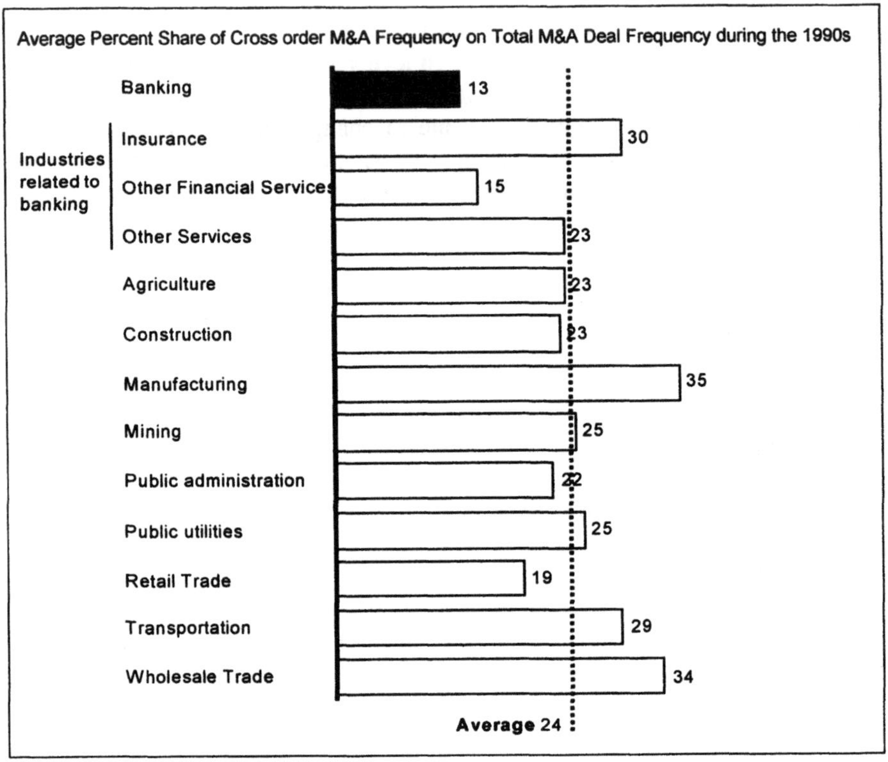

Source: Adapted from Focarelli and Pozzolo (2001)

ing and financial services industries, probably rather due to regulation than to the special role of information asymmetries, but that they were lowered at the end of the last decade. This may be related to intense banking deregulation in Europe as well as in the US in the respective periods.[17]

Thus, in a nutshell, while CBBM&A also became more important relative to domestic banking deals and compared to cross-border deals in other industries, it also developed from relatively low levels of relative importance.

17 See section 2.2.1 for details. However, Buch and DeLong (2004) also show that the growth in relative importance of CBBM&A is also due to a parallel decline in domestic banking M&A at the end of the 1990s. Thus, another explanation would be that it was not CBBM&A that became more attractive but domestic M&A that became relatively unattractive, maybe due to limits in domestic growth.

The numbers shown above all cover the period from the mid 1980s to the end of the century. However, the casual empiricism in the beginning suggested that there might be a "deal frenzy" going on in 2004 and 2005. Some recent figures on European cross-border banking from McKinsey (2005), a consultancy, shed some light on this, see figure 2.5.[18]

The numbers again show a cyclicality in deal flow that already became apparent in figure 2.2. The upward trend indicated there seems to have continued until 2001, followed by a decline until 2003 where the next upward cycle seems to have begun.

Figure 2.5: Development of European Cross-Border Bank M&A since 2000

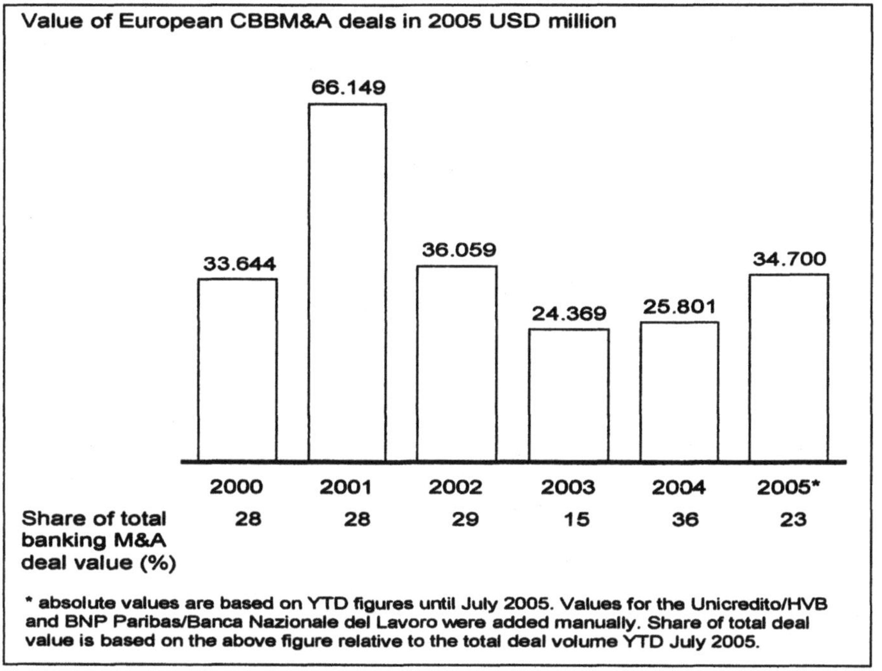

Source: Adapted from McKinsey (2005)

18 Values are again recalculated in 2005 dollars. The deal values for the Unicredito/HVB and the BNP Paribas/Banca Nazionale del Lavoro deal were manually added to the July 2005 year-to-date figures provided by McKinsey (2005). Caution is due in interpreting these numbers, since there is some intransparency with regard to the used CBBM&A definition.

Again, the development probably reflects the global economic downturn during the millennium and the recent recovery.[19] Thus, the numbers are in line with a continuing upward trend within an overall cyclical market.

Another point of interest is the split of CBBM&A deals into those that happened across borders but between commercial banks and those in which at least one transaction partner was a non-bank. Evidence on this is provided by Walter (2004) who gives an overview of the split of the total FI cross-border merger volume 1985 to 2002 by type of acquirer and target. Figure 2.6 shows the results. Interestingly, less than half of this deal volume involves commercial banks. Most deals are between insurers which links back to the high share of CBBM&A on total M&A in the insurance industry found by Focarelli and Pozzolo (2001).

Figure 2.6: Cross-Border Bank M&A Volume by Type of Bidder and Target

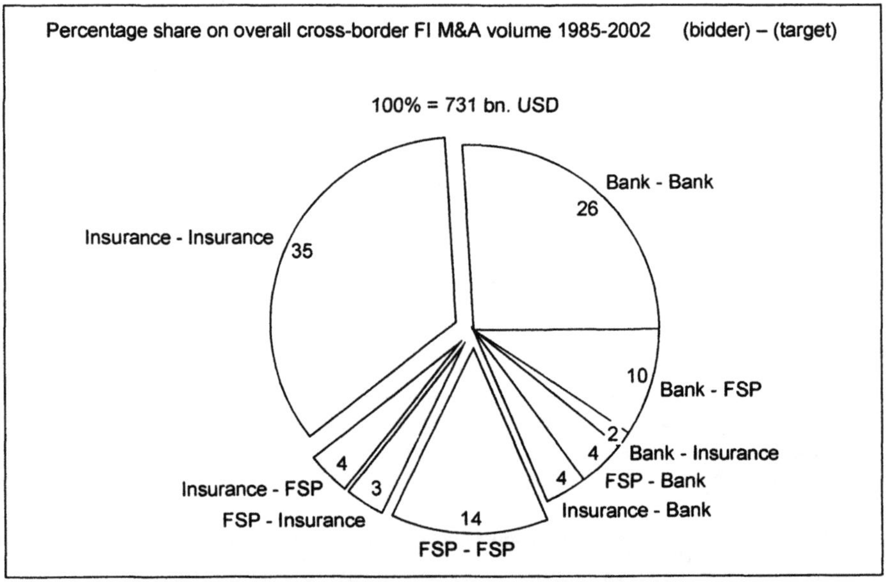

Source: Adapted from Walther (2004).

Even deals that do involve commercial banks happen about as often between banks as between banks and other types of financial intermediaries. The latter deals, therefore, need to be taken into account in any discussion of CBBM&A.

19 See Beitel (2002), Berger et al. (2004).

Finally, what about the geographical location of CBBM&A, that is, where do bidders usually come from and where do they prefer to acquire? The most detailed piece of evidence with regard to this question is provided by Berger et al. (2004) who provide an overview by geographical location of bidder and target for a large sample of cross-border mergers of FIs consisting of more than 1853 deals between 1985 and 2002.[20] An overview of the most important findings is provided in table 2.1.[21]

First, the table gives an idea about where, generally, bidders and targets come from. Here, the main impression is that cross-border bidding is a European domain, as European bidders perform almost two thirds of all such deals.

This is not surprising in the light of country size, the potentially large number of cross-border opportunities within Europe, the historically friendlier legal attitude to banking M&A compared to the US[22] and some indications that at least some European banks suffer from limits to domestic growth.[23] Some European countries, such as the UK, Germany, the Netherlands, France, and to an extent also Belgium and Spain are especially active acquirers. Berger et al. (2004) speculate that this could be due to a high degree of home clients that has likewise internationalized.[24]

Bidders from Australasia are much less important. African bidders are even completely absent, in line with the notion that banking FDI generally flows out of highly developed nations.[25] An exception to this rule, however, seems to be the US. Admittedly the US is, just before the UK, the single most important home country globally and by far the most important home country in the Americas. However, scaled by the size of its economy, the numbers seems surprisingly low. Possibly, the US market still offers relatively more domestic M&A opportunities and, primarily because of the historically restrictive regulation, banks may still lack the critical size for cross-border deals.

---

20 Berger et al. (2004, p. 351) report the number as 1849. This is neither consistent with the sum of the given country totals (which add up to 1867) nor the actually given country combinations (which add up to 1853), which is used here. The inconsistency in their figures between country totals and the actually given combinations stems probably from too many reported deals with targets in Greece (they report 11 but add up to 25).

21 For a summarized version of table 2.1 that highlights the main deal flows see table A.1 in the appendix.

22 See section 2.2.1.

23 See section 4.2.3 for a more detailed discussion.

24 This is the so-called follow-the-client argument, see section 4.3.2 for a more detailed discussion.

25 See UNCTAD (2000).

Table 2.1 Geographical Distribution of Cross-Border Bank M&A

		Continent of target																	
		Africa	Americas			Australasia			Europe										
Continent of bidder	Country/ Region	All	CDN	SA	US	JP	A	A/O	B	F	D	E	UK	NL	ROWE	ROEE	SCA	Sum	Sum Continent
Africa	All																	0	0
Americas	CDN			1	86	1		4		2			17		4	1	2	118	
	SA				2													2	489
	US		62	14		12		34	4	18	10	7	152	7	33	7	9	369	
Australasia	JP				28					2				1	6	2		39	
	A										2							2	99
	A/O				10	1		18		1			21	1	4	2		58	
Europe	B				11			1		11	3	5	5	15	9	5	2	67	
	F		5	1	26	3		4	14		10	12	35	7	29	4	4	154	
	D		3		29	1		10	5	27		6	28	15	39	11	8	182	
	E			4	5				1				2	1	10	1		24	
	UK		19	2	102	1		50	7	27	16	13		7	34	5	23	306	1265
	NL		6		37			13	12	12	8	8	22		9	10	6	143	
	ROWE		2	2	62	1		10	8	33	25	35	54	9	37	15	7	300	
	ROEE														1	3		4	
	SCA		1		9			1	1	2	2		16	4	10	3	36	85	
	Sum	0	98	24	407	20	0	145	52	135	76	86	352	67	225	69	97	1853	
	Sum Continent	0	529			165			1159										

Source: Based on Berger et al. (2004)

Legend: A= Asia, A/O = Australia/Oceania, B = Belgium, CDN = Canada, D = Germany, E = Spain, F = France, GB = United Kingdom, PL = Poland, ROEO = Rest of Eastern Europe, ROWE = Rest of Western Europe, SA = South America, SCA = Scandinavia, US = United States.

The geographical distribution of targets closely reflects that of bidders. Numbers generally back the hypothesis that the UK and US have comparative advantages at hosting foreign banks, e.g., due to due to high openness to foreign capital, transparent and fair "rules of engagement" for foreigners, and their roles as major financial centers.[26]

More interesting insights result from a look at specific bidder-target country combinations. Who are, e.g., the bidders from the Americas and where do they acquire? Next to some Canadian bidders that acquire in the US, most American acquirers are from the US.[27] While these also pursue some intracontinental deals, again, primarily in Canada, the vast majority of US bidders goes shopping in Europe. However, while American bidders, thus, seem to be willing to acquire even over large distances, they prefer cultural similarity, as more than half of their European acquisitions take place in the UK. This is very different from the Australasian, and especially the Japanese bidders that prefer to go shopping in the US, an economically comparable but geographically and culturally far distant country.

Europeans bidders show the most diverse behavior. Some countries such as Germany, France, and to an extent also the Netherlands acquire primarily within Europe but are also strong drivers of intercontinental consolidation, mainly by seeking targets in the US. However, they also seem to be up for the one or other occasional more exotic deal, be it in a culturally related region, such as some French acquisitions in Canada, or not, as witnessed by a remarkably high number of German acquisitions in Australia and Oceania or French acquisitions in Japan. Other bidder nations, such as Belgium, primarily stick to close-range intracontinental deals, seeking targets in neighboring countries such as the Netherlands and France. Scandinavians also prefer to stick with intraregional consolidation.

Other countries or regions, such as Spain and especially Eastern Europe – after the iron curtain came down – seem to be rather shopping malls than shoppers. However, Spain has made a significant number of acquisitions in South America, again showing signs that close social distance seems to be able to compensate for economic or geographic disparity. Close social distance is likewise visible in the choice of targets of UK bidders, that, like their US equivalents prefer related countries such as the US, Australia, and New Zealand.

One problem with the data of Berger and al. (2004) is obviously that it does not only include CBBM&A but also mergers between other FIs. However, industry dynamics might be different for other types of deals, as indicated by the

26 See Berger et al. (2004), Ben Salem (2006).

27 Note that all other American countries except Canada and the US are referred to as South American.

number for the insurance industry discussed above. Amihud et al. (2002), who focus exclusively on CBBM&A, provide more applicable evidence. However, their sample is both much smaller, probably due to the fact that they require bidders to be listed, and they only provide deal frequencies per country and no information on bidder-target combinations. Nevertheless, results are overall very similar.[28] The one significant difference is with regard to the US. Here, US targets seem somewhat more important than with Berger et al. (2004), while US bidders seem considerably less important.[29]

Summarizing, the historical development indicates that, in the period 1985 to 2005, CBBM&A grew in terms of deal frequency, deal volume and average deal size. It also grew in relative importance compared to domestic banking M&A as well as cross-border M&A in other industries. That growth, however, started at low initial levels. Furthermore, deals between banks and other FIs play an important part in the development of CBBM&A. Geographically, deals happen primarily within Europe and show some characteristic geographic patterns that seem (also) related to the development of banking regulation and social similarities between bidder and target countries.

2.2 Selected Trends Affecting the Market Development

Few discussions of CBBM&A forget to mention that deals have been influenced and, in fact, often made possible by a set of global economic trends. Among the most frequently mentioned of these trends are legal deregulation and harmonization, advances of IT, and globalization.[30] The role of some of these trends had already been hinted at in the discussion in the previous section. The following sections will discuss them in more detail.

---

28 Table A.2 in the appendix provides a detailed overview of the results of Amihud et al. (2002).

29 As discussed above, this is probably due to the historically restrictive banking M&A regulation and the resulting average size of US bidders which makes them better targets than acquirers, see Amihud et al. (2002) and section 2.2.1.

30 E.g., Berger et al. (2000), Buch and DeLong (2004), Berger et al. (2004), Walter (2004). Beitel (2002, p. 49) cites many earlier references. The Group of Ten (2001) published a survey of top decision makers in banking M&A that also identified primarily these factors as the drivers of cross-border consolidation. Note that the three are highly interrelated as technological change e.g., also fosters globalization and may induce the need for regulatory change.

2.2.1 Legal Deregulation and Harmonization

Legal deregulation refers to loosening or abolishing restrictions that, directly or indirectly, hinder or impede CBBM&A. Legal harmonization refers to establishing common standards in the regulatory environment. Since worldwide efforts to deregulate and harmonize are possibly as numerous and diverse as regulations themselves, the following discussion centers on the two geographic locations that have been identified as most important for CBBM&A: Europe and the US.[31]

In Europe, heavy restrictions on banking FDI and a large diversity in banking supervisory standards were quite common in the early 1980s.[32] Change was brought about through the Single European Act of 1986, the Single Market Programme, and a set of subsequent, FI-specific laws put in place in the 1990s. Of major importance were the EU Directive on Liberalization of Capital Flows in 1988, the Second European Banking Co-ordination Directive in 1989, the Directive on Deposit Guarantee Schemes in 1994[33] and the Financial Services Action Plan of 1999.

The *Directive on the Liberalization of Capital Flows* had a primarily deregulative character, aiming at a fully liberalized financial market in the European Economic Community, i.e., one without capital controls, by 1990. Despite some loopholes for a temporary reintroduction of such controls[34] and significant concessions with regard to implementation timing to some member countries, the last member state, Greece, abolished its capital controls in 1994.[35]

The *Second European Banking Co-Ordination Directive* was intended to bring about deregulation as well as harmonization. The introduction of a single banking license allowed banks to open branches in any member state, given that they owned a banking license in any other. Furthermore, the concept of "home control" was introduced which put foreign branches of domestic banks under home country control. This gave national governments fewer options to deny foreign banks entry by either withholding licenses or imposing stricter regulatory requirements on them than on domestic banks.[36] Furthermore, this fostered a harmonization of standards as countries with more restrictive regulations risked

31 Another worldwide effort to harmonize banking regulation, the Basle II rules, are discussed in section 3.1.2.

32 See the overview at Dermine (2002).

33 These are Directives 88/361/EEC, 89/646/EEC and 94/19/EC, respectively.

34 The Directive allows for a temporary reinstallation of capital controls by the European Commission or member countries in the case of speculative movements, which cause some uncertainty on the durability of the Directive, see Dermine (2002).

35 Moser et al. (2005).

36 Berger et al. (2000).

putting their own banks at a competitive disadvantage.[37] However, to prevent an ultimately harmful "downward competition" of regulatory measures, certain minimum standards, especially with regard to capital requirements were introduced. In this vein, the *Directive on Deposit Guarantee Schemes* required member states to implement deposit insurance and set the minimum amount covered to 20,000 euros per individual.

Finally, the *Financial Services Action Plan* was a wide-ranging set of measures, both harmonizing and deregulatory, to eliminate remaining barriers on the way to a fully integrated European financial market. It aimed at establishing a single European wholesale market for financial services, an open and secure retail market and state-of-the-art prudential regulation and supervision, closely aligned with the Basle II framework. For that purpose, it intended to introduce a total of 42 measures until 2004, many of which, e.g., corporate takeover rules or an extension of the "single banking license" and "home control" rules, directly affected CBBM&A.[38]

The potential effects of these efforts on CBBM&A are strong. Abolishing capital controls should lead to a higher and, more importantly, much more equal level of economic openness in Europe. The latter should, therefore, tend to play a less important role for CBBM&A. Harmonization of regulatory requirements, such as minimum capital requirements and deposit insurance, should likewise make regulatory characteristics of the relevant host countries less important. The "home control" approaches, in turn, increase the importance of the regulatory environment in the home country. Thus, deregulation and harmonization in Europe overall seem to facilitate CBBM&A. More concretely, they increase the importance of home country characteristics and decrease that of some host country characteristics, such as economic openness or regulatory frameworks, that have the power to impede or hold up deals. Beitel (2002, p. 55) even concludes that there are no further hurdles left for CBBM&A in Europe.

However, a closer look at the discussed regulation and evidence on its effects casts some doubt on this conjecture. First, with regard to economic openness, there have been several recent, well-documented cases in which host governments opposed large CBBM&A on the grounds of the bidder being "unsuitable" but allegedly to keep banks under national control and to prevent layoffs. Some

37 Berger et al. (2000) in that context note that the Second European Banking Directive factually made universal banking the norm in Europe.

38 Until the deadline, 39 of these, even though often in a different form than in the original proposal, had been introduced. In October 2006, an evaluation of the effect of these measures is still underway, see European Commission (2006).

governments even tried to organize alternative domestic deals.[39] While the EU sided with bidders in all cases, government intervention was possibly costly for bidders, in certain cases visibly so through concessions to host governments, and in some cases even led to the withdrawal of the offer. These incidents have recently led Charlie McCreevy, the EU Commissioner for the Internal Market, to propose wide-ranging amendments to the existing directives, because he noted that "until now EU rules have allowed national regulators to block proposed mergers in the financial sector. Unfortunately, these rules don't provide any clarity or specific criteria to assess the suitability of the proposed acquirers."[40] Seemingly, despite the abolition of capital controls, the openness of the host country remains an issue in Europe.

There are also two important caveats with regard to the effectiveness of the "home control" rule. First, there are several exceptions to this rule allowing host countries to regulate foreign banks in matters of liquidity, consumer protection, advertising, and monetary policy.[41] Second and possibly more important, "home control" does not apply to subsidiaries which are considered part of the host country. However, in CBBM&A subsidiaries are the rule rather than the exception.[42]

Also the introduced common requirements were mostly a means to prevent "downward" competition but intended to leave enough room for regulatory competition, their harmonizing effect is supposedly low.[43] In line with this reasoning,

---

39 One example is the acquisition of Banco Totta & Acores and Credito Predial Portuguese, both part of the Champalimaud Group, by Banco Santander in 1999. The Portuguese government strongly opposed Santander's acquisition, leading to an extended conflict with the European Union. Finally, Santander agreed to acquire only a smaller part of the Champalimaud Group, leaving the rest under Portuguese control, see Financial Times (1999). Other examples are the takeover of Banca Antonveneta by ABN Amro and the planned takeover of Banca Nazionale del Lavoro by Banco Bilbao Vizcaya Argentaria (BBVA), both in 2005. The Bank of Italy, despite formal clearance of the deals by the EU, continued to block them which played a large part in the later withdrawal of the offer by BBVA. The incident ultimately led to the arrest of the governor of the Bank of Italy for unlawful behavior, see The Economist (2005). Finally, despite EU intervention, the Polish government continues to block the mergers between Bank Prezemyslowo Handlowy (BPH) and Bank Pekao, supposedly on the grounds of large resulting job losses. The deal, even though domestic, is a direct consequence of the Unicredit/HVB deal.

40 MergerMarket (2006).

41 Dermine (2002), Buch and DeLong (2003).

42 See, e.g. Dermine (2002).

43 In the case of deposit insurance, the relevant Directive is for example silent on how the deposit insurance should be organized (public versus private) or how premiums

European CBBM&A activity is generally found to be far below the expected levels before the initiated measures and many empirical studies fail to find a link between CBBM&A or FDI activity and the Single Market Programme.[44] In the context of these results, Dermine (2002, p. 20) asks: "Single Banking License, Single Home Country Regulator, Single Bankruptcy Proceedings: A great illusion?" and the so-called "Ceccini Report" to the European Financial Services Roundtable concludes: "There is a huge gap between the *vision* of the EU as the most dynamic economy in the world and the *reality* of still fragmented EU markets."[45]

Effects from the implementation of the Financial Services Action Plan are still under evaluation. However, intermediate outcomes, such as the implementation of modified version of a European Take-Over Directive,[46] or the complaints of market participants with regard to vagueness the Markets in Financial Instruments Directive (MiFID), that affects the extension of the single banking license,[47] cast some doubt on the assumption that its effect will be much stronger than that of previous initiatives. Thus, it does not seem that the regulatory environment in the host country has lost much of its importance either.

With regard to deregulation and regulatory harmonization in the US, reference is usually made to two pieces of legislation that primarily affected domestic consolidation but had second-order effects on CBBM&A. One is the continuous deregulation of interstate banking, culminating in the *Riegle-Neal Interstate Banking and Branching Efficiency Act of 1994.* Another is the passing of the Financial Modernization Act, also known as the *Gramm-Leach-Blily Act*, in 1999.[48] This effectively removed many barriers to universal banking in the US which, based on the Banking Act of 1933 and especially its sections on the involvement of banks in underwriting, insurance and securities trading,[49] had been extremely high. Since many potential foreign targets are, in fact, universal banks themselves, this also affected CBBM&A.

Summarizing, legal deregulation and harmonization in the EU and to an extent also in the US affects CBBM&A through its effect on country-characteristics

---

should be calculated even though these are the defining features of a deposit insurance, see Huizinga and Nicodème (2002).

44 Buch and DeLong (2003), Berger et al. (2004).

45 See Heinemann and Jopp (2002), p. 15, italics taken over from the original.

46 The modified directive as been strongly criticized, especially by the designers of the original proposal, as too much of a concession to particular interest groups and having hardly any effect on harmonization, see Apeldoorn and Horn (2004).

47 See The Economist (2006c).

48 Krozner and Strahan (2005).

49 These are also known as the Glass-Steagal Act.

such as economic openness of the host country and the regulatory environment of the home and host country. Generally, deregulation and harmonization are aimed at increasing the level of CBBM&A. However, at least within the EU, they do not always seem to lead to the desired effects. Thus, the question whether and how the identified country-characteristics do (still) affect CBBM&A (and possibly its wealth effects) in the presence of deregulation and harmonization, remains open.

2.2.2 Advances of Information Technology

Berger (2003) presents a thorough literature review of the economic effects of IT advancements in the banking industry. According to his findings, progress in IT primarily affects banks through effects on monitoring costs, processing costs, and the possibility to create new products and services. These three effects and their implications for the identified determinants of wealth creation are discussed next.

With regard to *monitoring costs*, advances in IT have lowered the cost of collecting information about borrowers and increased the power to process it, especially in the traditional retail business with customers and small and medium enterprises (SMEs). As a result, the distance between borrower and lender has become less important, to the extent that some banking products, such as retail credit and credit cards, are nowadays sold via mail or e-mail, more or less independent of physical borrower-lender distance. Ceteris paribus, this should make CBBM&A relatively more unattractive to cross-border lending and borrowing. However, decreased monitoring costs should also decrease the cost involved in monitoring faraway subsidiaries or overseeing a post-merger integration process. While there is, to the knowledge of the author, no direct evidence from the banking industry which of the two effects prevails,[50] there is some evidence that in service-intensive industries, like banking, the net effect ultimately fosters M&A.[51]

However, independently of the net effect, Degryse and Ongena (2004) note that the decreasing importance of monitoring costs for lending and borrowing mainly relates to physical distance, as cultural and economic distance is much

50 In his analysis of the economic effects of technological progress in the banking industry, Berger (2003) devotes a section to the effects of IT on the consolidation process. While he hypothesizes a net positive effect of IT advancements on banking M&A, the cited evidence is mostly domestic studies that do not explicitely control for IT related efficiency effects.

51 See Bender (2002) who provides an empirical analysis of the effect of changing firm boundaries in a new information and communication environment.

harder to bridge with IT.[52] A similar argumentation holds for "internal" monitoring: new technologies certainly decrease but they can hardly bridge cultural bidder-target distance. Thus, IT advancements have probably lowered the transaction cost-reducing effect of physical but not of cultural or economic distance.

Berger (2003) also argues that monitoring-related IT advancements have made economies of scale in monitoring easier to obtain and, thus, ceteris paribus benefit large banks more than smaller banks and make bank size a more important potential determinant of wealth effects. However, the increased importance of size probably differs with the complexity of the risk-management tasks at hand. For simple tasks, size is of less importance as the technology in question, e.g., lender information databases or monitoring technology, is generally also available to smaller banks from a wide range of third party providers.[53] More complex risk-management tasks such as dealing with market risk and constantly changing the organization's risk profile on the portfolio level within profitability and regulatory constraints require more sophisticated technology and know-how. Even though there are also off-the-shelf technologies to facilitate these tasks,[54] proprietary knowledge and data play a much more important role in this field.

Turning to *processing costs*, banking also requires the processing of large amounts of data, e.g., related to payments, security exchanges or lender information. Next to allowing the electronic processing of this information on the "back end", IT advancements have also opened up several new transactional channels besides the traditional branch on the "front end", such as call centers, automated teller machines, and transactional internet websites. The evidence reviewed by Berger (2003) suggests that this has helped banks to shift the average U-shaped cost curve upwards, making cost scale economies also available to larger banks.[55]

---

52 Consequently, the authors also find that the credit products mentioned above are rarely sold across borders.

53 Credit information in the US is e.g., provided by a range of private companies such as Experian, Equifax, and TransUnion. In Europe, there are also private firms, e.g., Callcredit in the UK or the SCHUFA in Germany. In addition, there are also a significant number of central-bank administered services such as the "Evidenzzentrale" of the German Bundesbank or the "fichier national des incidents de reboursement des crédits aux particulières" of the Banque de France, see Jentzsch (2003). Well-known providers of "off-the-shelf" risk-management technologies are for example Fair, Isaac and Company or Dun & Bradstreet.

54 Some prominent examples include Risk Metrics Group Credit Metrics, Credit Risk Plus from Credit Suisse Financial Products, Credit Portfolio View from McKinsey and the Portfolio Manager of KMV now offered by Moody's.

55 Interestingly, the evidence discussed above also suggests that while banks have been able to capture the benefits of "back-end" innovations themselves, competition has forced them to pass most benefits of "front-end" innovations through to customers.

Thus again, this type of IT advancement increases the importance of large size for wealth creation. But, as with monitoring costs above, the possibility to outsource standard processes mitigates the increased importance of bank size, as outsourcing is also an option to smaller institutions.

Finally, IT advancements have created opportunities for banks to offer *new products, services, and activities*. The lender-information databases and risk-management software discussed above is just one example of this.[56] In addition, the introduction of new transactional channels effectively consists of a service innovation for retail customers. Similar innovations, such as e-based debt and equity direct issuance, exist for wholesale customers.[57] Finally and probably most importantly, IT advancements have also caused designing and trading derivatives to become a major new source of income for banks. This, again, is most beneficial to large banks, as many smaller institutions lack the know-how and capital required to engage in such transactions.

Summarizing, from a transaction cost perspective, IT advancements have lowered transaction costs on markets in that they lower the importance of physical borrower-lender distance, thus making the market solution, i.e., cross-border borrowing and lending, more attractive relative to a hierarchy solution, i.e., CBBM&A. However, they have also reduced transaction costs within hierachies, allowing them to grow larger and do so profitably. While direct evidence on the net effect is lacking for the banking industry, there is evidence of an M&A-fostering effect from other, comparable industries.

2.2.3 Globalization

Legal deregulation, harmonization, and advances in IT have not only affected FIs, but also other industries. This has led to a substantial increase in the internationalization of production, sometimes referred to as globalization. Figure 2.7 shows the development of one measure of globalization that compares especially well with the figures discussed above, namely the value of global cross-border M&A transactions across all industries.[58]

Overall, globalization through cross-border mergers has developed similarly to CBBM&A: strong increases until the 2000 "boom year", a steep decline during the following slowdown of overall global economic activity and a recent re-

56 Note that most of the risk-management products mentioned in footnote 54 were originally developed and sold by banks.

57 See Walter (2004) for an overview of recent IT-induced innovations in financial services in the wholesale segment.

58 Again, figures are given in terms of 2005 real dollar values.

Figure 2.7: Development of Cross-Border M&A Deal Value

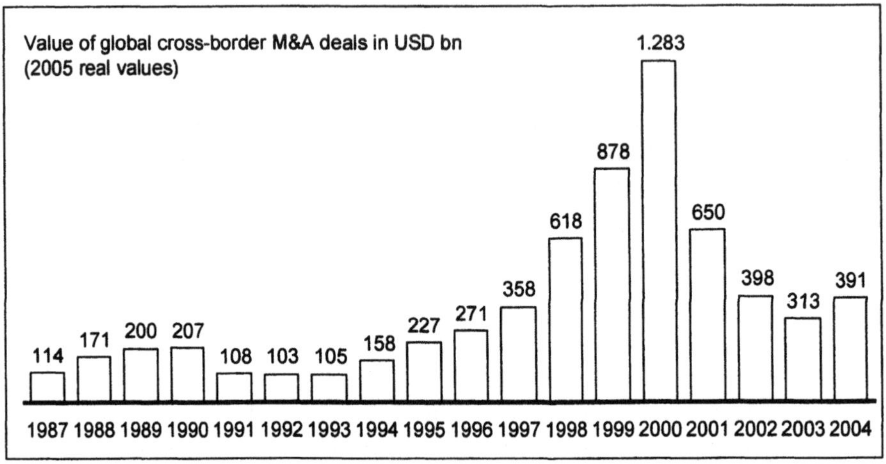

Source: Based on UNCTAD (2005).

covery in deal value are observable. Thus, from the perspective of banks, globalization causes an increasing number of home country clients to go abroad. Since some authors have argued that the presence of home country clients in the host country makes CBBM&A more attractive for banks,[59] it might be that globalization tends to make it even more important.

There is another aspect of globalization that industry participants find more and even most important for CBBM&A: the growing importance of capital markets.[60] These have indeed experienced significant growth in absolute terms and also relative to banks, the major alternative conduit of capital flows. Figure 2.8, based on Berger et al. (2003), provides some numbers for the US.[61]

---

59 This is the "follow the client argument", see section 4.2.2 for a more detailed discussion. While the latter section shows that empirical evidence with regard to this argument is mixed, it is nevertheless on the agenda of at least some industry participants: 17 percent of respondents in a survey conducted by the Group of Ten (2001) on important factors driving CBBM&A believed that non-financial internationalization was "important" or "very important".

60 44 percent of respondents in the Group of Ten (2001) survey found this factor to be an "important" or "very important" driver of CBBM&A.

61 While the US is rather a market-based economy, the results discussed in the context of figure 2.8 are also representative for rather bank-based economies such as Germany, see Allen and Santomero (1998, 2001).

Figure 2.8: Development of Bank and Capital Markets in the US

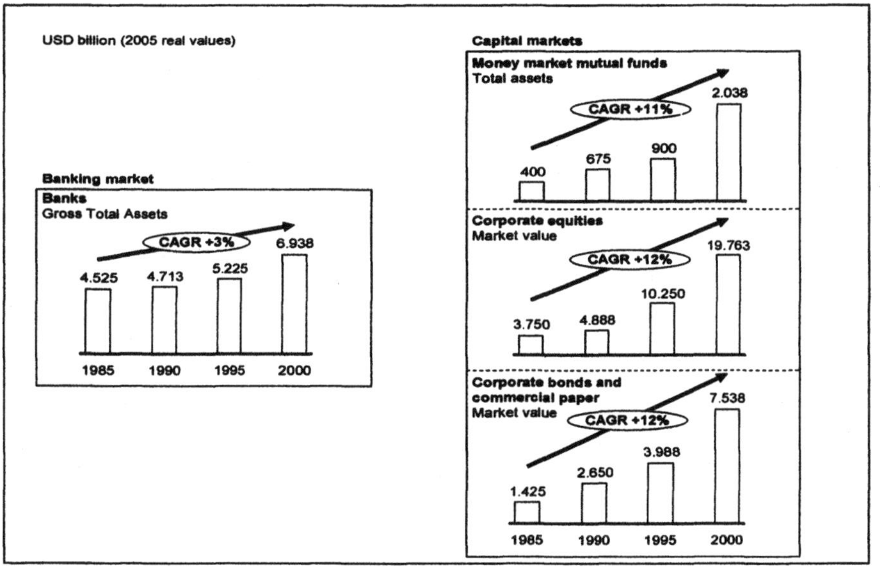

Source: Adapted from Berger (2003)

The numbers show that money market mutual funds, an alternative to bank deposits, and both equity and debt securities, an alternative to bank loans, have experienced a far higher annual growth between 1985 and 2000 than bank assets. Both equity and debt securities also overtook bank assets in importance by the end of the decade. Much of this growth has again been fueled by technological progress. Indeed, many of the innovations in financial services have been methods to link providers and seekers of capital directly with financial markets.[62] Thus, disintermediation poses a threat to banks, as it lowers the need for their core services, namely accepting deposits and granting loans. However, by observing the actual impact that globalization had on banks, some authors instead argued that it "only" leads to a shift in the activities of banks and even opens up new business opportunities, especially in the field of risk and portfolio management, and may even make deals between banks and insurers or other financial service providers more attractive.[63]

62 See the overview at Walter (2004).

63 See section 3.1.1 for a more detailed discussion of the core activities and the shifting role of banks relative to capital markets.

2.3 Summary

The first task of this chapter was to validate the growing importance of CBBM&A: it was shown that these deals have continuously grown in terms of size, value, and relative importance. Domestic deals were however still relatively more important than cross-border ones and the relation between the two in the banking industry has only recently reached that of comparable industries. The numbers also suggested a recent strong upturn in CBBM&A, especially driven by European transactions. Europe also generally turned out to be the most important location for CBBM&A as it hosts the majority of bidders as well as targets. The US, probably partly due to its legal legacy on banking regulation, lagged behind but was still the most important single country with regard to both bidders and targets. Results also indicated the importance of a consistent definition of CBBM&A deals and that, while most deals still happened between commercial banks, bank-nonbank deals are not to be disregarded in an analysis of CBBM&A.

The second task of this chapter was to review global forces of change affecting CBBM&A, namely regulatory harmonization and deregulation, advancements of IT and globalization. One finding was that, while all these factors are likely to affect CBBM&A positively, their effects are also probably less strong than they are intended to be (as in the case of harmonization and deregulation) or coupled with other, partly offsetting effects, as in the case of IT advancements and globalization. Given the frequent reference to these global forces as drivers of CBBM&A, there is also a surprising lack of empirical evidence on their actual net effect.

Insofar as these trends positively influence CBBM&A and given that CBBM&A is at least partly driven by the desire to create wealth, they are also first candidates for the sought-after determinants of wealth creation. However they seem conceptually too broad to be related to a specific wealth effects. What seems more promising, is to continue the search for determinants on the level of such firm- and country-level factors as firm-size and economic openness of the host country, that the above discussion also pointed at. This will be taken up again in the next chapter.

3. Theoretical Foundations of Banking and M&A

This chapter covers selected perspectives on banks (*section 3.1*) and on M&A (*section 3.2)*. This chapter also covers the primary methods to assess the wealth effects of M&A, including their specific advantages and disadvantages (*section 3.3*). These are event studies, operating performance (OP) and dynamic efficiency (DE) studies as well as case studies. *Section 3.4* summarizes the findings on the theorectical foundations of Banking and M&A.

3.1 Selected Perspectives on Banks

This section includes a characterization of banks as FIs including a definition of banks that is used throughout this study (section 3.1.1) as well as a discussion of the motives and consequences of banking regulation (section 3.1.2), which are later shown to be closely related to potential determinants of wealth effects.

3.1.1 Banks as Financial Intermediaries

Banks are FIs, i.e., economic agents that facilitate transactions between providers and seekers of capital. Depending on whether FIs directly interact with market participants, e.g., borrow capital from providers and lend it to seekers or just facilitate transactions between third parties, they are distinguished into FIs in a narrower and a broader sense.[64]

An example of a FI in a narrow sense is a commercial bank that accepts deposits and grants loans. Insurance companies are also often regarded as FIs in that sense, even though they have a stronger focus on risk management than banks.[65] FIs in a broader sense are, e.g., securities firms, sometimes also called investment banks, that offer such diverse services as capital market access, trading, brokerage, investment research and advice, risk management, CF advisory or principal investing.[66] Another, often separately mentioned class of FIs in a

64 Spicher (1997).
65 Walter (2004).
66 Walter (2004).

broader sense are institutions that provide asset management services for third parties, such as mutual or pension funds.

Real-world FIs are often active in both types of intermediation.[67] Almost every commercial bank, e.g., also offers limited investment advice. Asset management is also a core activity of insurers and many banks are so-called universal type institutions that offer both commercial and investment banking services.

In order to better understand the characteristics of FIs, one has to understand why such institutions exist, i.e., why market participants do not interact directly with each other and leave transformational functions to capital markets. This is explained by the theory of financial intermediation. Since many excellent overviews of this theory have been given elsewhere,[68] this effort is not repeated here. Instead, some key findings are highlighted that have special relevance for the research questions at hand.

Using a general equilibrium model with perfect and complete capital markets, Freixas and Rochet (1998) show that the welfare position reached through the interaction of households and firms via capital markets is Pareto-efficient and cannot be further improved by FIs. It follows that classical microeconomic theory cannot explain their existence.

Such an explanation only follows if market frictions and specifically transaction costs are introduced. Then, given market participants incur less transaction costs when interacting via FIs than directly via financial markets, FIs emerge as a more efficient alternative to the market solution. In that context, many early contributions of the literature have focused on transaction costs such as fixed trading costs that give hierarchical coalitions of borrowers or lenders, i.e., FIs, cost advantages through fixed costs digression – and, thus, ultimately economies of scale – over markets.[69] These early contributions usually do not consider other transaction costs, such as costs of searching or monitoring, nor do they explain them. Rather, these are assumed as exogenously given.

This has inspired a strand of literature that originated in the late 1970s and early 1980s to focus on the role of asymmetrical distribution of information and the costs that result from it.[70] One central contribution in this context is the work

67 As discussed in the previous chapter, US regulation until recently prohibited banks to be active in both types of intermediation at the same time. However, in other regions, especially in Europe, such a strict separation had not been forced upon market participants.

68 E.g., Santomero (1984), Bhattarcharya and Thakor (1993), Freixas and Rochet (1998).

69 Benston (1976) and Baltensperger (1980) provide surveys of this literature.

70 Some authors, such as Hellwig (1994) and Gorton and Winton (2002), refer to these theories as asymmetric-information approaches as opposed to the earlier transaction-

of Diamond (1984). The author focuses on ex-post information asymmetry, in the form of costly verification of the true outcome of an investment project. In Diamond's (1984) model, investment projects of entrepreneurs need to be financed by many small investors. Since the outcomes of investment projects are unobservable, entrepreneurs have an incentive to report too low outcomes and need to be monitored. Given that there are economies of scale in monitoring, delegating the monitoring to an FI would be more efficient than individual monitoring by each investor. However, this raises the problem of "monitoring the monitor," whose actions are also not costlessly observable. This leads to delegation costs. Here, diversification plays a central role. If the FI lends to and monitors multiple entrepreneurs with non-perfectly correlated ventures, delegation costs become neglible in the limit for a very large intermediary as risk gets diversified away and the FI can credibly guarantee safe returns. Banks can thus be looked upon as delegated monitors.

The paradigm shift in the theory of financial intermediation from FIs as mediators of monetary transaction costs towards mediators of information asymmetries has recently been critized by Allen and Santomero (1998, 2001). According to the authors, contemporary theory predicts that recent developments such as the dramatic lowering of transaction costs through new IT and the explosive growth of financial markets should decrease the importance of financial intermediation, leading to so-called disintermediation. Even though they find this to be true in some selected instances, e.g., for traditional deposit-taking and loan-granting institutions, the latter seem to have only shifted their activities towards more fee-producing activities such as trusts, annuities or mutual funds. Moreover, they observe that the overall importance of FIs has grown proportionally with the growing importance of financial markets and FIs even seem to be the most important participants in many of these markets. The authors conclude that the recent focus of intermediation theory on the costs of asymmetrical information is too narrow and instead propose to focus on so called participation costs, i.e., the costs of directly participating in capital markets. Their main argument is that both an increase in the complexity of financial markets and increasing opportunity cost of investors' time increases participation costs. FIs can lower these costs by building long-term trust based relationships and by "repackaging" risky income streams into new streams with different risk-reward profiles that market participants find less costly to monitor.

---

cost-based approaches. However, as Freixas and Rochet (1998, p. 16) point out, the costs induced by asymmetrical information can be looked upon as just another type of transaction cost.

The discussion above defined banks as FIs but also provided several examples of FIs that are not referred to as banks in practice. The question arises how banking differs from financial intermediation or how to define a bank. This study follows Freixas and Rochet (1998, p. 1), who define banks as FIs that grant loans and receive deposits from the public. Their definition is very close to what is in practice known as a commercial bank or closely related institutions and also frequently used by other authors.[71] All FIs that are not banks or insurers are henceforth referred to as financial service providers (FSPs).[72]

Summarizing, banks are FIs that grant loans and receive deposits from the public. Intermediation theory sees the primary role of these institutions as mediators of transaction costs, whereby the focus of interest has shifted from monetary transaction costs to costs originating from asymmetrical information. In that context, FIs are a hierarchical, sometimes more cost-efficient alternative to financial markets. More recently, a shift has been proposed to see FIs also as a conduit and not only as an alternative to financial markets.

3.1.2 Banks as Highly Regulated Institutions

Bankers have to deal with powerful regulators. In Germany, if regulatory obligations such as minimum capital requirements are not fulfilled, regulators may for example suspend the decisions of the bank's[73] management to distribute dividends, prohibit further granting of loans, and even temporarily take effective control of banks if there is a danger of default.[74] This is internationally not uncommon. Based on a World Bank survey of regulatory practices in 107 countries in 1999, Barth et al. (2001) report that more than 80 percent of the respondent countries had implemented rules that allow regulatory authorities to suspend some or all ownership rights of a problem bank.

Giving an overview of all or even only the most important banking regulations worldwide is beyond the scope of this study. Instead, a brief overview of the

---

71 E.g., Gorton and Winton (2002), Hartmann-Wendels et al. (2004). Greenbaum and Thakor (1995, p. 95) in a similar vein call commercial banks "the center of the financial intermediation universe."

72 Insurers are separated because of the above evidence on somewhat different M&A dynamics relative to banks and FSPs.

73 Legal definitions of banks differ across countries and are often broader than the definition of deposit-taking and credit-granting institutions given above, see e.g., § 1 Kreditwesengesetz (KWG) (2005) for the case of Germany. Nevertheless, banks in that sense are usually, and also in the specific case of Germany, included in regulatory banking definitions.

74 The relevant regulatory are norms are given by § 45 and 46 KWG (2005).

general reasons identified in the literature that can justify extensive bank regulation is provided.[75] Based on this, some frequently mentioned regulatory measures are reviewed. An understanding of these will later facilitate the understanding of some bank-specific motives for M&A.

According to the theory of market failure, regulatory action can be justified as a welfare-enhancing activity if there is a danger of market failure due to asymmetrical information, natural monopolies or external effects.[76] All three reasons have been used to justify bank regulation.

First, the *asymmetrical information* argument links directly to a bank's high degree of leverage and its role as a delegated monitor. Jensen and Meckling (1976) show that shareholders in highly leveraged firms have the incentives and means to expropriate creditors. Put simply, shareholders are incentivized to undertake investments, which promise high payoffs if successful, even if the overall probability of success is low. This is because if the investment is successful, shareholders have a theoretically unlimited upside while they enjoy limited liability in case of failure where most of the costs are borne by creditors.[77] Therefore, banks themselves need to be monitored. Since there is usually a large number of small depositors, no depositor is incentivized to actually perform monitoring due to the costs involved, leading to a free-riding problem. In that context, banking regulation can be justified as the public-choice solution to the "monitoring the monitor" problem that thus increases total wealth.[78]

---

75 See e.g., Dewatripoint and Tirole (1994), Bhattarchaya et al. (1998) or Freixas and Rochet (1998) for a more detailed treatment.

76 See e.g., Donges and Freytag (2001). Regulation may also be motivated (but not justified) by the self-interest of the agent who monitors (i.e., the regulatory body) or his principal (i.e., politicians), see Bittlingmeyer and Hazlett (2000). This issue is not unknown to the banking industry: Krozner and Strahan (2005) interpret US chartering restrictions and limitations on interstate banking in the US, in particular with regard to the McFadden Act of 1927, as rent-seeking measures of US States that could extract revenues only from banks chartered within their state territory. There are also recent allegations of regulatory self-interest in the context of CBBM&A in Italy, Portugal, and Poland. See footnote 39 for further details.

77 Jensen and Meckling (1976) refer to the option pricing model of Black and Scholes (1973) to make the effect even more transparent. The latter authors show that under certain circumstances the position of a shareholder of a firm that is leveraged is equivalent to the holder of a European call option on the firm value with the exercise price equal to the face value of debt and time-to-maturity equal to the maturity date of debt. The position of a bondholder is meanwhile equivalent to holding the firm plus the corresponding short call position. Since call option value increases with increasing volatility of the underlying, i.e., firm value, making the firm riskier benefits the shareholders at the expense of the bondholders.

78 Dewatripoint and Tirole (1994, pp. 31) refer to this as the "representation hypothesis."

Second, banks are sometimes argued to be *natural monopolies*.[79] The argument becomes more obvious within the model of Diamond (1984), in which there were economies of scale in monitoring and banks could diversify all risk away if they grew infinitely large. This, even though not discussed by Diamond (1984), effectively constitutes a natural monopoly. Thus, reduction of risk may come at the expense of excessive market power. The latter leads to social welfare losses and induces a necessity for regulation.

Third, it has been argued that bank failures lead to *negative external effects*.[80] If bank assets are opaque, i.e., not easily assessable by third parties, then bank failures may be interpreted by investors as signals of a bad quality of bank assets in general or of a general incentive problem of banks to adequately monitor lenders.[81] This may, in turn, cause runs on other banking institutions, even if they are fundamentally sound, leading to high liquidation costs and potentially an ultimate breakdown of the whole banking system.[82] Therefore, regulatory measures to prevent bank-runs may be required.

With regard to concrete regulatory measures that affect CBBM&A, a first interesting observation is that few countries have bank-specific antitrust laws.[83] However, several regulatory constructs, besides the general existence of a strong regulator that should act on behalf of lenders and the wider public, can have a second order effect on CBBM&A. Among the most frequently discussed are deposit insurance, minimum capital requirements, the existence of banking charters and a "lender of last resort" as well as market based monitoring measures. These are discussed in turn.

One way to prevent bank runs is to give depositors a credible guarantee that their investments are safe, even if their bank fails. Such a guarantee can be delivered via a system of *deposit insurance* that, even though the design varies, is in place in most countries.[84] While deposit insurance can prevent unfounded bank runs, it cannot mitigate the incentive effect that shareholders have to expropriate

79 See e.g., Dowd (1992) and the cited literature.

80 E.g., Freixas and Santomero (2003).

81 In addition, they may destroy firm-specific capital such as bank-client relationships and specific management knowledge.

82 Diamond and Dybvig (1983) show that bank runs need not be induced by the failure of another bank but can be simply a consequence of each investor's uncertainty about other investors' preferences.

83 Freixas and Rochet (1998) cannot identify a theoretical justification for bank-specific antitrust law. Consequently, Duursma (1999) only finds minor differences in bank-merger control relative to general merger control within Europe. In the US, however, such regulation is more prominent, see Baltensperger (1989).

84 Barth et al. (2001), report that less than 40% of the countries in the sample do not have some form of deposit insurance.

lenders. With deposit insurance in place, the problem persists but lenders cede their role to the wider public that ultimately pays for obligations of the deposit insurance. Thus, shareholders could now try to expropriate the wider public. If regulators want to prevent this, they need to price deposit insurance contingent on the riskiness of the insured assets and the level of a bank's own equity that absorbs first losses.[85] However, since the riskiness of a bank's asset is difficult to assess from the outside, this makes fair pricing of deposit insurance problematic.[86] Also, the more inclusive the deposit insurance guarantees, the less monitoring effort will be made by the market, i.e., single large lenders that would otherwise find monitoring worthwhile.

The discussion of deposit insurance has already pointed towards another regulatory measure that is well suited to address the asymmetrical information problem: the introduction of *minimal (equity) capital requirements* for banks, since the incentives for shareholders to increase risk decreases with decreasing leverage. The basis for such requirements in many countries is the agreements of the Basle Committee on Banking Supervision from 1988 (also known as "Basle I") of which an actualized and expanded version ("Basle II") is currently being discussed and has already partly been implemented.[87] One central pillar of this approach is, relative to Basle I, a more sophisticated calculation of the riskiness of specific assets and, on that basis, the calculation of the required equity necessary to absorb the potential loss of this asset.

Inducing minimal capital requirements is one way to make default more costly for shareholders. Another is to increase the value of the firm as an operating entity by restricting access to the banking market through government-granted *bank charters*.[88] However, this comes at the costs of creating monopoly rents which again lower social welfare.

Next, many regulators, or effectively the respective central banks, often explicitly or implicitly act as a "*lender of last resort*" for distressed banks. While the provisioning of such liquid facilities is in theory reserved for illiquid but solvent institutions,[89] Hughes and Mester (1993) find that in practice central banks

---

85 This can, in a similar vein to the discussion in footnote 77, again be interpreted in an option-pricing context, where the volatility of the underlying (the asset's riskiness) and the strike price (the bank's level of equity) determine the value of the "deposit-insurance option" held by the bank, see Acharya and Dreyfuss (1989).

86 Chan et al. (1992).

87 A detailed description of the new accord can be found in Basle Committee on Banking Supervision (2006).

88 See Marcus (1984) for a discussion and yet again a formal option-pricing model that shows how charter value counterbalances the moral-hazard problem of shareholders.

89 Freixas and Santomero (2003).

frequently come to the rescue of institutions that are considered too big to fail (TBTF), i.e., whose failure is supposed to lead to negative external effects for the whole economy. Obviously, shareholders may again try to take advantage of this by increasing a bank's size until it is TBTF and, thus, shift risk to the wider public.[90]

A last regulatory approach builds on the insight that, as many regulatory measures are difficult to implement, costly, and may create new problems not least because it creates the problem of efficiently "monitoring the monitor's monitor", more *market-based monitoring measures* may be needed. Measures proposed range from relatively simple approaches such as limited deposit insurance for large lenders and special disclosure requirements for banks[91] to more sophisticated proposals such as privately organized deposit insurance or to let banks hold a certain amount of subordinated debt.[92] Even though a more market-based system of bank regulation also has its critics,[93] the idea of more market-based monitoring has meanwhile become a central pillar of Basle II.[94]

Summarizing, banks are highly regulated institutions. Much of this regulation can be justified with the presence of asymmetrical information, external effects and maybe a tendency towards a natural monopoly. Hence, banks in most countries have to deal with such regulatory measures as deposit insurance, minimum capital requirements, banking charters, a "lender of last resort" and market-based monitoring. Most of these measures are designed to counter potential efforts of banks to expropriate other stakeholders and lower social welfare. However, some of the measures may cause new threats for social welfare through regulatory arbitrage by banks.[95]

3.2 Selected Characteristics of M&A

This section includes a clarification of the overall M&A terminology use in this study (3.2.1), the M&A process (3.2.2) as well as a discussion of general motives for M&A (3.2.3) and some specific considerations for cross-border M&A (3.2.4).

---

90 See O'Hara and Shaw (1990) for a more detailed discussion of the TBTF argument.

91 See e.g., the overview of market based regulatory measures in Barth et al. (2001).

92 See the literature overview provided by Harm (2002). The key idea of subordinated debt usage is to create incentives for bondholders to monitor banks and signal their monitoring outcomes to the market via bond prices.

93 Kane (1995) e.g., argues that holders of subordinated debt may well have an incentive but not the required tools to monitor banks effectively and that subordinated debt markets are usually much too shallow to give meaningful price signals.

94 Basle Committee on Banking Supervision (2006).

95 Or, alternatively, regulators that do not act in the public interest.

The latter sections also detail further the concepts of firm- and country specific characteristics as potential determinants of wealth creation.

3.2.1 Terminology

The term M&A broadly refers to a type of transaction in which two firms are combined. If a formal distinction is made between mergers and acquisitions and sometimes also other terms such as consolidation and fusion, it usually refers to whether the acquired firm (usually called the target) becomes part of the acquirer (usually called the bidder) or the two form a new entity. However, terminology is not homogenous: if the target becomes part of the bidder, this is a "merger" for Damodaran (2001, p. 835) but an "acquisition" for Grinblatt and Titman (1998, p. 666). If instead a new firm is formed, Damodaran (2001, p. 835) calls this a "consolidation" whereas the latter authors now speak of a "merger".[96] Practically, both terms are frequently used interchangeably since it is often practically difficult to distinguish between the two and distinctions usually lead to few if any insights with regard to wealth creation.[97]

What many authors consider important in an M&A definition is reference to a change in ownership in the sense of the bidder gaining effective control over the target.[98] This distinguishes M&A from other transactions such as portfolio investments or joint ventures. With regard to geography, mergers are generally considered cross-border if the headquarters of the target are not located in the same country as that of the ultimate parent of the acquirer.[99] This is to account for the fact that bidders often use previously founded or acquired institutions for a further "roll-up" of a foreign market.

Following the definition of banks given in section 3.1.1, it is tempting to define bank mergers as M&A in which one deposit-taking and loan-granting institution acquires another. Such deals, where bidders and targets are in the same industry and on the same level of the value chain, are referred to as horizontal deals.[100] However, the above discussion of the work of Piloff and Santomero (1998, 2001) and the frequent cross-border mergers between banks and others FIs identified in section 2.1 point to an intensifying convergence of loan-granting and deposit-taking institutions and other FIs. So called vertical M&A, i.e., deals in which bidder and target are still in the same industry but on different levels of

96 Grinblatt and Titmann (1998), p. 666.
97 Arnold (2005), Kerler (2000).
98 E.g., Beitel (2002), Buch and DeLong (2004), Berger et al. (2004).
99 E.g., Group of Ten (2001), Focarelli and Pozzolo (2001), Buch and DeLong (2004).
100 E.g., Arnold (2005).

the value chain,[101] are a natural means for banks and other FIs to perform such a shift and ignoring them would, hence, probably fail to account for an important motive for banks to acquire across borders.

Another common distinction of M&A refers to the target management's attitude to the deal and the means of payment used.[102] Thus, there are cash deals, in which the bidder pays in cash, and stock or cash/stock deals, in which the bidder pays fully or partly with his own stock, and friendly deals, in which the target management endorses the bid, and hostile deals, in which it rejects it.

Building on the above discussion, this study defines CBBM&A as transactions, in which two firms are combined and there is a change in ownership that leads to effective control of the bidder over the target. Furthermore, the headquarters of the target is not located in the same country as that of the ultimate parent of the bidder, both transaction partners are FIs, and at least one is a bank.[103]

3.2.2 The M&A Process

There are some specifics with regard to how CBBM&A comes about that have important consequences both on how to measure its effects and the relative importance of firm- and country-specific factors that determine its wealth effects. In particular, this is the way that a deal is phased, how information about it reaches the market, and how the target organization is legally integrated into the bidder.

With regard to the *deal phases and publicity*, deals usually start with a phase in which the potential bidder explicitely formulates his motives for an M&A and

101 See e.g., Arnold (2005) for a definition of vertical deals. These are distinguished from conglomerate deals, in which bidder and target are in entirely different industries. The nature of the financial intermediation business makes it somewhat hard to determine whether e.g., banks and brokers belong to the same industry (financial intermediation) but are on different levels of the value chain or belong to entirely different industries (e.g., banking and brokerage). Thus, there is some ambiguity with regard to distinguishing vertical and conglomerate deals. Some authors such as Seidel (1995) and Beitel (2002) have chosen to refer to deals between banks and other FIs as conglomerate deals. This study chooses the term vertical M&A in order to distinguish deals between FIs from FI-non FI deals. The acquisition history of the Australian Macquarie Bank illustrates that FI-non FI cross-border deals indeed exist, see Business Week Online (2005).

102 E.g., Grindblatt and Titman (1998) or Arnold (2005).

103 Similar definitions are used by Cybo-Ottone and Murgia (2000), Beitel et al. (2002) or Buch and DeLong (2004).

selects possible targets.[104] Knowledge accumulated in this phase is generally proprietary to the bidder. What follows is a phase of negotiation, in which the target's management is approached, positions are exchanged, and assessments adjusted. During this phase, information about the deal reaches the market. Most frequently, this happens for the first time with the official bid itself, in which the offer is officially communicated to the target's management that, in turn, informs its shareholders of the proposal and its own position on it.[105] If the – eventually adjusted – proposal is accepted, which in some cases might take months, what follows is the integration phase in which the operational integration of the two firms is conducted. While the market usually gets some information about this phase, it is often lagged and not too detailed, e.g., in the form of annual or quarterly reports that may or may not contain status reports on the integration.

With regard to the *legal integration* of the acquired institution, targets can become branches, a legal extension of the parent organization, or subsidiaries, separate legal entities incorporated under host country law.[106] The choice of organizational form depends on considerations with regard to the importance of control versus flexibility, regulation, and signaling effects.[107]

Turning first to the *control/flexibility tradeoff*, branches ceteris paribus allow for greater control over the newly acquired institution, thus facilitating wealth creation through X-efficiencies or economies of scale and scope.[108] Branches may for example only perform "front-end" functions, such as granting loans and accepting deposits, whereas "back-end" functions such as risk-management and processing are centrally delivered from the home country or a third location. Subsidiaries, however, facilitate flexibility, allow for better influencing of the environment in the host country and also sell-offs of parts or the whole of the acquired organization, should it become necessary in the future.

---

104 For the following short overview of a stylized deal process, compare e.g., Seidel (1995), Beitel (2002) and Arnold (2005).

105 However, bidder and/or target occasionally also communicate the approach before the actual bid, with or without making reference to a specific counterparty. If bidders do this and name their target, this is called an indicative or virtual bid, see Arnold (2005).

106 Other organizational forms sometimes discussed in the context of cross-border banking, such as affiliates, alliances or joint ventures, do not result in home bank control and, thus, are not related to CBBM&A. Representative offices, another sometimes discussed organizational form in the context of CBBM&A, are rather associated with small-scale greenfield investment, see Slager (2005).

107 For the following arguments and empirical findings, see Dermine (2002), Slager (2005) and the cited literature and also Miller and Parkhe (1998) and Focarelli and Pozzolo (2001).

108 See section 3.2.3 for a more detailed discussion of these motives.

Regulation, especially in the host country, usually grants subsidiaries the same rights as local banks whereas activities of branches are often severely restricted. Tax laws, despite wide variation among countries, also favor subsidiary structures as they facilitate the preservation of start-up losses, make evasion of capital gains easier and avoid tax liabilities that come about because of a conversion of a target into a branch. Furthermore, value-added taxes on (back-end) services delivered from abroad also make branch structures more costly.

Also affected are the possibilities for risk-shifting. If the intention of the deal is to exploit an unfairly priced deposit insurance system in the host country, this generally requires a subsidiary structure, since subsidiaries are covered by host country deposit insurance whereas branches generally fall under the home country system. Subsidiaries also mitigate eventual co-insurance problems as the parent organization has no legal obligation to assist a failing subsidiary abroad.[109] Greater possibilities to extract wealth from the host country are, however, countered by a larger degree of control that the host country regulators has over the bank. Also, it follows that this type of risk-shifting only affects the resources committed to the host country. If these are small compared to the total bank, total bank risk is not affected. Subsidiaries are, therefore, in practice rather considered as a tool to limit or "fence" risk increases resulting from CBBM&A.[110]

Another, potentially more rewarding, risk-shifting strategy is to assume liability for the bank in the host country (i.e., set up a branch), which will affect total bank risk, especially if the subsidiary is active in a country in which overall country risk is high. Risk-shifting inside a branch structure is also somewhat easier for banks, as branches require less public reporting and are, hence, more opaque to the outside world. This creates bidder wealth in case of an unfairly priced deposit insurance system in the home country and also facilitates wealth creation through becoming TBTF.

Another argument in the branch versus subsidiary discussion are *signaling effects*. As discussed above, shareholder have to worry about the opportunistic behavior of managers and thus are generally in favor of transparency. This favors subsidiaries, as they do not only have higher reporting requirements but also allow for a separate listing in the host country that conveys an even larger share of information to shareholders. A more subtle argument concerns asymmetric information between bidder management and incumbent target management as well as other host country stakeholders before the deal is completed. Target management may block deals or make them more costly for bidders because of oppor-

---

109 It may, nevertheless, do so because of potential reputational damage from letting a subsidiary fail.

110 Dermine (2002).

tunistic motives such as fear of job losses, loss of reputation or control. While uncertainty with regard to whether target management can stay or will be replaced is usually revealed in the negotiation phase, the exact degree of independency that an incumbent target management that stays on will retain is hard to pre-specify. Hence, target management may worry about a factual total loss of control even after being allowed to stay. Subsidiary structures are meanwhile a credible but costly signal by the bidder that he respects agreed-upon independency agreements. Similar arguments apply to other stakeholders, such as politicians or unions, that may resist takeovers by foreigners because of concrete adverse consequences such as job losses or national pride[111] and that have some power to impede deals. Again, establishing subsidiary structures that allow stakeholders to retain some control may lower resistance. In practice, the various pros and cons of the two organizational structures in sum seem to favor subsidiaries, since they are the organizational form of choice in the lion's share of all CBBM&A transactions.[112]

In summary, as a consequence of the general phasing of a deal, the majority of information about a specific transaction reaches the market, when the bidder first reveals his intent to acquire a target. This will have important implications for the methodologies of measuring the wealth impact of a deal that will be discussed next. Also, CBBM&A deals usually lead to subsidiary structures, which in turn will be important when interpreting the applicability of the results of IM studies on banking FDI.

3.2.3 General Motives

One might ask why M&A happen. This is not obvious since buyers generally pay hefty premiums, often in the 20 to 30 percent range, above the target's actual or estimated market value. Here, the literature offers several theories that identify such merger motives. Figure 3.1 gives an overview.[113]

---

111 One of the rare admittances that these factors play a role in CBBM&A has recently been given by Romano Prodi, the Italian Prime Minister. According to The Economist (2006b) and before the background of some recent CBBM&A deals in which Italian banks have been targets, Prodi noted: "Instead of always being the prey, I would like, once in a while, also to be the predator."

112 Miller and Parkhe (1998), Focarelli and Pozzolo (2001), Dermine (2002).

113 Note that a discussion of empirical evidence with regard to these motives is postponed to section 4.2, where it is analyzed in the context of determinants of wealth creation.

Figure 3.1: Motives for Banking M&A

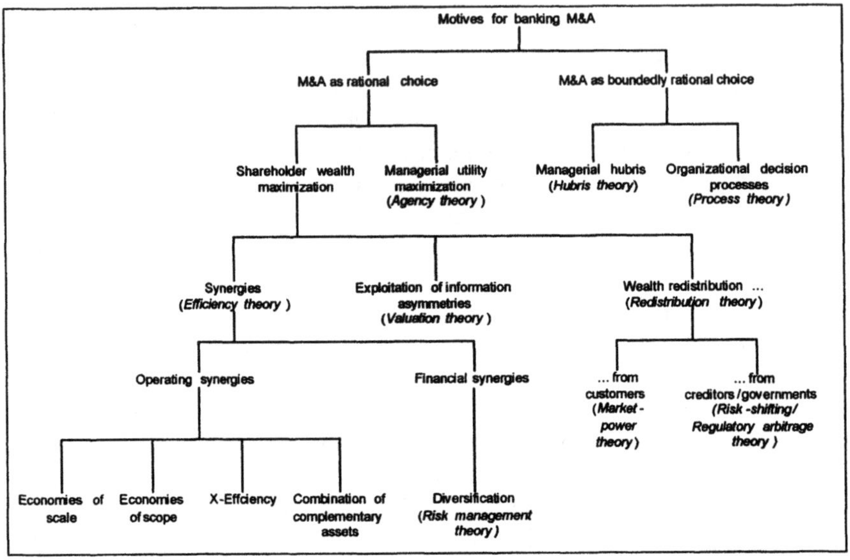

Source: Author

On the highest level of abstraction, one can distinguish between theories that regard M&A as the outcome of a decision process of actors that behave rationally and those that assume only boundedly rational decision makers. If M&A is a looked upon as a *rational choice*, approaches can be further distinguished by whom they consider the relevant decider, i.e., whose utility the decision is supposed to maximize. Possible alternatives are the firm's managers or the firm's shareholders.

Considering shareholders as the relevant decision makers, or more generally assuming that all corporate actions should be directed towards the maximization of shareholder utility, is a central assumption of the *shareholder value* approach, which has gained broad popularity in theory as well as in practice.[114] The central role of shareholders in this approach is justified with the incentives necessary to become a shareholder, i.e., a claimant of risky residual cash flows,[115] or the bene-

114 E.g., Rappaport (1998). Kürsten (2000) finds many practical shareholder value concepts to be, often erroneously, proposing firm- instead of shareholder-value maximization. In this study, shareholder value refers to the market value of equity.

115 Franke and Hax (2004).

ficial role that shareholder decision-making power has on allocative efficiency.[116] However, the shareholder value approach goes further than postulating shareholders' utility maximization to be the relevant corporate objective function. Using additional assumptions, it shows that the maximization of the market value of equity is an equivalent but much easier to act upon objective function on which all shareholders, and eventually also all creditors and other stakeholders, will agree. Since shareholder wealth maximization and related concepts are probably the most frequently named motives for banking M&A in practice[117] and because the research questions of this study imply its acceptance as a valid fundamental goal for banks, some further remarks on this concept seem due.

The additional assumptions of the shareholder value approach primarily regard the characteristics of capital markets. These are assumed to be perfect.[118] Perfect capital markets allow for the well-known Fisher Separation between consumption decisions based on individual preferences and investment decisions based on market values that holds even under uncertainty.[119] Perfect capital markets also guarantee the existence of a market value for all cash flows including all investment projects. Furthermore, market values can be easily quantified by proper discounting.[120] If corporate actions are, furthermore, assumed independent of the riskiness of cash flows to creditors (stakeholders in general) the maximiza-

---

116 Hellwig (1997).

117 See the survey results of Dalborg et al. (1999). Hartmann-Wendels et al. (2004) show that shareholder value maximization is consistent with risk-adjusted performance measures, such as "risk adjusted return on capital" that are frequently used in practical banking.

118 Perfect capital markets fulfill the conditions "competitivity" (single corporate actions do not change the valuation function used by market participants), "spanning" (cash flows resulting from corporate actions can be perfectly replicated using publicly tradable securities) and "information" (corporate actions, insofar relevant for valuation, are publicly and timely enough known to investors so that they can offset potential consequences by the means of securities trading). Additionally, markets need to be at least semi-strong efficient (public information is instantly incorporated into security prices), there are no taxes and transaction costs and securities are infinitely divisible. Jointly with assuming perfect capital markets, market participants are usually assumed to maximize expected utility, see Wilhelm (1983) or Franke and Hax (2004).

119 For this and the following, see Wilhelm (1983, 1985).

120 "Easy" is used in the sense of "easier" since many issues in properly discounting future risky cash flows, such as how to account for the value of corporate flexibility (so-called "real options"), are non-trivial. However, compared with the issues inherent in large-group decision making under uncertainty based on individual utility functions, the practical alternative to market value maximization, these issues seem well controllable, see Eisenführ and Weber (1999), for a discussion of the latter.

tion of the market value of equity leads to the same decisions as the maximization of firm (stakeholder) value.[121]

Obviously, real world capital markets are not perfect and some conditions for perfectness do not even seem close to being fulfilled. This complicates the justification of shareholder value as a reasonable fundamental goal for firms. The problem is even more severe for banks whose very existence, as discussed above, is usually explained with capital market not being perfect and whose intense regulation is (also) justified with the severe implications that management decisions can have on the riskiness of bank debt. Proponents of shareholder value maximization argue that the violation of the perfect-markets assumption should lead to a more careful application but not to abandoning the concept, especially because there is a lack of practicable alternatives.[122] This study generally agrees.[123]

It follows from the shareholder value paradigm that major corporate investment decisions, such as M&A, should primarily happen in order to increase the market value of equity. Here, with efficiency, valuation, and redistribution theory, the literature identifies three main motives how shareholder value can be created.[124] These are discussed in turn.

---

121 See Wilhelm (1983, 1985). Hartmann-Wendels et al. (2004) show that a similar logic is generally applicable to banks.

122 See Kürsten (2000) for a general argument with regard to shareholder value and Schmittmann et al. (1996), Uyemura et al. (1996), Walter, (1997) and Schuster (2000) for a bank-specific argumentation. However, many authors have also noted that, given the various necessities for banking regulation discussed above, instead of pure shareholder governance, banks may need multi-dimensional governance systems that also incorporate regulatory and therefore depositors' interests. See e.g., Harm (2002) and the cited literature.

123 While it considers shareholder-wealth maximization a reasonable fundamental goal for banks, it does not assume that other stakeholders, and especially creditors, are unaffected by a bank's actions. This allows for M&A motives that aim at increasing shareholder wealth through transfers from other stakeholders to be accounted for. Note that, while such motives and determinants related to them may play a role in practice and, thus, need to be identified, they are not socially justifiable with the usual Pareto- or Kaldor-Hicks-arguments. Also note that this is consistent with the concept of of multi-dimensional bank governance discussed in the previous footnote.

124 Trautwein (1990) also discusses Gort's (1969) disturbance theory that postulates that mergers, or rather merger waves, are caused by macro-level economic shocks that change the ordering of individual expectations and preferences leading preshock non-owners of assets to place a higher value on a specific asset then preshock owners which then leads to M&A. Next to various other theoretical issues with this theory (Trautwein, 1990), this does not seem a valid motive for M&A

Since it follows from the same assumptions that lead to the shareholder value paradigm that the acquisition of a company with a given market value only increases the acquirer's market value by the same amount and, hence, does not create value,[125] M&A only makes sense if the properly discounted present value of the cash-flows that result if the transaction occurs (including the premium paid for the target) is larger than that of the cash-fows that would have occurred in the absence of the transaction.[126] *Efficiency theory* shows how such new cash flows can come about in the form of *synergies* that can be further differentiated into operating synergies and financial synergies.

One way how operating synergies can come about are *economies of scale*, i.e., cost savings or revenue increases due to output expansion. The review of the theory of financial intermediation above has already shown that the assumption of cost economies of scale in monitoring is at the core of some approaches to explain the existence of FIs. Fixed costs digression with regard to overhead functions or branches might be other sources of cost scale economies. However, it seems less relevant for the cross-border case, as there are usually fewer if any redundant assets. Nevertheless, in practice, scale economies are one of the most frequently cited reasons for CBBM&A.[127] One explanation for this might be revenue scale economies. In that context, Berger et al. (2000) argue that wholesale customers might prefer larger over smaller banks, because they may need loan facilities or issue public debt or equity in quantities that smaller institutions cannot handle. Scale economies may also be brand-based, since brands of larger banks are generally more trusted by customers and, hence, attract more business.[128]

Another type of operating synergy stems from *economies of scope*. Such economies accrue when it is less costly or more revenue-generating to offer or produce two products jointly rather than separately. In banking, such economies are most important in the context of vertical M&A, whereby the literature puts special emphasis on the acquisition of banks by insurers (and vice versa) leading

---

since, in a shareholder value maximizing world, individual preferences are independent of investment decisions.

125 This is the value-additivity principle that states that if a given cash flow is divided up into n separate cash flows, the market value of the original cash flow equals the sum of the market values of the n cash flows. See Haley and Schall (1973) for a more detailed discussion.

126 E.g., Rappaport (1998).

127 The Economist (2006a).

128 Dermine (2002). However, to realize brand-based scale economies, the acquirer's brand value needs to be relatively higher than the target brand value in the specific host country, which is not necessarily the case.

to so-called bank assurances.[129] Cost economies of scope are usually also due to fixed cost digressions whereas revenue scope economies could stem from consumption or reputation complementarities. In the case of bank assurance, this could e.g., be the offering of bank and insurance products to customers that prefer to manage risk-reward tradeoffs with regard to their human and financial capital jointly and with the help of a single FI.

Next to economies of scale and scope, operational synergies can also come about through an improvement in the managerial quality of the new organization, e.g., by providing access to better people or processes or by changing its focus. Such efficiency changes, commonly referred to as *improvements in X-efficiency*, may happen because relatively more efficient bidders impose their supposedly superior management styles and techniques on targets or because M&A simply provides a good opportunity for restructuring.[130]

Finally, concluding the discussion on operational synergies, M&A might be a means to create wealth through *combining complementary assets* (other than products or management skills) of which at least one is scarce.[131] In the case of banking, this could be the combination of a set of products that investors value with a large branch network to distribute them (that is scarce because establishing new branches may be prohibited by law) or an advanced, proprietary risk management technology with a risky loan portfolio.

Turning to *financial synergies*, these are primarily attributed to *diversification*. Diversification with regard to bank M&A may happen because of differing, non-perfectly correlated loan portfolios[132] or generally because of non-perfectly correlated profits of the merging entities. This effect should be ceteris paribus stronger in horizontal deals and in deals where bidder and target are located in different geographies. Here, one also speaks of functional and geographic diversification. CBBM&A are obviously at least geographically diversifying.

According to risk management theory, diversification can increase firm value in various ways:[133] first and most simply, it could help investors to diversify their

129 Schierenbeck and Hölscher (1998).

130 Berger et al. (2000). A related argument can already be found in Manne (1965), who discusses the role of such transactions in the context of industry restructuring.

131 Damodaran (2001).

132 This is the type of diversification that was discussed in section 3.1.1.

133 For the following, see any of the various overviews of risk-management theory, e.g., Santomero (1985), Smith (1995), or Froot and Stein (1998). Smith (1995) notes that all of the following arguments require some sort of market imperfection since on perfect capital markets a firm's financing decisions, including changing the volatility of firm returns, do not affect firm value if the firm's investment decision are fixed, which is the Mondigliani-Miller Theorem. Nevertheless, as usual in most treatments of risk management, the authors see risk management primarily as a tool

non-systematic risk. However, such diversification at the investor level is usually dismissed as an invalid reason for M&A since individual investors, using securities markets, should be able to diversify their portfolio much more cost-efficiently than managers on a firm level.[134]

Second, lower volatility of returns lowers the probability of bankruptcy at the firm level. This creates value if bankruptcy is costly. Besides the standard arguments, e.g., legal expenses, loss of reputation or costs imposed by lenders because of anticipated distorted investment incentives of borrowers,[135] this has special relevance in banking. This is because of the potential loss of charter value that constitutes an effective loss of a monopoly position.[136] A related argument is that a lower probability of default increases a firm's debt capacity and, thus, increases the value of the tax shield.[137] This argument seems less applicable to banks as they usually have some minimum equity-capital requirement and, thus, a maximum debt level close to which they normally operate. However, simply lowering the probability of default without increasing the level of debt may effectively transfer wealth from shareholder to bondholders, which is known as the "co-insurance effect".[138] Thus, purely diversifying bank mergers can even lower shareholder value.[139]

Third, market imperfections might cause external financing of investment projects to be more costly than internal financing. Thus, investment projects that were wealth-creating using internal financing will be reduced in profitability or even be completely foregone if no internal funds are available and the firm has to resort to external funds. This makes volatility effectively costly and the reduction of volatility wealth-creating. In practice, banks indeed seem to use M&A to create such "internal capital markets", especially if outside capital markets are underdeveloped.[140]

---

to increase shareholder value, that in turn, as discussed above, presupposes perfect capital markets. This again shows that it is not unusual in finance to use the shareholder value paradigm even in situations where the necessary conditions are not strictly fulfilled.

134 Levy and Sarnat (1970). This argument holds less well if access to capital markets is extremely costly or in case of concentrated ownership. However, for the usually large and widely held banks that engage in CBBM&A, it applies well.

135 See e.g., Grindblatt and Titman (1996).

136 Allen and Santomero (1998) and the discussion in section 3.1.2.

137 Lewellen (1971).

138 See Lewellen (1971), Higgins and Schall (1975), and Galai and Masulis (1976).

139 Fabiana Penas and Unal (2004).

140 Houston et al. (1997).

Fourth, risk management can create value through reducing a firm's expected tax liability.[141] Here, the basic argument is that if the tax function is convex, which due to progressivity, limitations on the use of tax preference items etc. is true for many countries, in years when taxable income is low tax rates are low and they are high if taxable income is high. If the volatility of taxable income is reduced, tax increases in bad years will be less than tax decreases in good years, thus lowering the tax burden.[142]

While efficiency theory states that wealth increases come about through synergies, *valuation theory*, sometimes also called gold-mine-theory,[143] relaxes the assumption of symmetrical distribution of information on capital markets to show that wealth increases can also come about through the *exploitation of asymmetrical information.*[144] Banks may have more and/or better information to assess the future cash flows of other FIs than other market participants since they are industry-insiders or they may have information about them from previous interactions. If this private information suggests undervaluation, there is an incentive for better informed banks to acquire the undervalued institution and, thus, increase their own shareholder value. In the bid, the acquirer partly reveals his private information, which triggers the remaining market participants to adjust their own expectations upwards.[145] In practice, numerous references from bidder managers or other market participants to "bargain" deals support the intended exploitation of undervaluations as a deal motive.[146]

Redistribution theory, just as valuation theory, shows another way to increase bidder wealth without creating synergies. In this view, M&A is not a net-wealth increasing activity but simply induces a *wealth transfer* from other stakeholders to bidder shareholders. More concretely, wealth could be transferred from customers, bidder and target creditors or governments.[147]

---

141 See Smith and Stulz (1985).

142 Under special circumstances, such as the availability of losses that can be carried forward and made available to other firms, or the possibility to transfer profits to countries with lower tax rates, tax evasion can also looked upon as a non-risk-management related motive for M&A, see Grindblatt and Titman (1996). However, Kaplan (1989) finds the induced tax-effects usually not large enough to motivate transactions.

143 Seidel (1995).

144 Ravenscraft and Scherer (1987).

145 Note that therefore, according to this theory, bidder wealth only increases if the bidder's private information still indicates target undervaluation after the bid, the bid is successful, and the bidders expectations realize.

146 See e.g., Business Week (2004).

147 Trautwein (1990) also discusses raider theory which interprets M&A as a means to expropriate target shareholders. Since this seems somewhat far fetched in the con-

Market power theory is primarily concerned with *wealth transfers from customers*. For banks, this possibility has already been made explicit with the reference to a natural monopoly as one reason for extensive bank regulation in section 3.1.2 above. In the banking industry, the exercise of market power is usually discussed with regard to small retail customers, e.g., in the context of lower deposit or higher small business loan rates. This seems less relevant in the present context, since market power empirically only seems to be an issue if a bank can substantially increase its local market share, which is not the typical case in CBBM&A.[148] If one of the merging firms is an investment bank, there may also be the possibility to increase market power over wholesale banking customers through CBBM&A. The possibility to exert market power is diminished by general antitrust laws.

Risk-shifting theory is primarily concerned with *wealth transfers from creditors*. The discussion of the findings of Jensen and Meckling (1976) in section 3.1.2 that ultimately give rise to regulating banks in the interest of creditors have already made clear that this is a highly relevant topic for banks. It is obvious that CBBM&A can be a means to induce a risk-shift. On the one hand, the previous discussion has shown that because of this importance, banks are subject to considerable scrutinity from powerful regulators with regard to their risk profile. This obviously limits possibilities to increase shareholder wealth by risk-shifting. On the other hand, it was shown that regulation may open up new possibilities to shift risk at the expense of regulators. This is the subject of *regulatory arbitrage theory*. The above discussion on the misincentives that regulation can induce points to two concrete ways to do so. First, if there is unfairly priced deposit insurance, banks can try to increase risk and gain the potential upside while all

text of transactions in which bidders pay targets hefty premiums – which is also Trautwein's (1990) final conclusion – this theory is not taken up here. A similar argument hold for employees: while M&A in non-perfect markets can certainly have negative as well as positive consequences for them (e.g., layoffs without the prospect of future employment elsewhere, new career opportunities etc., see Beitel (2002) for a discussion), it is hard to see how wealth could be transferred from employees to bidder shareholders in M&A. Consequently, Jensen (1984) states that approaches featuring wealth transfers from employees have little factual importance.

148 Berger et al. (2000). Nevertheless, the authors also state that CBBM&A can have an indirect effect on market power in that it affects domestic consolidation (banks frequently cite a need to first grow domestically before engaging in or to deter CBBM&A), changes the competitive dynamics among cross-border institutions or enhances competitive rivalry by increasing the contestability of domestic banking markets. Since these are rather second order than first order effects of CBBM&A that do not directly translate into shareholder wealth increases, they are not discussed further.

downside is covered by the deposit insurance. Second, M&A might also make the resulting bank entity TBTF, i.e., increase their size into a range where default of the resulting institution would lead to adverse macroeconomic effects and force governments to act as a lender of last resort.

So far, shareholders and, in turn, shareholder-value maximization have been assumed to be the main drivers behind banking M&A. However, since banks, especially those that engage in cross-border M&A, are often large, widely held institutions, shareholders rarely exert direct control over decisions such as M&A. Rather, control is exerted via a professional management that shareholders appoint to act on their behalf. In a similar vein, the M&A market is frequently interpreted as a market for corporate control on which management teams rather than shareholders compete for control rights over a set of firms.[149] From this perspective, managers are the agents of mostly passive shareholders who are their principals. If management's and shareholder's incentives are perfectly aligned, this does not substantially change the above considerations. Shareholder motives simply become management motives. In practice, however, management motives might differ from those of shareholders.

From the perspective of *principal-agent theory*, it might be that *management utility maximization* is the driving factor behind M&A. External growth by the means of an M&A deal might increase managerial utility in several ways. First, firm size is often directly linked to management compensation, which is an incentive for managers to increase their level of compensation through external growth.[150] Second, growth generally implies an increase of the resources under management control. This in turn allows for an increase in indirect compensation, either through increased prestige and/or through facilitating the free consumption of perks within the managers' enlarged "private empire".[151] Third, growth might also help managers to hedge their firm-specific human capital by making third-party takeovers of their new, larger company, which might endanger management job security, more difficult to conduct.[152] Jensen (1986) shows that the risk of such management-utility-maximizing behaviour increases with the level of free cash flow available to a firm.[153] Hence such behaviour may be especially preva-

149 Jensen and Ruback (1983).

150 Bliss and Rosen (2001) present evidence for this for a sample of US banks. Interestingly, they can also show that increases in management compensation following an increase in firm size also happen independently of firm performance subsequent to the deal.

151 Roll (1986). Brickley and James (1987) present bank-specific evidence.

152 Morck et al. (1990).

153 Free cash-flow thereby is cash-flow in excess of that required to fund all projects available to the firm that have a positive net present value.

lent at banks, that are ultimately providers of liquidity. Management utility maximization as a driver of banking M&A is also consistent with frequent reports in the business press, which portray CBBM&A as the result of personal motives of top managers.[154] Finally, it is also a possible explanation for the merger paradox.[155]

In the above discussion, M&A has been considered as the consequence of a decision process by rational decision makers However, decision makers may only be *boundedly rational*. *Hubris theory*, like agency theory, stresses that M&A decisions are made by managers. These managers may try to maximize shareholder value, but they continuously overestimate their own or their organization's capability to do so successfully. In that view, M&A decisions are ultimately driven by managerial hubris.[156]

While hubris theory still presupposes a single decision maker e.g., the CEO, or a group of perfectly aligned decision makers, this is not true for *process theory*, sometimes also called organizational decision process theory. Process theory introduces two new elements into the discussion. First, firms are viewed as a complex system of deciders and deciding units, that each follow their own, often contradictory goals. This leads to the well-known problems of group decision-making under uncertainty.[157] In addition most elements of major corporate decisions[158] for complex investments such as M&A are regarded as too ambiguous and uncertain to be part of a rational decision process in the sense of prescriptive decision science.[159] Instead, heuristic organizational decision routines substitute for individual rational decisions and practically replace them.[160] Trautwein

154 See e.g., The Banker (2002).

155 Note that M&A can thus be looked upon as a mechanism to mitigate agency issues by replacing an inefficient management team by another but also as a consequence of managerial entrenchment in the bidder organization. Harm (2002), who provides a more detailed literature overview of these two perspectives, concludes that the latter effect probably prevails.

156 Roll (1986). However, Piloff and Santomero (1998) point out that the non-rational decision-making argument is not well-suited to explain a phenomenon as persistent as the merger paradox. They note (p. 72): "Perhaps managers have over-inflated egos and unrealistic views of their talents. However, elsewhere in finance we presume that reality impinges upon delusion and markets have a way of sorting things out. Why does this not occur here? The literature is silent on this point."

157 See e.g., Eisenführ and Weber (1999). Thus, implicitly, this approach regards the assumptions leading to market-value maximization as unrealistic.

158 Those are e.g., the goals of the decider, potential future states of the environment or the consequences of decisions, see Eisenführ and Weber (1999).

159 March (1994).

160 Schreyögg (1993) further differentiates this theory into organizatorial differentiation, political process and organized anarchy approaches. The first assume organi-

(1990) identifies elements of such approaches in many prevalent explanations of M&A activity. Some case studies of CBBM&A also support the general relevancy of complex organizational units with conflicting goals, political ambitions, and the power of organizational routines.[161]

What has so far not been considered are so-called *strategic motives* behind banking M&A that some author's theory explicitly add.[162] Here, one can distinguish between adaptations of strategy frameworks for banking purposes and rather ad-hoc generalizations from observed banking behavior.

Examples for adaptations of *general strategy frameworks* are Büschgen and Börner (2003) who develop generic bank strategies from the perspective of the market- and the resource-based view. This leads to an adoption of Porter's (1998) generic strategy types for banks from the market based view or a variety of strategic measures, including acquisitions, to develop a bank's "core competencies" in the resource-based view. Slager (2005) adapts Dunning's (1992) generic internationalization strategies to the banking case, leading to strategic motives such as "resource-seeking", "market-seeking" or "efficiency-seeking."

The very nature of *generalizations of observed banking behaviour* into strategic rationales makes an overview somewhat difficult. Some examples of the CBBM&A strategies identified by this approach are market entry strategies,[163] strategies to reap scale economies, foster transformation into universal banks or respond to changing regulation,[164] strategies that require following customers abroad,[165] or others that call to conquer, change or consolidate.[166]

How do these strategic motives fit into the set of motives developed above? A possible starting point is to note that the term strategy refers to both fundamental and instrumental goals of a firm.[167] In that sense, a shareholder value-maximizing strategy refers to a fundamental goal, namely shareholder value maximization.

---

zations to be complex systems of decision makers and decision-making units with partly conflicting goals and relatively simple decision-making routines. The second views decisions as the outcomes of political games played by the members of an organization in a constant struggle for scarce resources. The third and most radical views decisions as more or less random outcomes of an also more or less random interaction of problems, decision-making opportunities, solutions, and deciders.

161 E.g., Björkmann and Vara (2006).

162 E.g., Beitel (2002), Achleitner (1999). Note that since the strategy literature is rather broad, the following discussion focuses on bank-specific results.

163 Beitel (2002).

164 Canals (1997).

165 Williams (2002).

166 De Carmoy (1990).

167 See Grant (1998) for a discussion on the role of strategy and Eisenführ and Weber (1999) for a discussion of fundamental and instrumental goals.

Strategies such as "gaining market share" or "acquiring new resources" refer to instrumental goals as they implicitly assume a relationship between market share or resources and some fundamental goal, usually shareholder wealth maximization.[168]

Seen in this way, all of the identified strategic motives are ultimately instrumental goals for shareholder wealth maximization. This is obvious in those cases where the strategy exactly corresponds to a motive in figure 2.1 below the "shareholder value" level. This is, e.g., the case for the "scale economy" strategy. However, the only difference for the other strategic motives identified is that they either refer to a more concrete way, how the generic motives can be realized or are effective combinations of these generic motives. Thus, a strategy that requires "following the customer" effectively shows a way to realize scale economies.[169] Porter's (1998) generic "cost leadership" strategy can be shown to be one way of creating wealth by simultaneously leveraging scale economies and market power.[170]

Thus, the strategy perspective does not identify any new motives but shows ways how to realize different motives concretely and how to combine the different levers.[171] Since these arguments turn up again in the IM literature that tries to pinpoint what is specific to CBBM&A, their discussion is postponed to the next section which reviews these contributions.

3.2.4 Specific Considerations for Cross-Border M&A

The discussion above has provided various bank specific examples to illustrate the relevance of the identified motives for M&A. Some motives, such as regulatory arbitrage, were shown to be of special importance in the banking industry. Others, such as diversification, were also shown to be of special importance in cross-border deals. However, in general, the discussion was led from a CF perspective, causing the identified motives to remain somewhat generic. To add a cross-border banking perspective, attention is now shifted towards the IM litera-

---

168 Firms may certainly follow such strategies for their own sake, hence making them a fundamental goal. This is, however, hard to justify using economic theory.

169 See section 4.2.2 for a more detailed discussion of the "follow the client" argument.

170 Büschgen and Börner (2003).

171 However, note that strategic motives, especially if their impact on shareholder value is hard to quantify, may also be an effective veil that managers can use to disguise actions that maximize their own utility.

ture which is specifically concerned with banking foreign direct investment (FDI).[172]

Theories from the field of IM that aim to identify motives for banking FDI have generally developed in parallel as special cases of general FDI theories. In an early contribution, Aliber (1976) applies standard comparative advantage theory to the banking sector. In this view, some countries possess idiosyncratic comparative advantages in producing banking services and profit-maximizing banks from these countries will prevail over foreign banks, i.e., force them out of the market. This process is slowed down by barriers to trade in financial services, which cause banks to set up or acquire facilities abroad rather than trade services across borders.

Grubel (1977) adds three further motives for banking FDI. First, geographic diversification is assumed to enhance value. Second, in an application of Kindleberger's (1969) theory of surplus entrepreneurship, FDI is seen as a consequence of surplus managerial resources that can be cheaply leveraged abroad. Third, expansion is assumed to be triggered by the behavior of existing clients. If clients expand abroad, banks have an incentive to follow since existing knowledge about the client can be applied abroad at low marginal costs which allows the realization of scale economies.[173] This is the "follow the client" argument already encountered above that dates back to Brimmer and Dahl (1975).[174]

These discussed early approaches already offer some interesting insights. Reassuringly, this literature does not offer other motives than the ones discussed above. Instead, the usual suspects such as economies of scale or diversification turn up again and it becomes evident that the realization of these motives is determined by firm-level characteristics, e.g., managerial resources or existing clients abroad, and country- and market-level characteristics, such as "idiosyncratic comparative advantages" or "market deficiencies." This is not entirely new for CF theory that also relates motives, such as X-efficiency improvements or economies of scale, to characteristics such as firm efficiency or firm size. However the characteristics discussed by the IM literature are more cross-border-specific and there is a greater emphasis on the country- and industry-level, probably due to the origins of this literature in international economics. However, the identified firm level characteristics in this early IM literature rarely seem ex-

172 Therefore, it also covers motives for greenfield investments or joint ventures. However, as CBBM&A is by far the most important means of banking FDI (UNCTAD, 2000), this does not seem to be a serious issue.

173 Rugmann and Verbeke (1993), Williams (1997).

174 Some authors add that this expansion may also help to "defend" the client against capture by a foreign competitor, it has also been termed "defensive expansion", see Williams (2002).

haustive as, e.g., functional diversification, efficiency- or even agency-related motives are mostly left unconsidered. In addition, the corresponding country/industry-level characteristics seem somewhat vague as it remains unclear, what the specific country-characteristics are, that allow a country to develop a comparative advantage at im- or exporting financial institutions M&A. Both, a more thorough consideration of firm-level characteristics and more granular insights into the nature of country-specific comparative advantages are consequently at the core of the subsequent IM literature. Two prominent examples from this literature are internalization and OLI theory, which are discussed in turn.

One theory deemed able to frame the internationalization decision of banks is internalization theory that, in turn, draws upon the Coasian theory of the firm.[175] Within internalization theory, markets are imperfect due to transaction costs stemming from negotiating contracts. By owning complementary assets, a firm is able to internalize these externalities and, hence, reduce transaction costs. Internalization in the form of FDI happens whenever transactions can be more efficiently handled internally or cannot be conducted via markets at all. Rugman (1980) notes that banks as firms, for which exchange of information is key, have strong incentives to internalize, i.e., set up their own foreign locations or acquire foreign institutions as markets for the exchange of information are underdeveloped. More concretely, monitoring costs for bank are supposed to increase with distance to the lender, making banking FDI more cost-efficient than the export of financial services. In a similar vein, Williams (1997) interprets an earlier theory of banking FDI in an internalization context: in that view Aliber's (1976) "barriers to trade" are market failures in a Coasian sense which ultimately lead to internalization of comparative advantages rather than their export. These barriers are also identified as an unstated assumption behind Grubel's (1977) application of the surplus entrepreneurship theory. Finally, Williams (1997) also finds “the follow the client” explanation consistent with internalization theory, as trading information about existing clients is prohibitively costly in a market setting, leading again to internalization, i.e., to following the customer.

Overall, internalization theory shows why firm and market characteristics need to be considered jointly when identifying determinants of CBBM&A: both influence the relevant transaction costs. However, while providing a good frame for thinking about CBBM&A, internalization theory has also been criticized as difficult in the sense that it results in frameworks that either tend to be too broad, summing up all types of different determinants under the general label of "trans-

175 Coase (1937). Kutschker and Schmidt (2005) discuss the general application of transaction cost theory to FDI decisions.

action cost influencing", or too narrow, covering only a set of factors too specific for application to an individual industry.[176] Consequently, even proponents of the application of internalization theory to banking FDI concede that so far the theory has not been able to generate many empirically testable hypotheses.[177]

The OLI-framework, based on the work of John Dunning (1977) and subsequent adaptations,[178] is widely considered an alternative holistic approach to a firm's FDI decisions.[179] OLI states that three types of advantages that have their roots in industrial-organization-theory (ownership advantages), location-theory (location advantages), and internalization theory (internalization advantages) determine a multinational's decision to invest abroad and the mode of investment. Since it is grounded in different distinct theories, OLI is also called the eclectic paradigm.[180]

Ownership-specific advantages are equal to firm-specific characteristics which allow the disadvantage of being foreign to be overcome. Location-advantages are, in turn, grounded in host and home country and the industry characteristics of the multinational. Finally, internalization advantages stem from the internalization of activities that are too costly to be performed on markets. OLI-theory predicts that a firm will only choose to conduct FDI if it possesses all three types of advantages and location advantages favor the host relative to the home country.

A first comprehensive application of OLI-theory to banking is by Yannopolous (1983) who identifies e.g., a broad product portfolio, size or experience abroad as relevant ownership advantages.[181] Identified locational advantages consist of such factors as the regulatory and political situation in the host, non-financial-FDI from home to host countries (as a proxy for clients abroad) as well as physical proximity, whereas the main internalization advantage is the existence of information as an intermediary product that cannot effectively be traded on markets. Subsequent authors have added other variables for each type of advantage.[182]

---

176 Kutscker and Schmidt (2005).

177 Williams (1997).

178 See Dunning (2000) for an overview.

179 Williams (1997).

180 Dunning's work is generally rather viewed as a framework than a theory. In later contributions (Dunning, 2000), the author agrees.

181 An earlier application by Gray and Gray (1981) is generally considered too narrow. See Williams (1997) for a discussion.

182 See e.g., Cho (1986). Note that Yannopolous (1983) regards the existence of home country clients in the host as a country-specific factor, primarily because it is measured with a country-level variable. One might also argue that this variable is only a proxy for firm-specific relationships that are, however, more difficult to measure.

Dunning's approach has been widely praised for its integration potential that at least partly manages to overcome the strong partial character of earlier theories. It has been called the reigning approach, both for international business in general[183] and for banking internationalization in particular.[184] Nevertheless, it is also subject to some criticism. Much of this, especially in the context of international banking, has focused on the role of ownership advantages which especially proponents of internalization theory do not consider relevant. Their argument is that the concept of ownership advantages focuses on a single cost-benefit relationship, namely the cost of overcoming the disadvantage of being foreign. Instead, the trade-off should be between total costs and total benefits within a transaction cost framework.

Dunning's subsequent reaction to the critique, namely the integration of internalization-theory into his framework and, later, the distinction between two types of ownership advantages (asset-based ownership advantages and ownership advantages stemming from transaction advantages) has, in turn, led to a debate in the literature, whether this does not in fact make internalization and ownership-advantages indistinguishable, adding yet another inconsistency to the framework.[185] Most empirical IM work on banking FDI that uses OLI has responded to this debate by ignoring the notion of internalization advantages and identifying and testing only ownership and location advantages.[186]

In summary, IM theory stresses the importance of both firm- and country/industry-specific characteristics that determine how well a specific FDI motive can be realized. There is no predominant theory to identify such factors as early approaches only offer partial explanations and more holistic theories seem either too general or suffer from theoretical discrepancies. Therefore, it is not surprising that the identification of concrete factors together with their effect on FDI have been left to empirical studies. The latter generally use simplified versions of OLI or a wide range of – sometimes ad-hoc – theories and frameworks to identify specific firm- and/or country-level characteristics, that potentially determine banking FDI.[187] For that reason, a discussion of specific factors is postponed to the review of empirical evidence on determinants of CBBM&A in section 4.2.

---

183 E.g., Eden (2003), p. 280.
184 E.g., Focarelli and Pozzolo (2001), p. 2306.
185 Williams (1997).
186 Sagari (1992), Buch and DeLong (2004).
187 See Buch and DeLong (2004), Wezel (2004) and section 4.2.3, especially table 4.6.

3.3 Methods for Measuring M&A Success

In the following, the most frequent methodological approaches to measure M&A success including their specific advantages and drawbacks are discussed. The reviewed methodologies are event studies (section 3.3.1), OP and DE studies (section 3.3.2), and case studies (section 3.3.3)

3.3.1 Event Studies

Event studies are probably the most frequently used method to measure wealth effects. This method, sometimes also called residual analysis or abnormal performance index tests, is concerned with measuring the impact of the information content of an event on security price behavior up to and concurrent with the event-type in question. First applications can already be found in the early 30s,[188] but the methodological foundations for the research set-up still used today were laid in the seminal papers of Ball and Brown (1968) and Fama et al. (1969). Since then, the use of the method has flourished: Khotari and Warner (2004) estimate that a minimum of 565 event-studies have been published since the mid-70s, counting only a limited number of highly reputable journals. MacKinlay (1997) calls the field of CF perhaps the most successful application of the method and uses the field of value effects of M&A as a prominent example.

3.3.1.1 Description of Methodology

The basic idea of event studies is simple. It is assumed that capital markets are at least semi-strong efficient, i.e., that security prices react instantaneously and in an unbiased fashion to publicly available new information. The wealth effects of an unanticipated event will then immediately be reflected in security prices. Measuring this effect on security holder-wealth is achieved in the following steps:[189] first, the event in question, i.e., the point in time when information about the M&A deal reaches the market needs to be determined. Since, as discussed above, most information about a deal reaches the market at the announcement date of the deal, i.e., the day, when bidder and/or target announce the intent to merge in the press, this is usually also assumed to be the event date. The assumption of instantaneous incorporation of information in stock prices suggests analyzing the security price behavior of the bidder and/or target only at the time of information

188 See MacKinlay (1997) for a short historical overview.
189 See MacKinlay (1997).

revelation. However, this yields a set of potential problems in practice: accurate information about the event date might be lacking or, even if a particular day can be pinpointed, information might have leaked or market participants might only after some time be able or ready to trade on the information.[190] Therefore, the usual procedure is to define a time window of a few days around the event, the so-called event window. In the large number of domestic banking M&A studies, this event window typically covers about 21 days, including the event day itself.[191]

Second, a sample of deals, together with information on the event dates and the concurrent stock price information is selected. A typical sample used in studies on the effects of domestic banking M&A usually covers between 90 and 120 deals.[192] After the sample, together with information on the event dates and the concurrent stock price information, is selected, the focus of interest is to measure the unexpected change in shareholder wealth or abnormal returns (ARs) that can be attributed to the event. This is defined as the difference between the actual observed return and the expected return unconditional on the event, the so-called "normal return". Define t = 0 as the event date. For share i at date t relative to the event, the AR is given by

$$(1)\ AR_{it} = R_{it} - K_{it}$$

where R_{it} and K_{it} are the actual and normal or expected return. While the former is observable on securities markets, the latter needs to be calculated using an expected return model. Besides the choice of such a model, this also requires the estimation of model parameters.

Event studies are concerned with finding out whether a class of events, such as M&A is, on average, associated with changes in shareholder wealth. For that purpose, cross-sectional and/or time-series aggregation of abnormal returns becomes important and a specific aggregation method needs to be selected. One of the most frequent approaches to aggregate abnormal returns is first averaging abnormal returns over securities and then additively aggregating them over time.

190 Seidel (1995) in his analysis of bank-merger-related press announcements e.g., finds that many announcements are made on fridays with an explicit request for publication only after the end of the trading day to give investors some time to assess the information accurately.

191 This is the median number of days in the event window based on the review of 35 short-term event studies on domestic banking M&A reviewed in section 4.1.1.

192 The average number of bidders (targets) (joint bidder-target entities) in the 35 domestic banking M&A studies reviewed in section 4.1.1 is 89 (115) (119).

This leads to the so-called cumulative abnormal return (CAR) for a specific time window and a group of securities.[193]

Finally, for this aggregated return measure, a test statistic is computed and compared to its assumed distribution under the null hypothesis, e.g., that the event has no impact on the distribution of expected returns. Inferences can be drawn about target- and bidder-abnormal returns and the joint-target-bidder-entity.

Event studies can be further classified by the time-horizon investigated. Event windows that are much longer than the 21 days discussed above are obviously more difficult to reconcile with the standard assumption of semi-efficient capital markets. Nevertheless, there is evidence that certain events, among them M&A and specifically banking M&A, lead to systematic non-zero long-term abnormal returns. These studies back the hypothesis that markets can under- or overreact, only gradually and over time correct their estimates and are, hence, not generally efficient.[194] Based on this observation, some researchers have conducted event studies with post-event windows of 1 year or more which are commonly referred to as long-term event studies.[195]

3.3.1.2 Potential Drawbacks of Methodology

Event studies offer a theoretically sound, direct way to measure the wealth impact of M&A which allows effects on bidders, targets, and the joint entity to be separately estimated. In addition, they are based on market data which is less likely to be distorted by measurement problems, accounting conventions and one-time deal related transaction costs than accounting information.[196] This is even more relevant if, as in the case of CBBM&A, multiple countries with multiple accounting conventions are involved.

However, also the event study methodology has its drawbacks, which are mainly related to violations of the underlying assumptions. In order to understand the limitations of event studies and to later help model an adequate testing approach, these are reviewed next. Table 3.1 gives an overview of the relevant issues, that are discussed in turn.

---

193 Since returns are cumulated over time and averaged over securities, cumulative average abnormal return would probably be the more appropriate term. However, the former has become the standard term in the literature.

194 See section 4.1.2 for details.

195 Khotari and Warner (2004).

196 Piloff and Santomero (1998).

Table 3.1: Potential Drawbacks of Event Studies

Issue	Relevancey for... Short-Term Studies	Long-Term Studies
Market Efficiency	*Medium/High*: Results questionable if markets are not efficient	*None*: Approach is an implicit test of market efficiency
New information	*Low/Medium*: Results biased if event window does not suffice to capture leakage	*None/Low*: Leakage, if present, not too relevant since focus on post-event window
Confounding events	*Low*: Probability of confounding events in small window negligible	*High*: Confounding events in large windows almost unavoidable, potential impact high
Bad model	*Low*: Choice of model mostly irrelevant for results	*High*: Unavoidable model error becomes more relevant with increasing time horizon
Aggregation method	*Low/Medium*: Additive aggregation methods with favorable statistical properties applicable. Potentially some adjustments necessary	*High*: Multiplicative aggregation methods necessary to appropriately reflect investor experience, causing serious methodological issues
Event clustering	*Low*: Probability of simultaneous events in small window negligible	*High*: Event-clustering in large window almost unavoidable, results probably biased
Sample selection	*Medium*: Samples restricted to listed firms	

Source: Author

If capital markets are not semi-strong efficient and instead systematically underreact, e.g., to a bad investment decision by the bidder or overreact, e.g., to usually good pre-merger acquirer performance, inferences based on a short event window around the time of announcement deliver an incomplete picture.[197] Given the complexity, size, and time scale of mergers, such under- or overreaction seems at least possible. Furthermore, as discussed above, some studies of long-term acquirer performance[198] indicate long-term abnormal losses of bidders following M&A. Obviously, this is only an issue for short-term studies as long-term studies implicitly test for market efficiency.

Also primarily relevant for short-term studies is the "leakage" issue: if the information about the firms intending to merge is not completely new to the mar-

---

197 Fama (1998).

198 Studies usually restrict themselves to acquirer performance because targets tend to be delisted post-deal.

ket, the measured reaction only captures the delta between previous investor expectation and the realized action and not the wealth impact of the realized action alone. One possibility for this to happen is the leakage of information prior to the deal announcement.[199] But even if there is no leakage, investors will naturally form expectations about a firm's acquisition behavior. This is especially likely if the bidder follows a dedicated long-term acquisition strategy or the target has been "in the game" before.[200]

Another issue is the potential presence of confounding events. These are events other than the one in question within the analyzed time window which have a sufficiently strong effect on firm value. Because of these, the measured net abnormal return effect may no longer be attributable only to the original event.[201] The risk of confounding events is obviously dependent on the analyzed time horizon and the relative importance of the announced event: if a bank acquires another bank of similar size, the bidder share price reaction on the event day will probably entirely be driven by the acquisition. However, movements in the share price movements of a large multinational bank two years after it aquired a much smaller institution somewhere abroad are probably completely unrelated to this deal.

Next, all event studies are joint tests of the hypotheses posed, e.g., the absence of abnormal returns in the analyzed event window, and the model of expected returns used. This is insofar a problem, as finance theory currently cannot offer a commonly accepted model of the true return-generating process.[202] For short-term studies, this is not an issue: simulation experiments find that even simple normal-return models lead to well specified and powerful test statistics and that results are largely independent of model choice.[203] The reason for these at

---

199 Leakage does not necessarily imply unethical behavior. The majority of M&A-studies define the event date as the announcement date of the decision by the respective companies. It is meanwhile not unusual for companies to communicate that there are "merger talks" ongoing before an actual announcement which can also be interpreted as leakage.

200 Note that in the introductory Banco Santander/Abbey National example, both factors were given.

201 McWilliams and Siegel (1997).

202 Fama (1998).

203 Brown and Warner (1980, 1985). These studies use sample portfolios of randomly selected shares which are replicated using simulation methodology. Since randomly selected shares (and their replications) should on average not display abnormal performance, the null hypothesis of no abnormal performance is assumed true and the samples are used to assess the specification of standard t-tests. After that, abnormal performance is artificially induced so that, for a given level of significance and abnormal performance, the power of tests can be analyzed.

first sight surprising results is that, given short event windows, errors in calculating abnormal performance are unlikely to matter since daily expected returns are close to zero across all models.[204] The issue, however, becomes strongly relevant in long-term studies.

Event studies can also have issues with regard to the aggregation of abnormal returns. As discussed above, short-term studies usually average returns over securities and additively aggregate them over time. The resulting CAR-measure can be adjusted relatively easily for the violation of assumptions in the used normal return model, such as heteroscedastic returns, and has generally favorable statistical properties.[205] It does, meanwhile, not appropriately reflect actual investor experience as compounding effects and transaction costs are disregarded[206] and can lead to biased measures of appropriately compounded returns which more closely reflect actual investor experience.[207] If such appropriate compounding in the form of buy-and-hold abnormal returns (BHARs) is performed, this may lead to skewed return measures of abnormal returns. Various simulation studies[208] have shown this skewness bias to be so severe that the central limit theorem is not applicable even in very large samples, rendering traditional t-tests biased. Again, the issue of return aggregation is rather relevant for long-term studies, as multiplicative and additive aggregation of returns lead to similar results in short time windows.[209]

Event studies can also become problematic if the events under consideration are clustered, i.e., share the same event windows. This leads to cross-sectional dependence of returns of the firms involved which increases the variance of the sample mean return and biases test statistics, especially if the sample firms all

---

204 Khotari and Warner (2004) show that misestimation of securities beta, a parameter in one of the most commonly used normal return models, by 30% would lead to misestimation of abnormal returns in the order of 0.06 percent in a 3-day-window which is most likely to be unimportant, since typical bidder abnormal returns are in the order of 1 percent and target abnormal returns are several multiples higher.

205 See the more detailed, technical discussion in section 5.2.1.3.

206 To see the transaction cost argument more clearly, note that additively aggregated returns are equivalent to the proceedings from a trading strategy which invests equal amounts of money in all securities under consideration at the beginning of the trading period. Then, at the end of the trading period, the portfolio is rebalanced so that total wealth is again equally distributed across securities. In contrast, proceedings from multiplicative aggregation, i.e., compounding, are similar to a less transaction-cost-intensive strategy, that simply holds the selected securities until the end of the investment period, see Bowman (1983). This is also why multiplicatively aggregated returns are often referred to as buy-and-hold abnormal returns.

207 Barber and Lyon (1997).

208 E.g., Lyon et al. (1999), Erhardt and Koerstein (2001).

209 Fama (1998).

belong to the same industry. Again in the case of M&A, clustered events are highly unlikely if event windows consist of a few days but become almost inevitable if multi-year windows are used. Last but not least, event study methodology requires the security prices involved to be known which requires that the securities involved are publicly traded. This usually reduces sample sizes and the quality of the inference.

In summary, event studies suffer from a variety of issues that can bias their results. Overall, these issues are much more serious in long-term studies. Therefore, their results have to be interpreted with extreme caution.[210]

3.3.2 Operating Performance and Dynamic Efficiency Studies

While event studies are concerned with wealth effects based on investor expectations, OP and DE studies analyze actual changes in efficiency after M&A transactions based on publicly available accounting information. OP and DE studies, however, differ in the degree of sophistication with which changes in efficiency are estimated.

3.3.2.1 Description of Methodology

OP studies compare changes in profit-, cost- and sometimes also risk-ratios, i.e., simple relations of different types of accounting information, of a group of merging banks before and after the merger. Those changes are then interpreted relative to changes in a control-group of non-merging banks. Time periods, ratios used, and tests performed vary across studies. A look at the review of 25 bank-specific OP studies at Beitel (2002) and an earlier, comparable review of Rhoades (1994) gives a good idea of the usual setup: on average, data from approximately 2.5 years before the merger until 4 years after the merger is used. Most frequent ratios are return on assets (ROA), return on equity (ROE), and non-interest-expenses to total assets. Usually, studies then employ univariate t-tests to compare operating ratios before and after the merger or use multiple regressions to control for other factors in testing whether changes in performance can be explained by merger activity.

DE studies are structurally similar to operating performance approaches in that they use accounting information to infer merger related efficiency-changes.

210 Compare e.g., Kothari and Warner (2004). Lyon et al. (1999, p. 165) conclude that, even using the best available methods, "the analysis if long-run abnormal returns is treacherous".

However, they use methodology from production economics to get more differentiated results, such as separated market-power- and efficiency-effects and breakdowns in efficiency to different types, e.g., technical and allocative efficiency as well as scale and scope efficiencies. To calculate efficiency measures from production economics, the production function of the firm in question, or alternatively, using the duality-principle, its cost, revenue or profit function must be estimated. Since best-practice firms, relative to which estimation is usually performed, are said to operate on the "efficient frontier", DE studies are also called "frontier approaches".

DE studies are far less homogenous then the approaches previously discussed and, due to differing methodologies within the DE approach, the comparison of results is sometimes difficult.[211] Nevertheless, one large conceptual difference across methods is the way in which the cost and profit functions are estimated.[212] The methods used can be divided into nonparametric approaches, especially data envelopment analysis (DEA) and free disposal hull analysis (FDHA) and parametric approaches, which consist of the stochastic frontier approach (SFA), the distribution free approach (DFA), and the thick frontier approach (TFA).[213]

Nonparametric approaches require relatively little ex-ante specification of the production function, the efficient frontier or behavioral assumptions. Instead, the frontier is constructed piece-wise over observed "best-practice" firms, using linear programming methods. "Best-practice" firms are, in turn, those for which no other firm (or linear combination of other firms) has more output (input) per unit of input (output). Efficiency is then determined relative to firms on the efficient frontier.

A simple, bank-specific example of how DEA works based on Ramanathan (2003) might help to further illustrate the key concepts of DE methods. Assuming a simple banking production function with two inputs (labor and capital, measured in number of employees and units of currency) and one output (number of customer accounts), figure 3.2 shows the relative efficiencies of 4 banks (points

---

211 Berger and Mester (1997, p. 896) in this context state that DE approaches often seem to be a "black box".

212 Another criterion for differentiation is the way the production process in banking is principally interpreted and, therefore, what is regarded as typical input or output. Here, the production, intermediation, asset, value-added and the user-cost approach can be identified (Di Salvo et al., 2000). But with the possible exception of deposits, there is a broad consensus in the literature as to which inputs should typically be used in which estimation method (Berger et. al, 1997). Therefore, this differentiation is not taken up here.

213 The following draws on Berger and Humphrey (1997), Coelli et al. (1998) and Kumbhakar and Knox-Lovell (2000).

A-D) in a diagram, whereby the axes show how much one of the respective inputs is used to produce the respective units of output.

Since banks A and C have input/output mixes that are not dominated by other banks, they form the efficient frontier, i.e., the effective benchmark for the other banks (line ECAG). To measure the efficiency of one of the other banks, e.g., B, relative to the efficient frontier, its theoretical optimal performance (OF) is compared to its actual performance (OB), the ratio of which indicates how close the bank operates to its efficient frontier. In the case of bank B, the ratio of OF to OB (0.43) indicates that the bank currently operates at 43 percent of its theoretically maximal efficiency.

FDH-approaches are a special case of DEA. Other than DEA, it does not assume that substitution is possible between different input (output) combinations, thus leading to a more restricted efficient frontier.

Figure 3.2: Illustrative Dynamic Efficiency Approach

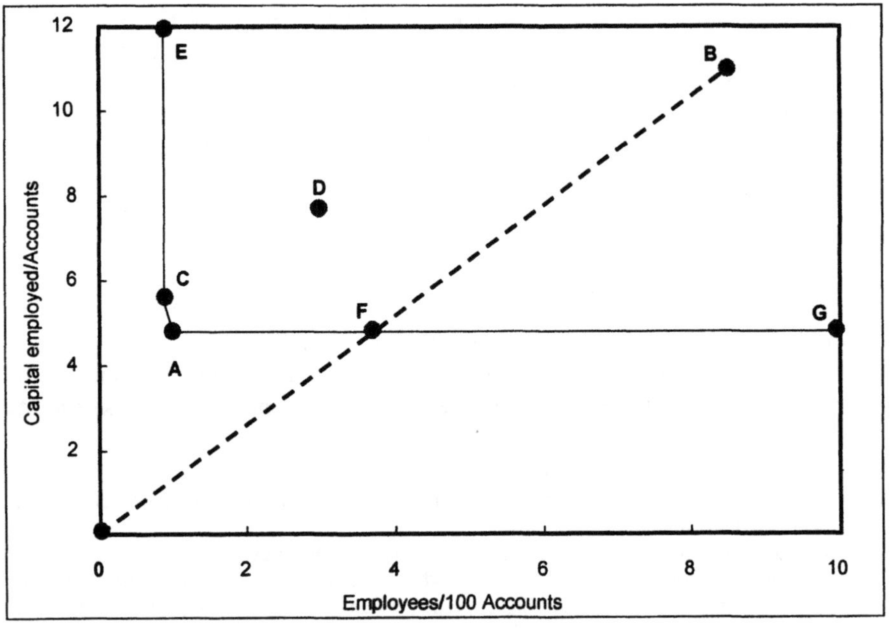

Source: Adapted from Ramanathan (2003)

Parametric approaches do pre-specify a functional form of the underlying production relationship but also account for noise, both in the form of stochastic efficiency and random error. Parametric approaches basically vary by the way in which this noise is accounted for. The SFA is based on a composite error model, where inefficiencies are assumed to follow an asymmetric distribution, usually the half-normal,[214] while random-error follows a symmetric distribution. Unlike the SFA, the DFA makes no strong assumptions regarding the specific distribution of the inefficiencies or the random error. Instead, it assumes that inefficiencies are stable over time, whereas random error averages out to zero. Finally, the TFA assumes that deviations from predicted performance values within the highest and lowest quartiles of the observations represent random error, while deviations between those quartiles represent inefficiencies.

Early DE studies of banking M&A almost exclusively focus on cost-efficiency. Cost-efficiency takes outputs as given and measures how close a bank's cost is to what a best practice bank's cost would be for producing the same output under the same conditions. This implicitly assumes that banking M&A have only cost-minimizing rationales which is not necessarily true. Minimum costs at any given output-level also do not necessarily imply cost-efficiency at the optimal output level. Standard profit efficiency addresses this by measuring how close a bank is to earning the profits of a best-practice firm that operates under the same circumstances, taking input and output prices as given. This then implies the more realistic assumption of profit maximization.[215] Similar to operating performance studies, changes in efficiency are usually measured relative to a control group of non-merging banks.

3.3.2.2 Potential Drawbacks of Methodology

Compared to short-term event studies, OP and DE studies focus on actual observed results rather than on expectations at the announcement date and, thus, have the advantage of "hindsight over foresight".[216] Nevertheless, they are also plagued by several issues. Analogous to event studies, the issues and the respective relevance for the two approaches, an overview of which is given in table 3.2., are discussed in turn.[217]

---

214 In order to let inefficiencies not become negative.

215 A third efficiency concept is alternative profit efficiency which also measures the degree to which profits are maximized, but, other than standard profit efficiency, takes output quantities as given while output prices are variable. This may, for example, be adequate when the quality of banking services differs greatly. The "price" of this alternative version are problems with controlling for market-power effects (since prices are not controlled for) or potential failure to capture efficiency increases from changes in the output mix (which is held constant), see Berger (1998).

216 Caves (1989), p. 1.

217 For the following, compare Rhoades (1994), Berger (1998) and Vittas (1991).

Table 3.2: Potential Pitfalls of Operating Performance and Dynamic Efficiency Studies

Issue	Relevancey for... OP studies	DE studies
Wealth measurement	*High*: No direct measurement of wealth changes or wealth distribution possible	
Confounding events	*High*: Confounding events in large windows almost unavoidable, potential impact high	
Accounting data	*Medium/High*: Comparability and adequacy of data, especially in cross-border context, questionable	*Medium*: Adequacy of input-data, especially in cross-border context, questionable
Assumptions on production function	*Medium/High*: Results biased by differences in capital structure/output mix	**Parametric approaches** *Low/Medium:* Depending on functional form assumptions. All approaches problematic in cross-border context.
		Non-parametric approaches *Medium/High*: Assumptions on functional form rather unproblematic, however no controls for stochastic effects and focus on technical efficiency.

Source: Author

First and foremost, both OP and DE approaches measure changes in efficiency but cannot measure changes in wealth directly, let alone for different groups of stakeholders. Undoubtedly, such changes are linked to wealth changes and may well be their most important driver. However, neither are they the only driver nor is the relationship between efficiency and wealth changes known.

Second, both approaches have a confounding event problem similar to event studies: while rather short observation periods of ratios after the M&A may not capture long-term efficiency changes, it is unclear if longer-term changes are still attributable to the original event in question or rather to an increasing level of noise.

Third, both approaches rely on accounting data which is per se not without problems. Accounting measures are inherently backward-looking, do not necessarily reflect economic values and, in addition, may differ across banks e.g., with respect to the treatment of inflation, asset- and liability-valuation, the level of provisioning, the use of "hidden reserves," and also leave individual banks a large discretionary freedom of how to use them. This issue is undoubtedly larger with OP approaches, which rely directly on accounting data rather than using it as an input. However, biased inputs can lead to biased outputs in DE approaches.

Fourth, some of the underlying assumptions when directly comparing efficiency measures for different banks, especially across countries, are problematic. With regard to OP measures, differences in capital structure e.g., easily distort some of the more frequently used ratios, e.g., operating-asset-ratios, which relate revenues and costs to average assets (e.g., ROA): banks with higher equity e.g., usually pay less interest expenses and, thus, have higher interest margins leading to a higher net income and a higher ROA. The production cost of a bank will also differ with the output mix which is usually all but homogenous across banks. The application of both operating-asset (e.g., cost-to-assets) and operating income (e.g., cost-income) ratios, thus, might compare apples with pears if the business mix of the banks compared differs significantly.

DE studies are much better at dealing with such problems in that they explicitly or implicitly model production functions. But they do have their own set of problems. Many parametric approaches make rather strong assumptions on the functional form of the production function modeled and are, thus, prone to misspecification. Advanced approaches, such as the use of Fourier-flexible functions, mitigate this problem but are also considered problematic in cross-country comparisons where they usually require the problematic assumption of homogenous banking production functions across countries or groups of countries.[218] Nonparametric dynamic efficiency approaches avoid strong assumptions on the form of production functions but, unlike parametric approaches, cannot account for noise in the data. Measurement error, luck that may temporarily increase or decrease efficiency, and accounting procedures that may cause deviations between measured and economic magnitudes are all assumed to be absent. Furthermore, many non-parametric approaches generally ignore prices and only focus on in- and outputs (and, hence, on technical efficiency) which is conceptually difficult to reconcile with the concepts of cost- and profit-efficiency.

3.3.3 Case Studies

Some authors have noted that wealth gains in mergers are often unique to specific transactions that can easily be overlooked using the standard cross-sectional tools discussed above.[219] Instead, they propose following the details of specific transaction with close scrutiny in a mostly qualitative analysis, which incorporates a

218 See e.g., Vander Vennet (2003).
219 Piloff and Santomero (1996), Calomiris and Karceski (1998).

much larger set of information on the deal than just market values or accounting numbers. This leads to the use of so-called case or clinical studies as a method to analyze the wealth effects of M&A. The obvious drawback of this approach is that, even though state-of-the art qualitative research methods are greatly concerned about creating transparency of results,[220] the generalization of findings is problematic. For that reason, they often rather complement than replace quantitative approaches[221]

3.4 Summary

The discussion of the theoretical foundations of CBBM&A firstly led to a definition of banks and CBBM&A for the purpose of this study. Based on a review of the CF literature, the study identified a set of firm-specific motives for CBBM&A, that translate into potential firm-specific determinants of wealth creation, such as firm size or firm efficiency. A review of the bank-specific IM literature identified additional, country-specific characteristics as potential determinants of wealth creation. However, the literature review also found that, so far, no single theory or framework had been able to deliver a consistent overview all or even the most relevant possible determinants. Instead, it was found that the concrete identification of determinants including a test of their relevance was generally left to the empirical literature. Hence, this study will proceed accordingly and identify the relevant determinants from the joint review of the empirical CF and IM literature.

The chapter also identified the available scientific methods for measuring the wealth effects of CBBM&A and their respective advantages and disadvantages. From the discussion it followed that event studies are the superior methodology to generate evidence on the posed research questions. This is because, despite various pitfalls with the use of this method, only event studies allow for direct inferences on shareholder wealth and can also capture wealth effects, that are not directly driven by efficiency related factors. OP and DE studies in turn can only capture changes in efficiency. While these will generally translate into wealth, it remains open, to whom this wealth accrues.[222] Also, insofar as wealth effects are driven by non-efficiency related factors, e.g., the discussed signaling effects that

220 See e.g., Yin and Campbell (2003) for a detailed discussion of the available methods and approaches.

221 See e.g., Mußhoff and Schiereck (2005).

222 This could be bidders, targets or even other stakeholders Remember e.g., that competition may force banks to "pass through" certain efficiency increases, notably those on the front end, to the customer.

are inherent in deals, they cannot be captured by OP and DE studies at all. The same is true for case studies, that might well capture the detailed circumstances of a single deal, but again ultimately cannot come up with a transparent measure for the overall wealth impact. The discussion of concrete results from the different types of methods in the next chapter will show if this notion can be substantiated.

4. Previous Empirical Evidence on Wealth Effects of Cross-Border Bank M&A

This chapter starts with a review of previous evidence on the general direction, size and benefactors of wealth effects (*section 4.1*). Next, the chapter turns to evidence on determinants of wealth effects as found in the previous literature (*section 4.2*). *Section 4.3* summarizes the findings, highlights gaps in the previous literature and concludes the literature review.

4.1 Previous Evidence on Direction, Size and Benefactors of Wealth Effects

This section reviews evidence gathered by all of the methods discussed in the previous section, namely short-term event studies (4.1.1), long-term event studies (4.1.2), OP and DE studies (4.1.3) as well as case studies (4.1.4). As also discussed in the last chapter, banks differ strongly from other firms, e.g. with regard to regulation, capital structure and corporate governance. Therefore, only bank-specific evidence is reviewed.

4.1.1 Evidence from Short-Term Event Studies

The majority of findings on the wealth effects of banking M&A in general is based on short-term event studies on domestic deals in the US. Due to an overall large and dynamic economy, a specific legal history that led to several large merger waves in the banking industry,[223] as well as the existence of several comprehensive databases on the issue, the US has been by far the most important laboratory for the production of such studies. Several authors have provided detailed reviews of the domestic banking M&A literature: Rhoades (1994) reviews results from studies done between 1980 and the early 90s, Piloff and Santomero (1998) discuss evidence from the 90s, and Beitel (2002) extends and summarizes the earlier reviews. Table 4.1 gives an overview.

223 Heavy restrictions on the number of branches a bank could own, the locations it could choose, and the type of banking activities it could perform, led to a large number of specialized banks in the US which were often of subcritical size. Massive industry consolidation was induced by continuous relaxation of these restrictions, see the next section for details.

Table 4.1: Overview of Short-Term Event Studies on Domestic Bank M&A

Study	Sample period	Location[1]	Event window[2]	Sample size[3]	Wealth effects[4]		
					Bidders	Targets	Joint
Lobue (1984)	n.a.	US	[-720;480]	n.a.	+	n.a.	n.a.
Desai and Stover (1985)	1976-1982	US	[0;1]	18/0/0	+	n.a.	n.a.
Dubofsky and Fraser (1985)	1975-1983	US	[-1;0]	110/0/0	0	n.a.	n.a.
Pettway and Trifts (1985)	1972-1981	US	[-10;5]	11/0/0	0	n.a.	n.a.
James and Wier (1987)	1973-1983	US	[-10;10]	79/0/0	+	n.a.	n.a.
James und Wier (1987b)	1972-1983	US	[-15;15]	60/0/0	+	n.a.	n.a.
Neely (1987)	1979-1985	US	[-50; 150]	26/26/0	0	+	n.a.
Sushka and Bendeck (1988)	1972-1985	US	[-14;14]	41/0/0	-	n.a.	n.a.
Bertin et al. (1989)	1982-1987	US	[-20;20]	33/0/0	0	n.a.	n.a.
Dubofsky and Fraser (1989)	1973-1983	US	[-49;20]	101/0/0	0	n.a.	n.a.
Kaen and Tehranian (1989)	1979-1987	US	[-10;10]	31/0/0	-	n.a.	n.a.
Wall and Gup (1989)	1981-1983	US	[-10;20]	23/0/0	-	n.a.	n.a.
Baradwaj et al. (1990)	1980-1987	US	[-5;5]	53/53/0	-	+	n.a.
Allen and Cebenoyan (1991)	1979-1986	US	[-5;5]	138/0/0	0	n.a.	n.a.
Houston and Ryngaert (1994)	1985-1991	US	[-230;-31]	153/153/153	-	+	0
Palia (1994)	1984-1987	US	[-5;5]	48/0/0	-	n.a.	n.a.
Seidel (1995)	1989-1991	US	[-20;20]	123/0/0	-	n.a.	n.a.
Zhang (1995)	1980-1990	US	[-5;5]	107/107/107	0	+	+
Piloff (1996)	1982-1991	US	[-20;0]	0/0/48	n.a.	n.a.	0
Siems (1996)	1995	US	[-1;1]	19/19/0	-	+	n.a.
Houston and Ryngaert (1997)	1985-1992	US	[-1;1]	209/0/0	-	n.a.	n.a.
Subrahmanyam et al. (1997)	1982-1987	US	[-1;1]	263/0/0	-	n.a.	n.a.
Bannerjee and Cooperman (1998)	1990-1995	US	[-50;0]	30/62/0	-	+	n.a.
Cyree and DeGennaro (1999)	1989-1995	US	[-1;0]	132/0/0	0	n.a.	n.a.
Kwan and Eisenbeis (1999)	1989-1996	US	[-20;1]	0/0/94	n.a.	n.a.	+
Wang (1999)	1990-1997	US	[-1;4]	177/177/177	-	+	0
Becher (2000)	1980-1997	US	[0;1]	558/558/558	0	+	+
Brewer et al. (2000)	1990-1998	US	[0;1]	0/327/0	n.a.	+	n.a.
Houston et al. (2000)	1985-1996	US	[-4;1]	0/0/64	n.a.	n.a.	+
Kane (2000)	1991-1998	US	[0]	110/110/110	-	+	0
Resti (2000)	1992-1997	I	[-120; 250]	12/12/0	+	0	n.a.
DeLong (2003)	1991-1995	US	[-10;1]	54/54/54	-	+	0
Akhigbe and Madura (2004)	1986-2000	US	[-1;0]	28/0/0	0	n.a.	n.a.
Caruso and Palmucci (2005)	1994-2003	I	[-30;0]	21/21/21	-	+	0
DaSilva and Diz (2005)	1995-2003	P	[-20;20]	30/30/30	0	+	0

Source: Based on Beitel (2002)

1 *I = Italy, P = Portugal, US = US.*

2 *Values in brackets indicate first and last day of the event window relative to the announcement date.*

3 *Values indicate number of bidders, targets, and joint bidder-target entities in consecutive order.*

4 *+ = significant positive effect; 0 = effect not significantly different from 0; - = significant negative effect; n.a. = not analyzed.*

The table shows properties and results from 35 previous studies. It is based on the work of Beitel (2002) but adds some contributions from earlier years and extends the period reviewed until mid 2006.[224] Since a more detailed discussion of individual studies is already provided in the above mentioned contributions, this study restricts itself to highlighting some overall patterns.

Almost all studies (89 percent) consider the wealth effects of bidders, while evidence on the wealth effects on targets or the joint bidder-target entity is much scarcer and only provided by less than a half (43 percent) and roughly a third (34 percent) of the studies, respectively.

With regard to results, the case seems clear cut for targets: all but one of the studies that consider target wealth effects find a significant positive effect.[225] For bidders, findings are mixed with results rather pointing towards negative wealth effects, which roughly half of the studies (52 percent) find, or neglible effects, found by roughly another third (32 percent), than positive effects, found by less than a fifth (16 percent). Finally, the net effect seems to be rather neutral, as found by roughly two thirds of the studies (67 percent), than positive, which the remaining third (33 percent) find.

The results are in line with the general M&A literature[226] but still somewhat surprising, given that deals are generally initiated by bidders, which are in turn generally assumed to maximize shareholder wealth. This is the merger paradox discussed above. Results are also consistent with bidders acting in a competitive acquisition market within which potential sources of wealth creation are rather target- than bidder-specific, leading to an erosion of bidder profits and their accrual to targets. However, this only explains deals that are wealth-neutral for bidders, not bidder-wealth destroying ones. The latter requires bidders to consistently overpay which, in turn, points to non-rational decision making or, more likely,[227] agency effects and managerial self-interest behind deals. The more neutral than positive net effects seem to indicate that deals do not create wealth but rather redistribute it from bidders to targets.

However, because cross-border M&A differs from domestic M&A and because it may be exactly these differences that drive wealth effects, various authors have proposed extreme caution with applying inferences based on domestic studies to the cross-border case.[228] Therefore, attention is now shifted to

224 However, note that the latest reviewed contribution is from 2005.

225 The diverging results of Resti (2000) are probably explained by small sample size and the unusually long event window.

226 See Bruner (2002) for an overview of the results of the latter.

227 See footnote 156.

228 E.g., Hudgins and Seifert (1996), Tourani Rad and van Beek (1999).

two other types of short-term event studies. The next section still considers domestic M&A but only reviews results of studies which cover a specific type of transaction that involves large geographic distances between bidders and targets. More specifically, findings on mergers between banks located in different US states, so called interstate mergers, are discussed. The following section then covers results of genuine cross-border studies.

4.1.1.1 Studies on US Interstate M&A

Until the 1980s, merging across borders of the US federal states was extremely difficult for banks. Section 3 (d) of the Bank Holding Company Act of 1956, also known as the Douglas Amendment, prohibited banks from owning branches outside the state where they were headquartered unless the target bank's state explicitly permitted such acquisitions. Since this was not the case in any state, interstate banking was effectively prohibited.[229] However, continuous passing of reciprocity laws in many states since the mid 1970s,[230] a US Supreme Court decision in 1985 that such laws did not violate the constitution,[231] and finally the passing of the Riegle-Neal Interstate Banking and Branching Efficiency Act in 1994,[232] led to record levels of bank mergers across state lines in the 1980s and 1990s.[233]

A large number of event studies subsequently analyzed the wealth effects of these transactions, leading to evidence on a type of banking M&A that involves bidders and targets that are often separated by large geographic distances and also somewhat differing market environments. Even though these within-country differences are most probably smaller than between-country differences, the evidence from interstate banking M&A might well be indicative for the latter.[234]

---

229 Kroszner and Strahan (2005). Possible exceptions were possible for banks that already had branches in other states as well as for mergers that resulted in subsidaries which conducted only limited banking activities, see De and Duplichan (1987).

230 The first such law was passed by the state of Maine in 1978. At first, other states were slow to follow: It took 4 years until two other states, Alaska and New York, did so. But the pace of reciprocity accelerated so that in 1992 all states except Hawaii had passed similar laws, see Krozner and Strahan (2005).

231 The concrete ruling was Northeast Bancorp Inc. versus Board of Governors of the Federal Reserve System, US Supreme Court, June 10th, 1985.

232 The law effectively allowed US banks to cross state lines without permission. Even though it was only fully implemented in 1997, many states opted in early, see Berger et al. (2000).

233 During the period 1980-1987, interstate bank mergers accounted for nearly half of all large bank mergers in the US, see Baradwaj et al. (1991). Numbers were comparable in the 1990s, see and Frame and Lastrapes (1998).

234 Vander Vennet (2003), Altunbas and Ibáñez (2006).

Table 4.2 gives an overview of findings from interstate studies. Here, most studies that analyze the average wealth changes of bidders find significantly negative effects.[235] Only two studies, both covering the first interstate merger wave in the 1980s, DeCossio et al. (1988) and Cornett and Tehranian (1992), cannot find a significant bidder impact. However, both feature small interstate samples of only 21 and 15 deals respectively which possibly also play a role in their failure to detect significant results. The odd man out is Cornett and De (1991) who find significant positive bidder returns but cannot provide conclusive reasons for this. For targets, interstate deals again turn out beneficial in all but one study, De and Duplichan (1987), that, however, suffers from problems of small size.

Results of the studies that also consider the net effect find this generally neutral[236] except for Toyne and Tripp (1998), who show that it can also become negative. While these results are based on an analysis of interstate deals on a stand-alone basis, some studies additionally consider the relative wealth effect compared to intrastate deals. With regard to targets or the joint entity, such differences seem nonexistent.[237] With regard to bidders, the evidence is inconclusive but suggests that interstate bidders rather perform worse, than similar to or even better than their intrastate companions.[238]

Thus, overall, while the direction and size of the target effect seems more or less unaffected by the geographical origin of their acquirer, the results tentatively suggest that bidders perform worse in interstate deals, which is, to a smaller extent, also reflected in the net effect. Therefore, potential benefits of deals across large distances, such as diversification or access to large or less competitive markets, seem to be smaller than their drawbacks, e.g., more complicated integration or lack of operational synergies. However the findings, especially the relatively strong variation of bidder results, indicate that wealth effects are probably also driven by other, non-controlled for factors that mix with the distance effect.

---

235 De and Duplichan (1987), Trifts and Scanlon (1987), Hawawini and Swary (1990), Baradwaj et al. (1992), Toyne and Tripp (1998), DeLong (2001), Cornett et al. (2003).

236 Hannan and Wolken (1989), Hawawini and Swary (1990), DeLong (2001).

237 See De Cossio et al. (1988), Hawawini and Swary (1990) and DeLong (2001) for targets and Hannan and Wolken (1989) and DeLong (2001) for the joint entity.

238 DeCossio et al. (1988), Hawawini and Swary (1990 and Cornett et al. (2003) find that bidders perform worse. Baradwaj et al. (1992) and DeLong (2001) find similar results and Cornett and Tehranioan (1992) find interstate bidders perform even better than intrastate bidders.

Table 4.2: Overview of Short-Term Event Studies on Interstate Bank M&A

Study	Sample period	Event window[1]	Sample size[2]	(Relative) Wealth effects[3] Bidd-ers	Tar-gets	Joint Entity
De and Duplichan (1987)	1982-1985	[-30, 30] D	44/22/0	-	0	n.a.
Trifts and Scanlon (1987)	1982-1985	[-40, 20] W	14/17/0	-	+	n.a.
De Cossio et al. (1988)	1982-1985	[-30, 20] W	21/11/0 (41/18/0)	0 (-)	+ (0)	n.a.
Hannan and Wolken (1989)	1982-1987	[-15, 15] D	17/17/17 (26/26/ 26)[4]	n.a.[5]	n.a.[5]	0 (0)
Hawawini and Swary (1990)	1971-1986	[-5, 5] W	48/46/46	- (-)	+ (0)	0
Allen and Cebenoyan (1991)	1979-1986	[-5, 5] D	138/0/0	n.a.[6]	n.a.	n.a.
Cornett and De (1991)	1982-1986	[-15, 15] D	152/37/0	+	+	n.a.
Baradwaj et al (1992)	1981-1987	[-5, 5] D	37/0/0 (71/0/0)	- (0)	n.a.	n.a.
Cornett and Tehranian (1992)	1982-1987	[-1, 0] D	15/15/0 (15/15/ 0)	0 (+)	+ (-)	n.a.
Toyne and Tripp (1998)	1991-1995	[-1, 0] D	68/68/68 (121/121/121)	-	+	-
DeLong (2001)	1988-1995	[-10, 1] D	159/159/159	- (0)	+ (0)	0 (0)
Cornett et al. (2003)	1988-1995	[-1, 1] D	196/0/0	- (-)	n.a.	n.a.

1 *Values in brackets indicate first and last period of the event window. D = days, W = weeks, M = months.*

2 *Values indicate number of bidders/number of targets/number of joint bidder-target entities with regard to interstate mergers in consecutive order, values in brackets are the corresponding number of intrastate deals if applicable.*

3 *If available, results are given for interstate deals only. + = significant positive effect; 0 = effect not significantly different from 0; - = significant negative effect. n.a. = not analyzed. Numbers in brackets indicate relative performance to intrastate deals (if available): + wealth impact significantly more positive, - wealth impact significantly more negative, 0 wealth impact not significantly different.*

4 *The original sample consists of 43 bidders and 69 targets. Analyses on intrastate M&A are only performed on the subsample of deals where both bidder and target information is available (43), that consists of 17 interstate and 26 intrastate deals.*

5 *Results for bidders and targets are only given for the full sample and are not split by interstate versus intrastate deals. 6 Results are only reported for bidders that have high insider shareholdings and a high shareholder concentration. These are not significantly different from zero.*

4.1.1.2 Studies on Cross-Border M&A

Considering the sheer size of the US and the rather moderate distances between some countries in Europe, interstate M&A might often be comparable to CBBM&A in terms of geographic distance. However, bidder-target differences with regard to e.g., culture, law or banking regulation are probably much larger between interstate and cross-border deals. Since these characteristics may matter with regard to deal success, this review next turns to studies study that cover genuine CBBM&A. Table 4.3 gives an overview of these studies.

Here, most studies have analyzed the wealth effects that result, when banks from one specific country acquire banks from a variety of other countries or vice versa.[239] One could thus speak of "from-one-to-many" or "from-many-to-one" studies.[240] In these studies, the US plays again a prominent role as a home and host country.

Target wealth effects are again consistently positive and do not differ from those observed in comparable domestic deals.[241] Bidder results are inconsistent, ranging from negative[242] to neutral and not significantly different from domestic deals[243] to even more positive than the latter.[244] Unfortunately all "from-one-to-many" and "from-many-to-one" studies skip the crucial calculation of the net wealth effect.

Variations in bidder and target returns again probably stem from other influencing factors. The results of Bessler and Murtagh (2002) give rise to the speculation that one such factor could be certain characteristics of the bidder's home country, as it is the only study to feature Canadian bidders and also the only study to feature extremely positive bidder results. However, their research approach does not lend itself to testing this explicitly as they only consider one bidder and one target country.

Better evidence is provided by the handful of studies that analyze the wealth effects of European banking M&A, including cross-border deals.[245] Again, all

239 Waheed and Mathur (1995), Hudgins and Seifert (1996), Gleason and Mathur (1998), Schiereck and Strauss (2000), Bessler and Murtag (2002), Bohl et al. (2004).

240 Clark et al. (2003).

241 See Hugins and Seifert (1996), Schiereck and Strauss (2000), Bohl et al. (2004) and Kiymaz (2004) for absolute and Hudgins and Seifert (1996) for relative results.

242 Waheed and Mathur (1995), Gleason and Mathur (1998).

243 Hudgins and Seifert (1996).

244 Bessler and Murtagh (2002).

245 Tourani-Rad and van Beek (1999), Cybo-Ottone and Murgia (2000), Beitel et al. (2004), Campa and Hernando (2005).

Table 4.3: Overview of Short-Term Event Studies on Cross-Border Bank M&A

Study	Regional focus	Sample period	Event window[1]	Sample size[2]	(Relative) Wealth effects[3] Bidders	Targets	Joint
Waheed and Mathur (1995)	US (bidders), Global (targets)	1963-1989	[-1,1]	80/0/0	-	n.a.	n.a.
Hudgins and Seifert (1996)	US (bidders, targets) Global (bidders, targets)	1970-1989	[-1, 1]	88/72/0 (88/72/0)	0 (0)	+ (0)	n.a.
Biswas et al. (1997)	Global	1977-1987	[-5, 5]	90/46/35 (117/32/42)	0 (+)	+ (0)	+ (0)
Gleason and Mathur (1998)	US (bidders), Global (targets)	1963-1996	[-1, 1]	135/0/0	-	n.a.	n.a.
Tourani-Rad and van Beek (1999)	Europe	1989-1996	[-40, 40]	26/0/0 (30/0/0)	0 (0)	n.a.	n.a.
Cybo-Ottone and Murgia (2000)	Europe	1988-1997	[-20, 20]	13/14/ 13 (33/47/33)	0 (0)	+ (0)	0 (0)
Schiereck and Strauss (2000)	Germany (bidder), US (target)	1999	[-20, 20]	1	0	+	n.a.
Amihud et al. (2002)	Global	1985-1998	[-10, 1]	214/0/ 12	-	n.a.	0
Bessler and Murtagh (2002)	Canada (bidder), Global (targets)	1998-2001	[-5, 5]	26/0/0	+ (+)	n.a.	n.a.
Beitel et al. (2004)	Europe	1985-2000	[-1, 1]	42/42/ 42 (56/56/56)	- (0)	+ (0)	+ (0)
Bohl et al. (2004)	Poland (targets)	1996-2002	[-20, 20]	0/51/0	n.a.	+	n.a.
Kiymaz (2004)	US (bidders, targets)	1989-1999	[-10, 10]	207/70/0	0	+	n.a.
Campa and Hernando (2005)	Europe	1998-2002	[-1, 1]	52/52/52 (120/120/ 120)	0 (0)	+ (0)	0 (0)

1 *Values in brackets indicate first and last day of the event window.*

2 *Number of bidders/number of targets/number of joint bidder-target entities with regard to cross-border mergers; values in brackets: Numbers for domestic mergers*

3 *N.a. = not available; + = significant positive effect; 0 = effect not significantly different from 0; - = significant negative effect. The assessment for the European studies is with regard to cross-border deals only, if available. Numbers in brackets indicate relative performance to domestic deals (if available): + wealth impact significantly more positive, - wealth impact significantly more negative, 0 wealth impact not significantly different.*

studies report positive target returns, which are albeit similar to target returns in domestic deals. Otherwise both bidder and the joint entity effect are generally neutral and comparable to domestic deals. Interestingly, the largest and most comprehensive European study, the work of Beitel et al. (2004), and most recent global study, the work of Amihud et al. (2002), both find negative bidder gains and positive or neutral net effects. The neutral net effects found in the work of Amihud et al. (2002) are, however, most likely attributable to the extremely small number of only 12 joint bidder-target entities. The other global study, the work of Biswas et al. (1997), also finds positive net effects, even though here bidder gains are neutral.[246]

Overall, genuine cross-border studies, like interstate studies, show some variation with regard to bidder returns but, contrary to interstate studies, paint a more positive picture of the bidder and net wealth effects. This is somewhat surprising as the distances involved, both geographically and culturally, are higher.

4.1.2 Evidence from Long-Term Event Studies

As discussed above, inferences on the wealth effect of M&A based on short-term event studies strongly hinge on the assumption of market efficiency: the abnormal stock price reaction in a short window around the event is only indicative for the total wealth effect if stock markets are at least semi-strong efficient. If markets under- or overreact to information about the deal and only gradually adjust their expectations over time, this may lead to long-term positive or negative abnormal returns and the total wealth effect of the deal will instead only become visible by summing announcement- and post-announcement period abnormal returns.[247] To explicitly test the assumption of market efficiency and the actual abnormal return following M&A transactions, some researchers have, therefore, performed long-term event studies on banking M&A. An overview is of these is given in table 4.4.

---

246 However, the results from Biswas et al. (1997) have to be interpreted with care. Somewhat unconventionally the authors also include deals where the bidder does not acquire a controlling stake in the target. However, they do not present separate results for such deals. This is especially problematic, as some of their other analyses provide evidence that bidder wealth effects are indeed significantly lower in deals where a controlling interest is acquired. Thus, their neutral bidder effect may in fact turn out to be ngative for all deals, in which a change in control takes place. This, however, is what CBBM&A is usually about.

247 Loughran and Vijh (1997).

Table 4.4: Overview of Long-Term Event Studies on Banking M&A

Name	Regional focus	Sample period	Post-event months covered	Sample size	Wealth effect[1]
Madura and Wiant (1994)	US	1983-1987	36	152	-
Cybo-Ottone and Murgia (2000)	Europe	1988-1997	12	72	0
Beitel (2002)	Europe	1985-2000	12	98	+[2]
Aggrawal et al. (2003)	US	1986-2001	36	271	-
DeLong (2003)	US	1991-1995	36	54	+
Akhigbe and Madura (2004)	US	1986-2000	36	28	-
Bouwman (2004)	US	1993-2000	24	333	-
Cagle and Nixon (2005)	US	1990-1999	36	50	+
Campa and Hernando (2005)	Europe	1998-2002	12	52	-
Leshchinskii and Zollo (2005)	US	1986-1995	48	320	+

1 + = significant positive effect; 0 = effect not significantly different from 0; - = significant.

2 No formal tests for significance.

Madura and Wiant (1994) were the first to apply this technique to the (US domestic) banking sector. Consistent with the early non-bank specific literature on long-term abnormal returns,[248] they find long-term abnormal bidder losses indicating that markets indeed seem to be inefficient with regard to bank merger announcements. However, Madura and Wiant (1994) methodologically stick with conventional short-term event study methodology and simply extend the event window. Given the findings on the potential biases of long-term studies discussed above, this approach is highly questionable as the application of short-term methods can easily led to the detection of abnormal returns where in fact none are present. Often, once more advanced methods of calculating long-term abnormal returns are used, such long-term anomalies vanish.[249]

Further evidence on the long-term wealth effects of bank mergers is provided by the European focused studies of Cybo-Ottone and Murgia (2000), Beitel (2002) and Campa and Hernando (2005) who, in addition to their short-term

248 E.g., Loughran and Vijh (1997).

249 See Fama (1998) for a discussion and e.g., Mitchell and Staffort (2000) for (non-bank-specific) evidence.

studies, analyze the bidder share price reaction one year post-deal and DeLong (2003) who analyzes the long-term effect of domestic US deals. While these studies tentatively suggest positive abnormal bidder gains,[250] they mostly cannot provide conclusive reasons why this is the case[251] and still use simple methodologies which are prone to the known errors in estimating long-term abnormal returns.[252]

The hypothesis that findings of long-term abnormal gains are only attributable to the use of inadequate methods is weakened by the results from a series of relatively recent working papers on long-term abnormal returns following banking M&A in US deals that use more advanced measurement methods. Here, findings are almost equally split between positive and negative abnormal returns.[253] The latter results are somewhat unsettling as they do not only cast some doubt over the findings of the entire short-term literature[254] but at the same time do not reveal a systematic pattern in apparent market over- or underreaction.

Fama (1998), in a discussion of the implications of the findings of the long-term-return-anomaly literature, notes that if different studies measure positive as well as negative abnormal returns, this may point to a random split between the two with no normal returns being the normal case which is, however, less "flashy" and, therefore, less frequently reported. Also, Khotari and Warner (2005) note that even the most sophisticated contemporary measurement issues for long-term abnormal returns, if used stand-alone, are not robust to the above-mentioned issues with long-term return measurement pointing to the possibility

---

250 Cybo-Ottone and Murgia report such gains, even though only for bank-insurance deals and without giving explicit results. Beitel (2002) reports that 56% of the transactions show positive abnormal gains but does not provide formal tests for significance. Only DeLong (2003) provides formal evidence of long-term abnormal bidder gains while only Campa and Hernando (2005) find long-term abnormal bidder losses.

251 DeLong (2003) attributes long-term abnormal returns to increasing systematic risk in the banking industry during her sample period which, even if correct, should not be relevant for abnormal returns since it would also affect her benchmark, a local banking index. Beitel (2002) does not discuss reasons or implications of his findings. Only Cybo-Ottone and Murgia (2000) speculate that abnormal returns following conglomerate deals could be due to the unfamiliarity of this deal type to the market.

252 All authors use bidder buy-and-hold-returns relative to banking index returns without any further methodological adjustments.

253 See Leshchinskii and Zollo (2005), Cagle and Nixon (2005) for positive and Aggarwal et al. (2006), Akhigbe and Madura (2004), and Bouwman (2004) for negative results.

254 Not to mention many other areas of finance that usually assume market efficiency.

of measurement errors even in the more sophisticated studies. Thus, results may still be consistent with overall market efficiency.

4.1.3 Evidence from Operating Performance and Dynamic Efficiency Studies

Similar to event studies there is a large body of literature that examines efficiency changes, either with OP or DE methodologies, of domestic banking acquisitions.[255] Here, the focus is on cross-border OP and DE studies. Table 4.5 gives an overview.

Peek et al. (1999) exclusively focus on American targets of foreign bidders and compare their performance to that of US institutions acquired by domestic bidders using operating performance methodology. They analyze 84 such acquisitions over the period 1984 to 1997 and primarily assess changes in ROA as well as various variables indicating risk and find that foreign-owned banks target less healthy and less profitable banks relative to the peer group.[256] The foreigners then implement significant changes in business policy indicated by changes in the asset-liability-mix which seem to help to solve issues with problem loans.

However, the overall below-average target profitability remains unchanged, leading to a worse efficiency outcome relative to comparable domestic transactions. In the context of other studies reporting poor performance of foreign-owned banks relative to domestically-owned banks, they interpret this as evidence that problems were partly acquired and partly created.

Vander Vennet (1996) comes to different conclusions based on his study of European banking M&A between 1988 and 1993 that also contains a subsample of 70 cross-border deals. Using mainly operating performance but also a simple dynamic cost efficiency measure, he shows that while bidders enjoy unchanged above average profit- and cost-efficiency pre- and post-deal, targets are able to improve far below average cost-efficiency to average levels through the deal. Changes in bidder efficiency and target profit efficiency turn out insignificant. Since all deals are majority acquisitions that do not involve full integration, he

---

255 Results for domestic studies are summarized by Rhoades (1994), Berger et al. (1999), Beitel (2002), and Amel et al. (2004). Essentially, the discussed OP studies cannot detect any significant wealth changes following M&A. The discussed DE studies on the other hand do find some efficiency increases, often stronger with regard to profit than to cost efficiency. However, they also find that the size of these gains is far below the levels that seem theoretically obtainable from the mergers.

256 Note that this might partly be related to a "winner's curse" effect as the author's only consider transactions that have been carried out.

Table 4.5: Overview of Operating Performance and Dynamic Efficiency Studies on Cross-Border Bank M&A

Study	Regional focus	Methodology	Efficiency measures[2]	Sample period	Time window[1]	Sample size[2]	Efficiency effects[3]: Bidders	Efficiency effects[3]: Targets
Vander Vennet (1996)	Europe	OP and DE	Profitability ratios, cost ratios, cost efficiency	1988-1993	-3,3	70/70	0 (all measures)	0 (profitability ratios), + (cost ratios), + (cost efficiency)
Altunbas et al. (1997)	Europe	DE	Cost efficiency	n.a.	n.a.	n.a.	0/-	n.a.
Peek et al. (1999)	US (targets)	OP	Profitability ratio, risk ratios	1984-1997	-3,3	0/82	n.a.	- (profitability ratio), + (risk ratios)[4]
Vander Vennet (2003)	Europe	DE	Profit efficiency, cost efficiency	1990-2001	-1,1	62/62[5]	0 (all measures)	+ (profit-efficiency), 0 (cost efficiency)
Altunbas and Ibáñez (2004)	Europe	OP	Profitability ratio	1992-2001	-2, 2	55/0[6]	+ (profitability ratio)[7]	n.a.
Ayadi and Pujals (2005)	Europe	DE	Profit efficiency, cost efficiency	1997-2000	-3,3	7/7	0 (all measures)	+ (profit-efficiency), 0 (cost efficiency)
Campa and Hernando (2005)	Europe	OP	Profitability ratios, cost ratio, risk ratios	1998-2002	-1,2	172/0[6,8]	0 (profitability ratio), + (cost ratio), 0 (risk ratios)[9]	n.a.

1 First (second) value indicates date of first (last) efficiency measurement. Measurement in years relative to deal year.

2 First (second) value indicates number of bidders (targets) in the sample.

3 Wealth effects are generally measured relative to a control group of non-merging peer banks. + = increase in efficiency, 0 = no change in efficiency, - = decrease in efficiency, n.a. = not analyzed.

4 Changes are measured relative to domestic mergers rather than non-merging peers.

5 In cases where targets cease to exist, pro-forma efficiency effects for targets are calculated.

6 Target effects not analyzed since all targets seemingly cease to exist.

7 Effects are not measured relative to a control group of non-merging banks but are higher than those for domestic M&A. However, this difference is not tested for significance.

8 The samples contain 52 cross-border transactions for which, however, no separate results are given.

9 Results are not tested for significance.

speculates that cost-efficiency improvements must be mainly due to X-efficiency changes.

This more positive assessment of CBBM&A efficiency effects is supported by two recent European OP studies, that, however, point more towards increased profit- than cost efficiency. Altunbas and Ibáñez (2004) find an improvement of the ROE after mergers in their subsample of 55 cross-border deals that is even larger than the (also positive) ROE improvement in domestic deals. Campa and Hernando (2005) who analyze a sample of 172 European deals between 1996 and 2002, which contains 52 cross-border transactions, also find ROE improvements following the deal, albeit only for targets and not for bidders.

The findings of improved target profit efficiency after CBBM&A are further substantiated by two Europe-focused studies that use more advanced DE methods. Vander Vennet (2003) analyzes changes in cost and profit efficiency following 62 European CBBM&A deals using SFA and finds no effect on bidder efficiency or target cost efficiency but a significant increase in target profit efficiency. This leads him to speculate that efficiency barriers in cross-border consolidation, e.g., distance, make cost-efficiency improvements much harder to realize than profit-efficiency improvements. Ayadi and Pujals (2005) come to the same conclusion using DEA in a comparison of the efficiency effects of 7 cross-border and 26 domestic deals between 1997 and 2000. The work of Altunbas et al. (1997), who perform a simulation of various large cross-border mergers of European banks, also supports limited opportunities for cost improvements. According to their results, European CBBM&A can even lead to increases in total costs of the merging banks.

Summarizing, both OP and DE studies, despite some negative results, paint an overall more positive picture of CBBM&A than event studies. The analyzed ratios of the operating performance approaches, with the exception of Peek at al. (1999),[257] all indicate higher efficiency, especially for the target institutions,[258] following the deals, even though findings differ with regard to the nature of these improvements, i.e., changes in cost versus changes in profit efficiency. These differences might, in turn, stem from the ambiguous nature of most operating performance measures discussed above. The methodologically more advanced dy-

257 The authors, however, measure differences against domestic M&A and not against non-merging banks.

258 This is not inconsistent with the positive impact on bidders found by Altunbas and Ibáñez (2004) and Campa and Hernando (2005) since, as discussed above, these studies only consider bidder performance, presumably because targets cease to exist. The result is, thus, rather that of the joint entity that might well be driven by the target effect. All studies that analyze actual or pro-forma bidder performance only find positive effects.

namic efficiency studies consequently do not show such variations and rather consistently find CBBM&A to improve target profit efficiency. Target cost or bidder efficiency do not seem to be affected which also fits with the simulation evidence.

Thus, it seems that targets manage to become more profitable through the acquisitions, even though they rarely manage to do so by cost savings. This evidence is in line with cross-border deals being generally unable to reap the "usual" cost scale-efficiencies that result e.g., from branch closures in domestic deals. Rather, they seem to benefit from diversification benefits or revenue-increasing efficiency effects, such as sales of new products or better processes and leadership.

4.1.4 Evidence from Case Studies

Again, case studies on banking M&A primarily cover domestic deals.[259] However, more recently some authors have also turned to CBBM&A. The relevant studies are reviewed in turn.

Bruckner and O'Shea (2002) investigate the Hypovereinsbank/Bank Austria deal. In 2000, Hypovereinsbank, then Germany's second largest bank with a focus on retail and real-estate finance, acquired Bank Austria that even though much smaller, was Austria's second largest bank. It also had a strong retail banking position in the Austrian market and strong retail as well as wholesale operations in central and Eastern Europe. Bruckner and O'Shea's (2002) study highlights the various motives behind the deal and their importance. One was market power, as Central and Eastern Europe was at that point in time still relatively free from competition. Since the bidder planned to combine its own broad product portfolio with the target's specialized regional knowledge and branch network, combination of complementary resources also played a role. Finally, there were also diversifying motives in the form of allowing Bank Austria access to the bidder's internal capital market.[260] In addition, the authors highlight the influence of the host country's institutional environment by describing the crucial role that the Austrian Take-Over Commission played. With regard to wealth or efficiency effects, the authors claim that the transaction helped the companies involved to

259 See e.g., the work of Calomiris and Karceski (1998) or Walter (2004).

260 To a lesser extent, the authors also identify targeted scale economies (closure of some redundant branches), X-efficiencies (Bank Austria's former CEO became the bidder's head of operations in Central and Eastern Europe) and possibly sometraces of managerial hubris (a former executive of BA warned that treating central and Eastern Europe as a homogenous region would probably be a mistake).

maintain or improve their competitive positions in the market place. This claim, however, is not substantiated further.

Abraham and van Dijcke (2002), instead of focusing on specific CBBM&A deals, present case studies on large banks that have been particularly active in the European CBBM&A business, namely ABN-Amro, ING, FORTIS and NORDEA. Again, the cases highlight the importance of "classical" CF factors for M&A success such as cost efficiency and the choice between focusing versus diversifying acquisitions. However, they also stress the importance of cultural distance that seems to impede growth and the competitive situation in host countries of the targets. On wealth and efficiency effects, the authors again remain silent.

Most instructive with regard to wealth effects is the study of Mußhoff and Schiereck (2005) who combine a case study of the Unicredito Italiano/Bank Pekao deal with a short- and long-term event as well as an operating performance study of the transaction. At the end of 1998, Bank Pekao had emerged from the liberalization of the Polish banking market as the country's second largest universal bank, mainly due to a government-induced merger with three other regional banking institutions. However, it was still predominantly state-owned and had problems with realizing the targeted synergies from its domestic mergers, mounting loan loss provisions, and increasing foreign competition. In a bidding competition for a controlling stake, Unicredito managed to prevail over other foreign bidders such as Citigroup, Deutsche Bank or Allied Irish Bank, acquiring the target for a 14 percent premium. The authors identify targeted X-efficiencies (the bidder had ample experience in banking integration due to its own merger history in Italy and a widely admired governance model) and market power (further access to Eastern Europe where, compared with Italy, competition was still relatively mild) as the main deal motives. Also again, the authors stress the role of host country characteristics: these include the friendly attitude of the host government towards acquisitions by foreign bidders, caused by EU privatization-requirements, and a need for cash and foreign expertise in the banking sector. With regard to wealth effects, they find no significant effects for either party in a short-term study[261] but bidder gains in the long-term and operating performance study,[262] indicating that the market had underreacted to a wealth-creating deal and only gradually corrected this assessment.

261 The surprising target reaction is probably due to leakage, see the discussion in section 5.2.1.1.

262 Results are albeit not tested for their statistical significance.

4.2 Previous Evidence on Determinants of Wealth Effects

This section first makes some comments on the general approach chosen to identify determinants from the empirical literature (4.2.1). Then, findings on both firm (4.2.2) and country- and industry-specific factors (4.2.3) are reviewed.

4.2.1 Approach for Determinant Identification

The second research question of this study is the identification of determinants of wealth creation in the sense of publicly available ex-ante information that can explain wealth effects. A first step in identifying such determinants are the deal motives identified in section 3.2.3, as every deal should be driven by one or a set of these motives. However, deal motives are not observable. What is observable, though, are firm- and country-level characteristics that make the realization of motives more or less likely and that were already hinted at in previous sections. Thus, in order to identify determinants of wealth creation, both the IM and the CF literature is screened for theory and evidence on such characteristics. As suggested by IM theory, firm- and country-/industry characteristics will be considered separately.[263]

The CF studies reviewed for that purpose are a subset of those discussed in the previous sections. More concretely, these are the studies that also analyze the causes of the observed wealth effects. To ensure the applicability of the CF results, the review is restricted to studies with significant distance between bidder and target, leading to the exclusion of "pure" domestic studies.[264] As discussed above, this literature primarily covers firm-specific factors. To identify also country- and industry-specific factors and determinants that are more specific for the cross-border case, this review also covers a set of influential, i.e., frequently cited empirical IM studies. Table 4.6 gives an overview of this literature.

263 This approach is similar to the "simplified" application of OLI theory discussed above. Note that the approach therefore will also suffer from the discussed drawbacks of OLI theory. More specifically, it will also be strongly eclectic and not allow to derive determinants from one consistent, "hard" theorectical frame. However, since there is a large potential benefit from incorporating findings from the IM literature in the analysis, this is unavoidable and in line with the current standard approach in the banking-related IM literature.

264 However, US interstate studies are included.

Table 4.6: Overview of Reviewed International Management Studies

Study	Paradigm choice for determinant selection	Home country focus	Host country focus	Sample period	Dependant variable	Level of independent variables
Goldberg and Saunders (1980)	Eclectic	US	UK	1961-1978	Value of bank deposits	Country
Ball and Tschoegl (1982)	OLI	International	Japan, US	1978	Number of bank subsidiaries	Firm and country
Nigh et al. (1986)	OLI	US	Inter-national	1976-1982	Change in value of bank branch assets	Country
Sabi (1988)	OLI	US	Developing Countries	1975-1982	Value of bank FDI	Country
Hultmann and McGee (1989)	Eclectic	International	US	1973-1986	Value of bank subsidiary assets	Country
Goldberg and Johnson (1990)	Eclectic	US	Inter-national	1972-1985	Value of bank branch assets	Country
Budzeika (1991)	Eclectic	International	US	1973-1989	Value of bank subsidiary assets	Country
Grosse and Goldberg (1991)	Eclectic	International	US	1980-1988	Value of bank assets and number of bank offices	Country
Sagari (1992)	OLI	US	Inter-national	1977	Value of bank FDI	Country
Ursacki and Vertinsky (1992)	OLI	International	Japan, Korea	1986	Value of bank branch assets	Firm and country
Goldberg and Grosse (1994)	Eclectic	International	US	1981-1988	Value of bank subsidiary assets and number of subsidiary offices	Country
Brealy and Kaplanis (1996)	Eclectic	International	Inter-national	1992	Number of offices of large banks	Country
Fisher and Molyneux (1996)	Eclectic	Intern-national	UK	1980-1989	Number of banks	Country
Miller and Parkhe (1998)	OLI	US	Inter-national	1987-1995	Value of bank subsidiary assets	Country
Yamori (1998)	Eclectic	Japan	Inter-national	1951-1994	Value of bank FDI	Country
Buch (2000)	Eclectic	Germany	Inter-national	1981-1998	Value of bank FDI	Country
Focarelli and Pozzolo (2001)	Eclectic	OECD	OECD	1998	Number of bank subsidiaries	Firm and country
Buch and DeLong (2003)	Eclectic	OECD	OECD	1985-2001	Number of CBBM&A	Country
Gallindo et al. (2003)	Eclectic	International	Inter-national	2001	Percentage control of bank assets	Firm and country
Piscitello (2003)	OLI	Italy	Inter-national	1989, 1992, 1995, 1999	Number of bank branches	Firm and country
Tschoegl (2003)	Internal-ization theory	International	US	2000	Number of bank subsidiaries	Firm and country
Berger et al. (2004)	OLI/compara tive advantage theory	International	Inter-national	1985-2000	Number of CBBM&A	Country
Buch and DeLong (2004)	Eclectic	International	Inter-national	1985-2001	Number of CBBM&A	Country
Buch and Lipponer (2004)	Eclectic	Germany	Inter-national	1996-2000	Value of bank FDI	Firm and country
Wezel (2004)	Eclectic	Germany	Developing Countries	1994-2001	Value of bank FDI	Country
Buch (2005)	Eclectic	France, Germany, Italy, UK, US	International	1983-1999	Value of bank assets	Country
Buch and DeLong (2005)	Eclectic	OECD	OECD	1985-2001	Number of CBBM&A	Country
Focarelli and Pozzolo (2005)	Eclectic	OECD	OECD	1998	Number of bank subsidiaries	Firm and country
Ben Salem (2006)	OLI	EU	EU	1987-2004	Number/Value of CBBM&A	Country

As the nature of this research differs somewhat from the CF literature, some remarks are necessary before the actual discussion on relevant determinants of wealth creation. First, it was already noted above that these studies have taken a fairly eclectic approach in identifying determinants of banking internationalization.[265] Table 4.6 substantiates this: most contributions identify determinants using a mix of references to earlier empirical findings, formal frameworks or theories, and ad-hoc speculation, indicated as an "eclectic" approach in the column "paradigm choice".[266] Second, there are two caveats in applying the findings of IM studies to CBBM&A which refer to the geographical scope of the studies and to what is actually measured. With regard to geographical scope, just as with the event studies discussed above, internationalization does not necessarily equal internationalization. While only roughly a third of the studies consider a multitude of home and host countries, the remaining ones are again "from one-to-many" or "from many-to-one" studies. Also again, the US is the most frequently researched single home or host country. Therefore, not all studies can control for differing home and host country characteristics.[267] With regard to what is measured, the focus of this literature is not on the determinants of wealth effects, but on determinants of the internationalization decision per se. While the two should be closely related, especially if banks internationalize in order to increase shareholder wealth, they are not identical.[268] In that sense, the reviewed evidence from IM studies is less applicable than that from CF studies.

Even within the IM literature, the applicability of the findings to CBBM&A differs as only 5 studies explicitly consider the number of CBBM&A deals as the dependent variable.[269] Frequent other choices are the amount of banking FDI from the home to the host country or the (branch) banking assets in the host country that have owners in the home country. However, such measures may also

---

265 Eclectic is, thereby, not to be interpreted in the sense of OLI as only roughly a third of the studies refer to this framework.

266 The table also confirms that internalization theory is less well suited to guide empirical work as only one study, the work of Tschoegl (2003), refers to it.

267 Also note that none of the studies controls for differing regulations within the concerned US states, that can be significant.

268 Berger et al. (2004, p. 335), in the context of studying country-level determinants of CBBM&A decisions in the years 1985 to 2000, e.g., note: "While the data does not permit analysis of the ex-post financial performance of each of these M&A, we argue that the patterns of repeated export and import M&A over these 16 years are good indicators of country-based and/or country-pair based advantages at managing financial institutions. Presumably, financial institutions engage in M&A because they believe it is advantageous to do so and would not keep doing it over a long period of time if it turned out to be disadvantageous."

269 Berger et al. (2004), Buch and DeLong (2003, 2004, 2005), Ben Salem (2006).

cover greenfield investments or acquisitions without a change in ownership. For the purpose of this study, the evidence based on assets of foreign subsidiaries seems much better applicable, since, as discussed above, subsidiaries are the most frequent organizational form following CBBM&A.

Finally, most studies only analyze the impact of country-level determinants and only relatively few studies also cover firm-level indicators. This, however, is not because the latter are not considered important[270] but probably rather because the use of country- and firm-level data for a large number of home and host countries significantly increases the data needs and complexity of the analyses. With these caveats in mind, this study proceeds with the discussion of theory and evidence of specific firm- and country-level factors.

4.2.2 Firm-Specific Factors

The reviewed literature identifies 11 factors on the firm-level, that can potentially help to explain wealth effects of CBBM&A: bidder size, relative target-bidder size, the presence of home country clients of the bidder in the host country, relative target-bidder efficiency, target efficiency, geographical and social distance between bidder and target, functional differences between bidder and target, bidder acquisition experience, the existence of mechanisms to reduce agency conflicts in the bidder organization and the share of acquisition price paid in cash. Theory and evidence on these is reviewed in turn.

As discussed above, scale economies that can have an effect on costs and/or revenues are one of the most frequently cited reasons from practitioners for CBBM&A. Research on bank's cost functions in the 1980s revealed relatively flat U-shaped cost curves that reach a minimum at an asset size in the range between USD 100 million and 10 billion.[271] Consequently, some domestic studies have hypothesized *bidder size* to be positively related to wealth gains for relatively small banks and negatively related to wealth gains for relatively large banks.[272] However, all interstate or CBBM&A studies have simply assumed a negative relation to bidder size, probably because banks that acquire over large distances tend to be large.[273]

---

270 Williamson (2002) strongly argues for the use of firm-level data in modeling banking FDI decisions. Buch and DeLong (2004) present a similar argument for CBBM&A.

271 See Berger et al. (2000) and the cited literature.

272 Seidel (1995).

273 Hawawini and Swary (1990), Tourani-Rad and van Beek (1999).

There is also evidence that technological change since then may have affected the shape of cost curves, making cost scale economies also available for larger banks.[274] Moreover, revenue scale economies, which are probably at least as important in cross-border mergers, may also be available for larger banks, pointing rather to a positive relation between bidder size and bidder gains.[275]

The reviewed IM literature rather supports this positive relation, since results across different approaches almost all find that large banks are far more likely to expand abroad than small banks.[276] However, results need not be related to scale economies[277] and are not direct evidence of the wealth effects resulting from bidder size. The latter is only provided by the CF study of Hawawini and Swary (1990), who find bidder size to be inversely related to bidder gains. However, once they control for other factors, the relationship is no longer significant. Tourani-Rad and van Beek (1999) also cannot find a relation between bidder size and gains. Thus, while theory justifies both a positive and a negative relation between bidder size and bidder gains, the IM literature supports the notion of a positive relationship. The latter evidence is tentative since it presupposes that actual bank behavior is wealth-maximizing and is not supported by the scarce applicable event study findings that rather do not show a significant relationship.

Other authors suggest that it is the *relative size* of the merging partners rather than the absolute bidder size that has explanatory power with regard to the wealth effects. Hawawini and Swary (1990) use a similar line of argumentation as for bidder size: since scale economies are only realized at low levels of output, wealth increases should be inversely related to relative (i.e., target to bidder) size. Beitel et al. (2004) assume the same, albeit with the argument that relatively large targets require a more complex post-merger integration, which is also more likely to lead to failures. Altunbas and Ibañez (2004) do not find this convincing: first, they assume CBBM&A rather to be driven by revenue scale economies that are not limited to small banks. Second, they assume that distant targets need not be integrated in the same ways as domestic targets, making the integration-complexity argument irrelevant. Thus, they expect relative target-bidder size to be positively related to bidder gains. DeLong (2001) assumes the same, but on the basis of a TBTF argument: bidders could acquire relatively large targets in

274 See the discussion in section 2.2.2.

275 Evidence on (domestic) revenue scale economies, however, is ambiguous, see Berger et al. (2000).

276 Ursacki and Vertinsky (1992), Focarelli and Pozzolo (2001), Piscitello (2003), Tschoegl (2003), Buch and Lipponer (2004), and Focallarelli and Pozzolo (2006). Only Ball and Tschoegl (1982) cannot find a relationship which may be due to their limited geographical scope and/or somewhat outdated sample.

277 The causality could even be reversed: banks are large because they expand abroad.

order to gain a TBTF status, thus effectively getting access to government subsidies.[278] A final point on relative size is made by Cornett and De (1991), who speculate that the smaller the target relative to the bidder, the more likely the bidder is to enjoy no wealth effect at all, the simple reason being that any resulting wealth would simply be too small to be reflected in bidder returns.

With regard to evidence, some studies support the notion that the acquisition of relatively larger targets has positive wealth effects for bidders.[279] However, most studies cannot find a significant impact of relative size, indicating that the different effects may offset each other.[280]

One of the oldest and most frequently used arguments to explain bank internationalization is the "follow-the-client" argument: banks expand abroad because their home country customers do. As discussed above, this is also an economies-of-scale argument, namely related to economies of scale in monitoring: existing information about domestic clients can be used to attract further business abroad at low or zero marginal costs. Based on this hypothesis, the IM literature has frequently tested the explanatory power of the *presence of existing (home country) clients in the host country*, using the amount of non-bank FDI from the home to the host country as a proxy. The resulting evidence indeed strongly indicates that clients abroad foster FDI abroad.[281]

However, research that uses firm-level data casts some doubt on the "follow-the-client" story. Stanley et al. (1993) and Seth et al. (1998) find foreign banks to be more heavily engaged with host country customers than home country clients. Berger et al. (2003) even show that foreign affiliates of multinational non-banks prefer to do business with host rather than home country banks which leads them to speculate that the latter may serve them as "door openers" abroad or mitigate a

278 However, the author concedes that many international bidders probably already enjoy this status as they belong to the largest banks worldwide. This is also reflected in the sample used in this study, see section 6.1. Also, this is only a valid argument for branches, whereas most targets become subsidiaries.

279 See Trifts and Scanlon (1987) and DeLong (2001) for the joint entity. Altunbas and Ibañez show that the ROE the merged entity increases after the deal if targets are relatively large.

280 Cornett and De (1991), Baradwaj et al. (1992), Hudgins and Seifert (1996), Beitel et al. (2004). Campa and Hernando (2005), Vander Vennet (2003) cannot find evidence that relative size determines post-merger changes in efficiency. Hawawini and Swary (1990) find bidder gains to decrease with relative target size. However, the relationship becomes insignificant when they control for other factors.

281 Nigh et al. (1986), Sabi (1988), Hultmann and McGee (1989), Goldberg and Johnson (1990), Grosse and Goldberg (1991), Sagari (1992), Brealy and Kaplanis (1996), Fisher and Molyneux (1996), Miller and Parkhe (1998), Yamori (1998), Buch (2000), Piscitello (2003), Wezel (2004).

hold-up problem that multinationals may face with their home country banks. From that perspective, following the client should not have an important impact on shareholder wealth. Waheed and Mathur (1995) provide direct evidence on this by regressing the impact of home clients abroad, also proxied by home country FDI in the host country, on bidder CARs in CBBM&A. Surprisingly, they find a negative impact. It is, however, unclear whether this effect eventually cancels out with target gains (the study takes only a bidder perspective), is due to some factors they do not or cannot control for (the study e.g., only features US bidders) or indeed hints at a yet unknown negative relationship between wealth effects and the presence of home country clients.

If CBBM&A is a means to create value through improvement in X-efficiency, the *relative efficiency* of bidder and target, with regard to costs or to profits, would be a likely determinant of wealth changes. It is frequently found that more efficient bidders take over less efficient targets, giving rise to the assumption that bidders intend to create value by imposing their superior managerial processes and expertise onto targets.[282] Consequently, lower relative target efficiency should be associated with subsequent wealth increases. Even though the interstate study of Hawawini and Swary (1990) cannot find evidence for this domestically, the two relevant cross-border event studies find supportive evidence: the takeover of less efficient targets creates bidder wealth[283] and increases subsequent increases in efficiency of the joint entity.[284] Interestingly and in line with the earlier discussed findings from the efficiency literature, results only apply to relative profit efficiency, while relative cost efficiency does not seem to have a significant effect.

Berger et al. (2000) note that M&A may not so much be an opportunity for "better" bidders to bring "worse" targets up to their efficiency levels, but simply a good general opportunity for restructuring.[285] In that view, bidder efficiency is relatively irrelevant for wealth creation: even inefficient bidders can "start afresh", at least within the target organization.[286] This possibility to start afresh is sometimes assumed to depend on absolute *target efficiency*: it might either be that targets need to be sufficiently inefficient ex-ante in order for bidders to improve their performance, for which some studies find evidence[287] or that targets

282 E.g., Berger et al. (2000), Vander Vennet (2003).
283 Beitel et al. (2004).
284 Vander Vennet (2003).
285 Compare section 3.2.3.
286 This is also in line with the central role that outside consultants often play in post-merger management, see e.g., Hellgren et al. (2003).
287 DeLong (2001), Vander Vennet (2003).

need to be sufficiently efficient and well-managed in order for the increase in efficiency to succeed which Beitel et al. (2004) find.[288]

Another frequently discussed determinant in CBBM&A is the degree of relatedness of bidder and target. This is not surprising since one indicator of relatedness is *geographical distance*, which is by definition high for CBBM&A. In theory, the effect of large distance should be twofold:[289] first business cycles in the banking industry, even over relatively small geographical distances, are not perfectly and often even negatively correlated.[290] Thus, acquisitions in distant areas may create wealth through diversification.[291] Second, distance generally increases transaction costs and creates and effective efficiency barrier in CBBM&A.[292] This is especially important for banks, whose primary function, monitoring, becomes rapidly more costly with increasing distance.[293] It is, however, not the host-bank – borrower distance that increases. Since it is the newly acquired target that will monitor host country clients, this distance rather decreases which may be one reason why CBBM&A is usually preferred to cross-border lending, at least in the retail and small and medium enterprise (SME) business.[294]

The IM literature finds banking FDI to be generally strongly negatively related to distance and, thus, concludes that the (negative) monitoring effect prevails over any positive diversification effects.[295] Evidence from the CF literature

---

288 It is important to note that the argument is not that more efficient targets create more wealth because of their higher efficiency, since target efficiency should already be reflected in the acquisition price. Rather, more efficient (or sufficiently efficient) targets could be more likely to become even more efficient because of the change in management control, independent of the bidder efficiency. Note also, that it may well be that both high and low target efficiency are determinants of wealth effects, e.g., in the form that deals create most wealth when targets are inefficient but above a certain efficiency hurdle. There is, however, no evidence on this in the previous literature.

289 Buch (2005).

290 See also the evidence presented in Berger et al. (2000).

291 As discussed above, shareholder-wealth creation through diversification may be more difficult for banks as they have a regulation-induced maximum level of debt, close to which they usually operate, which might lead to a co-insurance effect. However, other diversification arguments, such as the creation of an internal capital market, or avoiding costly bankruptcy, seem well applicable.

292 Buch and DeLong (2004).

293 See e.g., Degryse and Ongena (2004) and the reviewed literature.

294 Degryse and Ongena (2004).

295 Ursacki and Vertinsky (1992), Buch and DeLong (2003, 2004, 2005), Gallindo et al. (2003), Berger et al. (2004), Buch and Lipponer (2004), Buch (2005), Focarelli and Pozzolo (2006).

exists in the form of comparisons between interstate and intrastate or domestic and cross-border deals, sometimes controlling for a variety of other factors. The resulting rather mixed findings have already been discussed: while interstate versus intrastate studies slightly suggest a negative net effect of increasing geographic distance, domestic versus cross-border studies usually fail to find significant differences between the two. Finally, Berger and DeYoung (2001) show that while there are some distance-related efficiency losses in bank mergers, these tend to be modest.

Next to geographic proximity, distance may also be defined in terms of *social distance between bidder and target culture*, reflected in such items as language, legal tradition or values. This type of distance, while it may also indicate the acquisition of important new cultural sensivity skills through the deal, is often regarded as an efficiency barrier and, thus, assumed to have a negative impact on wealth creation.[296] However, if targets are acquired precisely because they have experience in how to deal with customers from a different culture, such differences might also have a positive impact. IM studies generally confirm that social distance lowers a bank's propensity to expand abroad and, thus, probably has a negative impact on wealth creation.[297] However, Kiymaz (2004) explicitly tests the impact of cultural similarities on the CARs of US bidders and targets in international acquisitions and cannot find a significant impact.

Relatedness between bidder and target is also reflected in the degree of *functional relatedness* that is especially low in vertical cross-border deals which in turn foster diversification. Additionally, low relatedness may indicate possibilities for economies of scope. On the other hand, such deals may create diseconomies of scope, especially if different businesses require different types of expertise or combining them creates conflicts of interest. Empirical evidence shows either a significant negative impact of functional bidder-target differences[298] or no significant impact,[299] indicating that either negative effects from diseconomies of scope prevail or the two effects offset each other.

Since planning and conducting deals and integrating targets are complex tasks that require some experience, the odds of a successful deal should increase with *bidder M&A experience*. There is indeed strong evidence from the IM literature that previous internationalization experience significantly increases the chances

296 Buch and DeLong (2004).

297 Grosse and Goldberg (1991), Fisher and Molyneux (1996), Buch and DeLong (2003, 2004, 2005), Gallindo et al. (2003), Tschoegl (2003), Berger et al. (2004), Buch and Lipponer (2004).

298 DeLong (2001), Cornett et al. (2003), Altunbas and Ibañez (2004).

299 Cybo-Ottone and Murgia (2000), Vander Vennet (2003), Campa and Hernando (2005), Beitel et al. (2004).

of further internationalization.[300] However, event studies that account for this factor either cannot find an impact of bidder experience[301] or even find a negative impact,[302] which leads Gleason and Mathur (1998) to speculate that frequent previous acquisitions are an indicator of agency problems in the bidder organization.

If such agency effects are indeed relevant and come at the expense of shareholders, the *existence of mechanisms to reduce agency conflicts* on the side of the bidder may be positively related to wealth creation, at least as far as bidders are concerned. Allen and Cebenoyan (1991) and Cornett et al. (2003) provide evidence that measures such as insider shareholdings, a high level of ownership concentration, CEO's pay-performance-sensitivity or a high number of outsiders on the board of directors make acquisitions that create bidder wealth more likely.

Finally, the *share of the acquisition price paid in cash* could have a wealth effect, at least for bidding banks.[303] First, there is again an agency effect at work: if management has a tendency to use free cash-flows to conduct unprofitable but manager-utility-maximizing investments, diverting free cash flow away from management potentially reduces wealth-destroying agency effects and, thus, increases bidder wealth.[304] Second, bidders are assumed to be more inclined to make stock offers when they believe their shares are overvalued and cash offers when they believe their shares are undervalued. If investors see through this, they will reevaluate bidder shares upward following a cash offer and downward following a stock offer. Thus, cash-offers can be looked upon as a signal of bidder undervaluation. Baradwaj et al. (1992) and Cornett et al. (2003) confirm this effect in interstate acquisitions. Other authors, however, cannot find a significant impact.[305]

Table 4.7 summarizes the discussion on theory and evidence on firm-level determinants and also shows the M&A motives related to each of the identified determinants.[306]

---

300 Ball and Tschoegl (1982), Ursacki and Vertinsky (1992), Piscitello (2003), Buch and Lipponer (2004).
301 Waheed and Mathur (1995), Hudgins and Seifert (1996).
302 Gleason and Mathur (1998). Beitel et al. (2004).
303 See e.g., Hawawini and Swary (1990) and the cited literature.
304 Compare the discussion of Jensen's (1986) free cash-flow argument in section 3.2.3.
305 Cornett and De (1991), DeLong (2001), Beitel et al. (2004).
306 For a more detailed overview of results, see table A.3 in the appendix.

Table 4.7: Firm-Level Determinants of Wealth Effects

Determinant	Related M&A motive	Impact on shareholder wealth according to theory[1]	Impact on shareholder wealth according to evidence[1]: CF Literature	IM Literature
Bidder size	Economies of scale	-/+	0	+
Relative (target) size	Economies of scale, risk-shifting	-/+	0/+	n.a.
Presence of existing (home country) clients in the host country	Economies of scale	0/+	-	+
Relative (target) efficiency	X-Efficiency	-	0/-[2]	n.a.
Target efficiency	X-Efficiency	-/+	-/+	n.a.
Physical distance between bidder and target	Diversification	-/+	-/0	-
Social distance between bidder and target	Diversification	-/+	0	-
Functional differences between bidder and target	Diversification, Economies of scope	-/+	-/0	n.a.
Bidder M&A experience	All	+	-/0	+
Existence of mechanisms to reduce agency conflicts at bidders	Managerial utility maximization	+	+	n.a.
Share of the acquisition price paid in cash	Managerial utility maximization, private information	+	0/+	n.a.

1 *+ = positive, 0 = neutral, - = negative*
2 *Only with regard to profit efficiency, neutral effect of relative cost efficiency.*

4.2.3 Country- and Industry-Specific Factors

The literature review also reveals 9 country- and industry-specific factors that supposedly have some predictive power with regard to wealth effects. These are: host market size, host market growth, the degree of competition in the host market, exchange rates between bidder and target country currencies, the "temperature" of the equity capital market at the time of the bid, economic distance between home and host country, the economic openness and the intensity of bank regulation in the host country as well as specific geographic deal constellations. Again, theory and evidence on each factor are discussed in turn.

Banks may enter foreign markets in order to diversify or to follow their clients. However, an even more intuitive reason is to acquire new business with new customers, i.e., seeking profitable growth abroad. Following Buch and Lipponer

(2004) this is again an economies-of-scale argument: increasing the output by expanding into a large or growing new market is wealth-creating, because it allows the application of existing resources, such as management capability or risk-management technology, at low or zero marginal costs. A similar argument holds for X-efficiency: given that target efficiency can be increased, acquisition of a target in a large and/or growing market should ceteris paribus be preferable to one in a small and/or shrinking one. Seeking profitable growth abroad might also be of great importance to banks that face limits to domestic growth, either because the home market is already "overbanked" or because further domestic growth might face regulatory opposition on the basis of market power.[307]

The IM literature considers *host market size* or *host market growth* as good indicators for the presence of profitable growth opportunities from new customers. IM evidence is indeed strongly in favor of a positive effect of host market size,[308] indicating that "follow the client", if relevant at all, "is not the only game in town", as Degryse and Ongena (2004, p. 580) put it. Event studies again paint a somewhat less bright picture: Waheed and Mathur (1995) cannot find evidence of an impact of host market size on bidder wealth and Gleason and Mathur (1998) even find a significantly negative impact, leading them to speculate that large host countries may again generally be "overbanked".[309] Market growth is, in turn, not found to affect either market entry,[310] or subsequent joint entity efficiency changes.[311]

If CBBM&A intend to shift wealth from customers to shareholders by increasing market power, the *competitive situation in the host banking market* could be a good determinant of wealth creation. Lower levels of competition should indicate better possibilities to exploit market power. Evidence does mostly not support the relevance of the competitive situation, neither as a deter-

---

307 The European Central Bank (2000) provides evidence that this is indeed the case for a number of European countries. Tschoegl (2003) shows that limits to domestic growth foster CBBM&A. Bessler and Murtagh (2002) link a series of CBBM&A of Canadian banks to a home government decision to block further domestic consolidation.

308 Sagari (1986), Goldberg and Johnson (1990), Goldberg and Grosse (1994), Brealy and Kaplanis (1996), Miller and Parkhe (1998), Yamori (1998), Buch (2000), Berger et al. (2004), Buch and Lipponer (2004), Buch (2005), Focarelli and Pozzolo (2006).

309 See Focarelli and Pozzolo (2006) for a similar argument.

310 Berger et al. (2004), Ben Salem (2006). Kiymaz (2004) finds some – counterintuitive – evidence that host country growth negatively affects US bidders. His results are, however, not consistent across countries.

311 Vander Vennet (2003).

minant of the decision to expand into a specific country[312] nor of wealth creation[313] or efficiency changes.[314] This might be because market power is rather an issue in domestic mergers[315] or because of generally effective antitrust regulation.[316]

Another potential determinant is the *(real) exchange rate between bidder and target country currencies.* In the context of banking FDI, several hypotheses on the impact of this factor have been put forward. Some authors have argued that an appreciation of the home country currency relative to the host country currencies increases the relative wealth of bidder banks and allows them to acquire foreign assets more cheaply.[317] Hultmann and McGee (1989) instead argue that it is not actual exchange rates but expectations with regard to exchange rates that count. In that context, the authors argue that an appreciating foreign currency may well be looked upon as an indicator for future further appreciations and thus increase inward FDI.[318] Buch (2000) and Wezel (2004) build on the latter notion and argue that it is uncertainty with regard to exchange rate development, measured as exchange rate volatility, that determines FDI.[319]

Empirical results from the IM literature rather point to insignificance of this factor: Goldberg and Saunders (1980) and Hultmann and McGee (1989) find inconsistent results for the real exchange rate for differing indices. The most recent study of Goldberg and Johnson (1990), that tries to settle the issue, cannot find any significant results. Likewise, results by Buch (2000) that show negative significance of exchange rate volatility could not be replicated by Wezel (2004). With regard to CF studies that analyze this factor the work of Gleason and Mathur (1998) also does not find a significant impact. The results of Kiymaz

312 Sagari (1992).

313 Hawawini and Swary (1990), Cornett and De (1991).

314 Vander Vennet (2003).

315 Berger et al. (2004). However, as the case studies discussed above showed, market power played a role in at least some historic cross-border deals.

316 Note that results might also be related to a measurement problem as market power is generally measured in terms of asset concentration on local markets, which might not always be appropriate.

317 E.g., Goldberg and Saunders (1980), Goldberg and Johnson (1990). A more formalized, non bank-specific version of this argument can e.g. be found in Froot and Stein (1991).

318 Hultmann and McGee (1989), p. 385.

319 However, they do not predict a specific sign of exchange rate volatility. Wezel (2004) refers to a real options context in which increasing volatility of exchange rates may increase the (real option) value of a foreign subsidiary whereas he, like Buch (2000), also mentions that greater volatility may lower the rate of return on a foreign direct investment in a portfolio model-context. He simply concludes (p. 17): "In sum, there is no reason to be agnostic about the sign of the volatility measure."

(2004) are inconsistent across countries, also indicating that there is no general effect from exchange rate changes.

Rhodes-Kropf and Viswanathan (2004) show that managers have incentives to acquire when their stocks are overvalued, i.e., in "hot" equity markets which then coincide with "hot" merger markets. It follows that if investors are rational, *equity "market temperature"* should be negatively related to bidder wealth effects.[320] Beitel (2002) finds evidence that bidder and joint entity gains in bank mergers were indeed lower in "hot" deal phase around the turn of the last century.[321]

Berger et al. (2004), in addition to geographical and social distance between bidder and target, note the importance of *economic distance between home and host country* as a determinant of CBBM&A. Referring to a general equilibrium model of Markusen and Venables (1996), they test the so-called convergence hypothesis. This states that FDI in the form of CBBM&A is fostered by a similar level of development in the home and host country. The intuition behind this is that in economically dissimilar countries FDI from the higher developed country into the less developed country becomes too costly due to too low market demand and high production costs caused by poor factor endowments in the host and/or low technological expertise. The authors indeed find support for this. The CF study of Kiymaz (2004), however, cannot find support for this.

The *general economic openness* of the host country with regard to banking FDI is usually measured by the existence and intensity of capital controls or level of freedom provided to foreign FIs. Supposedly, less openness complicates both the transaction and the integration phase of a deal, lowering the level of wealth creation. Evidence is again exclusively based on the IM literature and is supportive of this notion.[322]

Since regulation plays a special role in the banking industry, the *level of bank regulation* may also be driving expected wealth creation. As discussed above, the relative importance of the regulatory environments of the home versus the host country largely depends on the choice of organizational form for the newly ac-

---

320 If investors rationally assume that managers are less concerned with deal fundamentals in phases of easy access to capital, this would likewise lead to bidder losses.

321 In a recent (non-bank) specific study, Kotzen et al. (2003) present evidence that is also in line with this hypothesis.

322 Nigh et al. (1986), Goldberg and Johnson (1990), Sagari (1992), Goldberg and Grosse (1994), Miller and Parkhe (1998), Buch and DeLong (2003, 2005), Berger et al. (2004), Buch and Lipponer (2004), Wezel (2004). Note that some of the above studies explicitly consider the European market after the implementation of the harmonization and deregulation efforts discussed above. This is in line with the notion that, despite harmonization and deregulation, economic openness of the host country is still of importance for CBBM&A.

quired institution. Since this is usually a subsidiary structure, the regulatory environment in the host country is of primary importance.

The discussion in section 3.2.3 showed that shareholder wealth increases through risk shifting are facilitated by "unfair" deposit insurance, a propensity of the regulator to act as a "lender of last resort", "powerless" regulators, and a lack of possibilities for market-based monitoring of banks. On the other hand, fair deposit insurance may increase the overall attractiveness of the market. Also, a strong regulator and ample possibilities for market based monitoring may make target institutions less opaque to bidder banks. This decreases the chances of bidder wealth losses through overbidding.[323] Evidence strongly supports that both "powerful" host country regulators and high host country market transparency in the banking sector attracts foreign banks,[324] while "fair" deposit insurance systems neither attract nor repel.[325] While the CF literature has not yet tested the wealth effects of these factors, it nevertheless finds that bank risk, both idiosyncratic and systematic, remains unchanged after CBBM&A, which is in line with risk-shifting being not a primary motive and/or realizable motive, the "risk-fencing" effect of subsidiary structures and also with the mostly negative results discussed above with regard to diversification benefits.[326]

While the above industry and country characteristics are frequently discussed as determinants of banking FDI or CBBM&A, the list is probably not exhaustive. Non-bank specific research has found other factors such as the strength of the rule of law, the level of corruption, the level of shareholder rights protection etc. to be related to cross-border M&A activity[327] and it seems at least possible that they are as well relevant for CBBM&A. Instead of individual analyses of these factors – that obviously strongly increase the data availability requirements in any empirical analysis – some authors have instead focused on the analysis of the effect of the involvement of specific home or host countries or country combinations. These countries are in turn assumed to posses a unique specification with

323 Degryse and Ongena (2004). Admittedly, this also decreases the chances of wealth gains through underbidding which should on average chancel out. However, empirically, overbidding seems to be more of an issue than underbidding.

324 Buch and Lipponer (2004), Buch and DeLong (2005). Note that the results of the former authors can also interpreted differently in the sense that more powerful regulators can create more opportunities for rent-extraction and are therefore attractive to foreign bidders.

325 Buch and DeLong (2005). The impact of capital requirements is usually much less tested, since, due to the efforts of the Bank for International Settlements (BIS) and the Basle rules, these are much more harmonized than deposit insurances rules.

326 Amihud et al. (2002), Buch and DeLong (2005).

327 E.g., Moeller and Schlingemann (2005).

regard to all these factors, that are especially conducive to banking FDI.[328] The most frequently *specific geographic deal constellations,* that are assumed to influence wealth, are deals with bidders and targets from the EU, deals with targets located in Eastern Europe and deals with targets located in the US or the UK.

The hypothesized effect of deals with *bidders and targets from the EU* links back to the discussion on legal deregulation and harmonization in section 2.2.1: Deliberately lowered regulatory hurdles are assumed to make these deals more attractive and, hence, wealth creating. If true, this could also be a reason for Europe being a CBBM&A "hotspot", as discussed in section 2.1. However, with the exception of Focarelli and Pozzolo (2005) who find a positive impact of EU membership and the number of bank subsidiaries between the respective countries, most IM research cannot find a significant impact of joint EU membership.[329] This may reflect the, on closer inspection, not entirely successful story of European financial market integration reviewed in section 2.2.1.

The hypothesized effect of deals with *targets being located in Eastern Europe* links back to market power deal motives or, more generally, the exploitation of market imperfections. Such deals may allow bidders, at least temporarily, to exploit monopoly gains in less competitive business environments, that were supposedly present in these countries shortly after they opened up their economies to foreign acquirers.[330] This is also consistent with the relatively large number of M&A deals in this region that occurred shortly after their economies opened up.[331] Indeed, the IM studies of Buch and DeLong (2003) and Wezel (2004) do find a positive relation between banking FDI intensity and targets being located in these regions.[332]

Finally, the notion of deals being more attractive and hence more wealth creating if *targets are located in the US or the UK* goes back to the large scale

---

328 See e.g. Berger et al. (2000, 2004), Ben Salem (2006).

329 Buch and DeLong (2003, 2004), Buch and Lipponer (2004), Berger et al. (2004).

330 This motive also became apparent in the review of the case study literature on CBBM&A.

331 See Soussa (2004) and section 2.1.

332 Some authors have argued that the consolidation process in Eastern Europe is over or at least considerably slowed down, e.g., Buch and DeLong (2003). In that context, one may further argue, that the impact of the target being located in Eastern Europe on shareholder wealth is of rather historic interest and not primarily relevant for present-day decision makers. Even if that was true, this study argues that insights drawn from deals with targets in markets that have only recently opened up to foreign bidders and still show significant imperfections are generally applicable to future deals with similar characteristics, e.g. deals with Chinese or Indian targets.

analyses of determinants of CBBM&A by Berger et al. (2000, 2004).[333] Controlling for a variety of other factors, the authors find support for such an hypothesized comparative advantage of the US or the UK at importing financial institutions M&A, which the authors explain by the joint impact of a transparent and open, capital-market oriented business environment in the respective countries.[334] Table 4.8 summarizes the findings on country- and industry-level determinants.[335]

4.3 Summary and Implications from the Previous Literature

The initial research questions developed in chapter one, whose practical relevance has been strongly supported by chapter two, adressed the wealth effects of CBBM&A and their determinants. Obviously, the previous literature had not been silent on these questions. What, therefore, is it that we do already know on these questions and what, if anything, is it that we still don't know?

Evidence with regard to wealth effects was gathered by event studies, both short- and long-term, OP and DE studies as well as case studies. The first, event studies, were the most numerous. Their findings are recapped in figure 4.1.

The figure shows the reported wealth effects by type of deal (domestic, interstate or cross-border) and type of entity under consideration (bidder, target, joint entity). Obviously, almost all studies pointed to abnormal gains for targets. Even though results for bidders and the joint-entity were less homogenous, it generally seems that the interstate literature finds strongly negative results for bidders, resulting sometimes in a negative net effect. This could suggest that the drawbacks of deals over large distances prevail over their advantages.

However, genuine cross-border deals painted a more positive picture of bidder and net wealth effects, which was even more positive than that of domestic deals. Overall, they suggested that bidders in cross-border deals do rather not

---

333 The findings of Ben Salem (2006) also support the notion of a comparative advantage of importing CBBM&A for the UK.

334 More detailed mentioned factors that could form such an environment are e.g. an active market for corporate control, access to well developed securities markets, access to a well educated labour force, possibilities to establish universal banks, relatively relaxed prudential regulation, reliable institutions, etc. see Berger et al. (2000). Walter (2003) shows that a comparative advantage of the US may be due to a relatively consistent system of banking regulation that covers a large and economically important area.

335 Compare again table A.3 in the appendix for a more detailed overview of findings in previous studies.

Table 4.8: Country- and Industry-Level Determinants of Wealth Effects

Determinant	Related M&A motive	Impact on shareholder wealth according to theory[1]	Impact on shareholder wealth according to evidence[1] CF Literature	IM Literature
Host market size	Economies of scale, X-Efficiency	+	n.a.	+
Host market growth	Economies of scale, X-Efficiency	+	0	0
Competitive situation in the host banking market	Market Power	+	0	0
Exchange rates between bidder and target country currency	Relative Wealth	+/-	0	0
"Temperature" of equity market	Private Information	-	-	n.a.
Economic distance between home and host country	All	-	0	-
General economic openness of the host country	All	+	n.a.	+
Intensity of bank regulation	All	+/-	0[2]	0[3]/+[4]
Specific geographic deal constellations (bidder and target in the EU, target in Eastern Europe, target in US or UK)	All	+	n.a	0[5]/+

1 + = positive, 0 = neutral, - = negative, +/- indications for both positive and negative effects.

2 findings show that bank risk, both systematic and non-systematic, does not change following a CBBM&A

3 No impact with regard to the "fairness" of host country deposit insurance

4 Positive impact on the "power" of the host country regulator and the possibilities for market based bank monitoring in the host.

5 Evidence with regard to EU membership of both bidder and target does mostly not show a significant impact.

gain but often break even, depending on circumstances that are more complex than just a linear decrease in wealth with distance. The resulting net wealth effects seem to be as often neutral as positive.

The review of the long-term event studies added an interesting, if somewhat alarming perspective, as most of these studies found significant long-term abnormal returns in the post-acquisition period. However, it remained unclear if deals on average over- or underperform, as the literature found evidence for both. It might be that results are outliers, with no long-term abnormal performance being the "normal" case, which would be in line with the findings of over- as well as underperformance and the presence of methodological issues, that are known

Figure 4.1: Summary of Previous Short-Term Event Study Outcomes

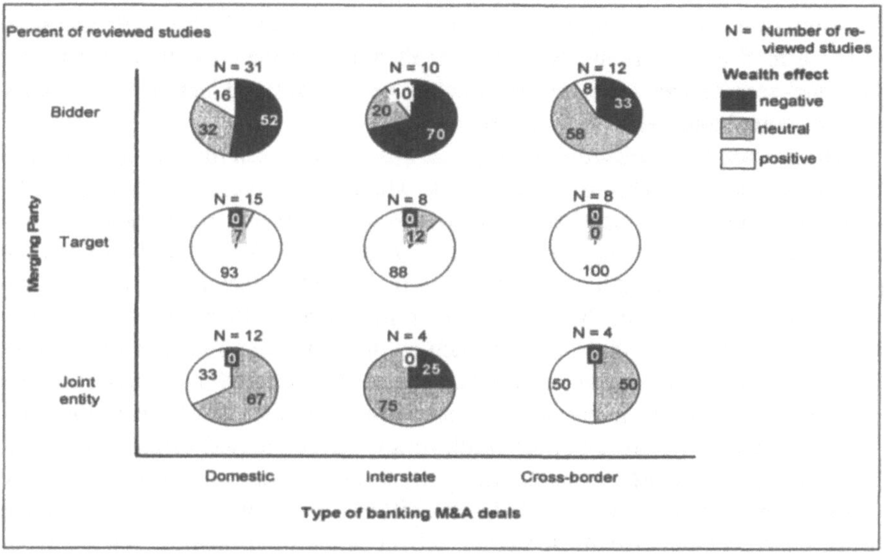

to lead to the detection of abnormal returns when in fact none are present. However, it might also be that results are indeed representative for CBBM&A, which would call into question the entire findings of the short-term literature, as the wealth effects found there would then only be a fraction of the total wealth effects.

OP and DE studies proved quite instructive, as they more or less clearly indicated that cross-border deals lead to profit-efficiency enhancements for the acquired institutions. Various reasons can explain why these do not show up as net gains in the event studies. Efficiency gains might e.g. be "passed through" to customers or clients or might be offset by losses that OP and DE studies cannot detect. It might even be that markets consistently fail to anticipate these gains and later correct their assessment, which would reconcile the OP and DE findings with the findings of positive abnormal returns from the long-term literature. However, the also found long-term abnormal losses do not fit into this picture. Thus, despite their instructiveness and as expected after the general discussion of the advantages and disadvantages of these methods, OP and DE studies can only offer limited insight with regard to the research question, as they cannot measure wealth effects directly. This is even more true for the reviewed case studies that rather helped to identify potential determinants of wealth creation than wealth effects.

What also follows from the literature review is that all previous studies, that allow for some inference on the wealth effects of CBBM&A, suffer from at least two and often multiple of the following five problems: inability to measure wealth effects comprehensively, lack of applicability to the cross-border case, insufficient sample size, lack of a "net wealth" perspective and lack of a methodologically sound long-term perspective.

The *inability to measure wealth effects* has already been discussed above. As discussed there, OP, DE and case studies, while instructive, could only provide indications but not a comprehensive answer to the posed research questions.

The *lack of applicability to the cross-border case* links to the discussion on the determinants of wealth effect, that identified a set of factors, for which there was some evidence, that they indeed determine wealth effects. However, since the impact of many of these factors, such as the economic openness of the host country or cultural bidder-target distance, cannot be captured in domestic studies or even in from-one-to-many or from-many-to-one studies, this leads to the conclusion that all non cross-border studies may deliver biased estimators of the "true" average CBBM&A wealth effect. Or, to turn things around, since there is evidence that wealth effects in CBBM&A differ significantly from those in other deals, only genuine CBBM&A studies deliver unbiased estimators for the average wealth effect. Unfortunately, despite the large number of previous event study work, the only genuinly global previous studies are the contributions of Biswas et al. (1997) and Amihud et al. (2004). The work of Beitel et al. (2004) also qualifies to an extent, since they choose a very broad definition of European deals.[336] The "next best" candidates, e.g., the European event- and OP/DE studies, are already more problematic, since, as discussed above, deals within Europe may systematically differ from deals in other geographic locations.

Insufficient sample size is another problem. Many of the studies discussed above use samples sizes of below 30 cross-border deals, which makes inferences on average wealth effects somewhat problematic.[337] Unfortunately, this is also true for the otherwise well suited studies of Biswas et al. (1997) and Amihud et al. (2004), that draw inferences on the critical net wealth effects based on a sample of only 35 and 12 deals, respectively. However, for some studies, there is even a complete *lack of a net wealth perspective*, and thus no assessment of the overall economic viability of the deals.[338]

---

336 More concretely, they define as European deal as any deal with a European bidder.

337 E.g., Trifts and Scanlon (1987), De Cossio et al. (1988), Hannan and Wolken (1989), Cornett and Tehranian (1992), Tourani-Rad and van Beek (1999), Cybo-Ottone and Murgia (2000), Akhigbe and Madura (2004), Ayadi and Pujals (2005).

338 E.g., De and Duplichan (1987), Trifts and Scanlon (1987), DeCossio (1988), Allen and Cebenoyan (1991), Cornett and De (1991), Baradwaj et al. (1992), Cornett and

Finally, given the findings from the long-term studies above, the *lack of a long-term perspective* in event studies is problematic, since short-term abnormal returns might only reflect a fraction of the relevant wealth effects. Only three studies, Cybo-Ottone and Murgia (2000), Beitel (2002),[339] and Campa and Hernando (2005) take such an additional long-term perspective. Even more problematically, the methodology used in these studies seems not suited to address identified common problems in the analysis of long-term abnormal returns.[340]

Thus, in a nutshell, there is a gap in the literature with regard to evidence on the average wealth effects of CBBM&A, that (also) takes a net wealth perspective, considers long-term effects and is based on a large, global sample of deals.

With regard to the second research question after the determinants of wealth effects the literature review resulted in a variety of factors, ranging from firm size to the level of power assigned to the host country banking regulator. However, the review again revealed some gaps in the previous literature. One, obviously, is that an adequate empirical assessment whether and how these factors determine wealth effects needs to be based on the abovementioned broad, global sample of CBBM&A deals, that is currently lacking in the literature. However, this is not the only issue.

Another is that all previous studies have analyzed only subsets of the identified set of factors. Even the most comprehensive earlier studies, do not cover even half of the them, and, consequently, also ignore potential interactions.[341] Another is that, with regard to some factors, evidence provided by the IM and the CF literature is contradictory and there is no effort to reconcile or explain these marked differences. Examples are e.g., the findings of the CF literature that the presence of home country clients in the host country and the level of bidder M&A experience rather decrease bidder gains whereas it is a generally accepted notion that these are key success factors for bidders in the IM literature.

Finally, with regard to some factors, e.g., host economic openness, there is so far no direct evidence on wealth effects at all since all evidence is provided by IM studies, that test the impact of these factors only on such proxies as the frequency of deals or the volume of FDI.

Tehranian (1992), Cornett et al. (2003), Waheed and Mathur (1995), Hudgins and Seifert (1996), Gleason and Mathur (1998), Tourani-Rad and van Beek (1999), Schiereck and Strauss (2000), Bessler and Murtagh (2002), Bohl et al. (2004).

339 Note that Beitel (2002) is an earlier, working paper version of Beitel et al. (2004), that other than the latter, does include a long-term perspective.

340 Compare footnote 252.

341 See table A.3 in the appendix for a comprehensive overview of which earlier IM or CF studies analyzed the impact of what factor. The table also displays the respective findings.

Thus, again, there is a need for further research on the joint wealth impact of all analyzed factors, optimally based on the large, global sample of CBBM&A deals described above.

This study will try to close the identified gaps in the literature. It already became apparent in chapter 3 that event study methodology may be the best available choice to do so. First and foremost, this is because only event study methodology allows to directly measure the impact of CBBM&A on shareholder wealth. Shareholder wealth maximization was in turn shown to be the practically most important and, moreover, theoretically valid, "desireable" goal for the primary decisionmakers in such deals. Also, other than efficiency-related methods, it also lends itself well to cross-country comparisions, the analyses of deal motives that are not related to efficiency enhancement and detailed inquiries on the split of effects between bidders and targets. Capturing these general advantages seem well worth accepting the drawbacks of event studies, including the fact that probably only a small fraction of CBBM&A deals can be analyzed. This, however, requires that adequate measures are taken to address the identified potential pitfalls of event study usage and that the analyzed CBBM&A sample still seem representative of the overall market. This is discussed in more detail in the following chapter on research design.

5. Design of Analysis

In order to fill the research gap identified in the previous section, this chapter describes a framework to empirically test the wealth effects of CBBM&A and their determinants. For that purpose, the findings from chapter 2 are first transformed into testable hypotheses in *section 5.1*. *Section 5.2* then selects and if necessary modifies an array of methods developed in the earlier literature to measure the wealth impact of CBBM&A. Following the implications from the literature review, the general method of choice will thereby be event studies.

Sample selection criteria and data sources are discussed in *section 5.3*. Next, *section 5.4* is concerned with how to measure the identified determinants and how to determine their impact on shareholder wealth. *Section 5.5* summarizes the developed framework for analysis.

5.1 Development of Testable Hypotheses

Based on the large majority of previous evidence, targets are expected to gain from acquisitions. Forming expectations for bidders and the joint entity is somewhat more difficult, as results differ across studies. However, assuming that the "true" CBBM&A event studies are the best applicable evidence and that the frequency of findings is indicative for their correctness, it is expected that CBBM&A does not affect bidder or the net bidder-target wealth. Following Fama (1998), markets are furthermore assumed to be semi-strong efficient, even in the presence of some documented anomalies. Thus, no long-term abnormal returns following CBBM&A are expected.

With regard to the 11 identified firm-level determinants,[342] only 10 will be tested for their impact on shareholder wealth. Unfortunately, the existence of mechanisms that reduce agency effects such as CEO pay-performance sensitivity, the number of outside directors etc. is not available for a sufficiently large number of firms to be empirically tested. Of the 9 identified country/industry-level determinants,[343] the growth rate of and the competitive situation in the host market are not tested, since previous evidence from both the CF and the IM literature

342 See table 4.7, p. 119.
343 See table 4.8, p. 126.

does not corroborate their relevance.[344] The same is true for exchange-rate induced effects. This leaves 6 country/industry-level determinants for testing.

The literature review showed that the impact of some of the potential determinants is in line with the theoretical considerations discussed for these factors above.[345] This is true for host market size, the temperature of the equity market, the general economic openness of the host country, and special geographic deal constellations, more concretely deals with targets in the US and the UK, deals with both bidder and target within the EU and deals with targets in Eastern Europe, on the country-/industry-level.[346] Accordingly, for these factors effects are assumed to be as predicted by theory or as found in earlier research. More concretely, the temperature of the equity market at the time of the bid is expected to affect shareholder wealth negatively while the size of the host country market, its level of economic openness and deals with one of the three abovementioned geographic constellations are expected to have positive effects.

For other factors, evidence, either within the CF or IM literature or across the two types, is split with some studies providing evidence that supports theory while other studies are unable to find a significant impact. This is true for bidder size, relative target size, relative target efficiency, functional differences between bidder and target, share of the acquisition price paid in cash and social and economic distance. Therefore, it is expected that results in this study are either in line with the previous significant evidence or not significant at all. More concretely, if significant at all, bidder size, relative target size, and the share of the acquisition price paid in cash are expected to have a positive impact on shareholder wealth.[347] If relative target efficiency, functional differences between bid-

344 Note that there is some chance that these determinants show some relevance in the current, adjusted research setup. However, also note that the number of determinants needs to be limited due to most probably very restricted sample size. Here, the irrelevance of determinants is selected as a suitable indicator of irrelevance also in future research.

345 This holds at least for one of the theories if there are several, see the overview in tables 4.7 and 4.8. Note that for all factors where evidence is unambiguous, it is either provided by the IM or the CF literature alone, i.e., there is no factor which both the IM and the CF literature have tested and both found evidence that pointed in the same direction.

346 Note, however, that evidence on the targets being located in Eastern Europe or in the US or UK is somewhat stronger than that of bidder and target being located in the EU.

347 Expectations on the impact of size are not further differentiated (e.g., positive for small banks and negative for large banks), as could be inferred from the findings of a U-shaped cost curve. This is, firstly, because it is assumed that banks that perform CBBM&A are large anyway which is, in turn, supported by the sample properties. Secondly, the discussion showed that size related effects in CBBM&A are probably

der and target and social or economic distance have an impact at all, it is expected to be negative. This is also true for geographical distance between bidder and target, despite some earlier discussed arguments that IT advancements had lowered the importance of this factor.[348]

Some determinants do not fit in either of these categories. With regard to the existence of bidder home country clients in the host country and bidder M&A experience, the evidence is mixed in the sense that empirical studies find both positive and negative results. A significant negative impact, however, cannot be explained by the existing theories. Thus, for those factors, a significant positive impact is expected.[349] With regard to target efficiency, theory justifies both a positive and a negative impact and evidence indeed supports both. Accordingly, this study also expects the effect to be either significantly negative or significantly positive. This leaves the intensity of bank regulation in the host country. Here, differentiation with regard to the different aspects of regulation is necessary. From these, this study will focus on the general level of power attributed to the host regulator and the existence of market-based monitoring measures. For both, there is empirical evidence that supports the notion of a positive impact on wealth creation. Thus, similar results are expected in this study.

On the firm level, this study has so far intended to test the impact of a set of factors that are more or less easily observable or can at least be reasonable well proxied. While there is a relation between each of these factors and one or multiple of the identified deal motives, the impact of deal motives is not tested directly. Obviously, this is because motives are difficult to observe private information. They are, however, not completely opaque, as bidders usually offer some explanation to their shareholders and the public as to why an acquisition is performed. Remember that the case study literature argued that quantitative analysis may sometimes fail to capture the often very specific considerations which drive a deal. Against this background, it may well be that actual management announcements much better reflect the true deal motives than accounting relations.

---

more strongly related to revenue than to cost scale economies, for which no U-shaped curves are found. Thirdly, also as discussed above, even if cost scale economies are relevant, there are also findings that support the notion that technological progress in the 1990s had a significant impact on cost curve shapes and made cost scale economies also available for larger banks.

348 See section 2.2.2.

349 In the case of bidder M&A experience, some previous evidence also indicates a neutral effect. Thus, neutral results are also considered a possibility in this study.

Thus, there is a case for directly testing the impact of the announced deal motives on shareholder wealth.[350]

From the previous discussion, three broad classes of deal motives are expected to be reflected in actual bidder announcements: operational synergy creation, geographical diversification and functional diversification.[351] Here, the literature review found that determinants related to both geographical and functional diversification were rather negatively related to shareholder wealth effects, while the opposite was true for determinants related to operational synergies. Thus, this study hypothesizes a negative (or possibly neutral) wealth effect for deals in which bidders intend to either geographically or functionally diversify while a positive (or again possibly neutral) effect is expected for deals in which bidders announce an intent to create operational synergies.

What has been ignored so far are IT advancements as a potential determinant of CBBM&A. While section 2.2.2 provided some arguments that these may affect the attractivity of CBBM&A, none of the various reviewed studies had supported this. Here, in line with the arguments provided in section 2.2.2, especially the hypothesis that the net effect of IT advancements in service-intensive industries is probably rather conducive for M&A, it is hypothesized that shareholder wealth effects increase with the level of bidder IT sophistication.

A final word on expectations with regard to the distribution of wealth effects across bidder and target seems due. With the exception of the share of cash in the acquisition price and the temperature of the equity market that should both primarily affect bidder and thus also net wealth, and as usual in the literature, no expectations with regard to the distribution of wealth effects across bidders and targets are formed. This is heavily dependent on relative bargaining power and ability, which is difficult to assess with the available information. Thus, a thorough analysis requires the analysis of the impact of each factor on the wealth of bid-

350 However, these announcements could be biased towards shareholder wealth-increasing and specifically synergy-creating motives, as the admittance of other reasons would likely lead to adverse consequences for management. Thus, the analysis is not well suited to identify the presence of agency related motives. However, since there is no reason why managers should systematically disguise agency related motives with a specific other class of motives, the overall results should nevertheless be instructive.

351 Note that the above discussion showed that operational synergy creation can be broken down into various more granular motives such as scale economy creation etc. However, the information available on announced motives is based on press clippings and not on analyst presentations and, thus, does not allow this level of detail to be captured. Nevertheless, the information does allow motives related to the creation of financial synergies to be broken down into those that relate to geographic-, and those that relate to functional- diversification.

ders and targets as well as the joint entity. Table 5.1 summarizes the developed hypotheses.

Table 5.1: Hypotheses on Determinants of Wealth Effects

Level of determinant	Determinant	Related M&A motive	Impact on shareholder wealth... ...according to theory[1]	...according to evidence[1] CF	...according to evidence[1] IM	...expected in this study
Firm	1. Bidder size	Economies of scale	-/+	0	+	0/+
	2. Relative (target) size	Economies of scale, risk-shifting	-/+	0/+	n.a.	0/+
	3. Presence of existing (home country) clients in the host country	Economies of scale	0/+	-	+	+
	4. Relative (target) efficiency	X-Efficiency	-	-/0[2]	n.a.	-/0
	5. Target efficiency		-/+	-/+	n.a.	-/+
	6. Physical distance between bidder and target	Diversification	-/+	-/0	-	-/0
	7. Social distance between bidder and target		+/-	0	-	-
	8. Functional differences between bidder and target	Diversification, Economies of scope	+/-	-/0	n.a.	-/0
	9. Bidder M&A experience	All	+	-/0	+	0/+
	10. Share of the acquisition price paid in cash	Managerial utility maximization, Exploitation of private information	+	0/+	n.a.	0/+
	11. Bidder intent to create operational synergies	All motives related to operational synergies	0/+	0/+	0/+	0/+
	12. Bidder intent to diversify geographically	All motives related to financial synergies	-/+	-/0	-/0	-/0
	13. Bidder intent to diversify functionally		-/+	-/0	-/0	-/0
	14. IT sophistication of bidder organization	Economies of scale, X-Efficiency	-/+[3]	n.a.	n.a.	+
Country/ Industry	15. Host market size		+	n.a.	+	+
	16. "Temperature" of equity market	Private Information	-	-	n.a.	-
	17. Economic distance between home and host country		-	0	-	-
	18. General economic openness of the host country		+	n.a.	+	+
	19. Intensity of bank regulation in the host country[4]		+/-	n.a.	+	+
	20. Host country is US or UK		+	n.a.	+	+
	21. Bidder and target are in the EU		+	n.a.	0/+	0/+
	22. Target is located in Eastern Europe		+	n.a.	+	+

1 + = positive, 0 = neutral, - = negative.
2 Only with regard to relative cost-efficiency.
3 Some tentative, non-bank-specific evidence for a net positive effect in service-intensive industries.
4 With regard to overall power assigned to regulator and possibilities for market -based monitoring.

5.2 Selection of Measurement Approach for Wealth Effects

A focus of this section will be to select and modify methods in a way, that the potential pitfalls in the use of event study methodology will be addressed. One such issue was the potential violation of the market efficiency assumption. Since the literature review showed that there is evidence that strengthens the notion of markets not being efficient in the context of CBBM&A, this issue becomes critical. Therefore, market efficiency and the size of possible positive or negative long abnormal returns following CBBM&A need to be explicitly tested. For that purpose, the methodology to be used in this study needs to include a long-term event study as well as a traditional short-term approach. The latter is outlined in section 5.2.1, while the former is developed in section 5.2.2. Section 5.2.3 summarizes the suitability of the selected methods with regard to the identified issues.

5.2.1 Short-Term Event Study Methodology

As discussed in section 3.3.1, the building blocks of an event study methodology are the definition of the event in question and the event window, a model of expected returns including the estimation of its parameters and, finally, a method to aggregate abnormal returns and measure their significance. Selections within these building blocks are discussed in turn.

5.2.1.1 Definition of Event and Event Window

The revelation of information about CBBM&A can be a process instead of a one-time event that can be pinpointed exactly. This poses a challenge for the optimal choice of event date and event window. The acquisition of the Polish Bank Pekao by the Italian bank Unicredito in 1999 is an instructive example of this issue. Mußhoff and Schiereck (2004), in their case study about the deal, show that the Polish government in September 1998 publicly announced that it was seeking an acquirer for its majority stake in the bank. This is a piece of information on which market participants could have traded. More specifically, since acquisitions usually lead to significant premiums for targets and there was now some likelihood that Pekao would be acquired, this news probably led investors to buy Pekao shares, thus driving their price up. Later, on October 20th, Unicredito's CEO, in the context of an interview on future growth opportunities for his bank, noted that "Poland is a very interesting market."[352] Since Pekao was up for sale and Uni-

352 Dow Jones International News (1998).

credito was interested in Poland, this suggested some chance of a deal between the two. Again, market participants had a chance to trade on this information and the resulting share price reaction depended on the assessed likeliness and impact of the deal.

After a bidding process in which some domestic and many foreign banks were assumed to participate, Reuters News titled on April 23rd, 1999: "Italy's Unicredito in final phase for Pekao buy" and referred to information from inside Unicredito that the deal was now all but formally completed.[353] Other news agents came up with similar reports on the same or the following day.[354] Again, market participants had the possibility to trade on the news. The official announcement by the Polish government that Unicredito was indeed the selected buyer followed 8 weeks later, on June 23rd.[355]

This chain of events makes the selection of a single event date a somewhat ambiguous task. As discussed above, empirical studies tend to select the "official" announcement date, in this case June 23rd, as the event date. This is also what Mußhoff and Schiereck (2004) did.

Leakage, slow information processing by market participants or simply errors in date estimation are usually accounted for with the use of an event window that covers a few days around the deal. Methodological guidance on the choice of this event window is scarce: most researchers choose a window of similar length to windows in earlier studies in order to make results comparable. Also, most researchers refrain from choosing windows that are much longer than 1 to 2 trading months, since there is evidence that in such windows the disadvantages of including noise start to outweigh the advantages of capturing leakage and slow information processing.[356] It was shown above that these considerations frequently lead to event windows opening roughly 10 days before the event and closing 10 days after it with the event defined as the official announcement date. In the above example, Mußhoff and Schiereck (2004) used an even larger window opening 20 days before the event date and closing 20 days after it.

This procedure has a good chance of capturing press reports about upcoming deals that precede the official announcement by a few days. However, as the example shows, that might not be enough: if there was a wealth effect caused by the Reuter's story that came out 8 weeks before the official announcement, Mußhoff and Schiereck (2004) failed to capture it. One may argue that such stories are rare. However, if there were wealth effects caused by the even earlier announce-

---

353 Reuters News (1999a).

354 See e.g., Dow Jones International News (1999), Neue Zürcher Zeitung (1999).

355 Reuters News (1999b).

356 Peterson (1989).

ments, i.e., that Pekao was to be sold or that Unicredito was generally interested in Poland, these were likewise not caught. Such bidder- or target specific leakage is, however, not uncommon.[357]

If previous relevant information and subsequent price reactions are missed, this can lead to biases in measured abnormal returns in the sense that much of the effect in which the researcher is interested is already incorporated in the stock price at the event date. In the case of Mußhoff and Schiereck (2004), their finding that Pekao suffered slight losses on the announcement day, which seems highly unusual in the context of the above discussion of the typical target reaction, might be such an instance. It is possible that market participants were already quite sure about the occurrence of the deal due to the previous stories and only reacted to the actual acquisition price, which may have been below their expectations.

What implications follow for the choice of methodology in this study? First, with regard to the definition of the event date, this study follows a similar approach to the domestic banking M&A studies of Houston and Ryngaert (1994, 1997) and Houston et al. (2000) for leakage detection. The event date is defined as the trading day on which credible information about the intent of a specific bidder to acquire a specific target reaches the market via the financial press.[358] Information is considered credible if the news agency in question cites sources inside the company. The "financial press," in turn, is considered to be appropriately reflected by the agencies covered in the Factiva Database, such as Reuters and Dow Jones International as well as various newspaper publications including e.g., the Financial Times. Concrete event dates are determined by starting with the official announcement date provided by the databases used to draw the sample and then starting a press search with Factiva covering a period 3 months before the announcement date until the announcement date. If references to earlier news are found, the press search is extended for another 3 months and so forth until the "true" event date is detected.

This procedure does, however, not account for bidder- or target-specific leakage. To address this issue also, for each deal in the sample, another press search, similar to the one described above, is executed that screens for information about either the bidder intending to acquire in the host country or the target being up for sale, independent of any reference to the other transaction partner.[359] As a

357 Remember e.g., the introductory example of the acquisition of Abbey National by Banco Santander Central Hispano.

358 If the day in question is not a trading day, the next possible trading day is considered the event day.

359 Other than with the search above, this information does not need to come from inside the company. This is to account for targets that, even though they do not de-

consequence, for each deal, there will be at least one (the event date, if it is identical to the announcement date) and maximal four dates that have some relevance for market participants and wealth effects (the bidder-specific leakage date, the target-specific leakage date, the event date and the announcement date). This procedure allows an analysis of whether wealth effects in deals in which there is bidder- or target specific leakage differ from those where there is none. There is some speculation in the event study literature that such previous bidder- or target-specific leakage generally lowers the wealth effects measured at the official announcements dates.[360] However, to the knowledge of the author, there is no previous evidence on this.

With regard to the event window analyzed, this study follows the advice of Peterson (1989) and selects a window that allows results to be compared with as many earlier studies as possible. As table 4.1 above indicates, an event window that opens 20 days before the event day and closes 20 days after it is well suited for these purposes, as it allows sub-windows to be formed identical to those in almost all previous studies.[361]

5.2.1.2 Model of Expected Returns

As discussed above, calculating abnormal returns according to (1)[362] requires a model of expected returns. The literature proposes a wide variety of such models, which MacKinlay (1997) broadly groups into statistical models, that mainly make statistical assumptions about the behavior of stock returns and economic models that, in addition, rely on general assumptions about an investor's behavior.

Statistical models usually assume that asset returns are jointly multivariate normal and independently and identically distributed (i.i.d.) through time.[363] A

---

clare themselves as such, are widely believed to be a takeover target or bidders from which the market believes that they are bound to acquire in a specific country.

360 E.g., Dittmann and Ulbricht (2004).

361 The exception is the event window used by Tourani-Rad and van Beek (1999) that opens 40 days before the event and closes 40 days after it. However, most evidence in the latter study builds on a smaller 3-day window symmetrical to the event date.

362 See page 79.

363 This may seem a very strong assumption. Indeed, by definition, negative returns are limited to -100 percent and positive returns are (theoretically) unlimited, which indicates positive skewness of returns. There is also strong empirical evidence for the non-normality of returns, especially if daily data is used (e.g., Fama, 1976) and that the same problems are relevant for excess returns, see e.g., Brown and Warner (1985). However, event studies are concerned with the cross-sectional sample mean of excess returns. The central limit theorem states that the distribution of this sample mean, given that the excess returns in the cross-section of securities are i.i.d. draw-

simple statistical model is the index model which assumes that, over any time period of length t, the expected share return is the market rate of return R_{mt}:

$$(2)\ K_{it} = R_{mt}$$

Another simple model, sometimes called the average return model, assumes that expected share returns are equal to the average returns of a share during an estimation period (R_i):

$$(3)\ K_{it} = R_i$$

Finally, in the so-called market model, one hypothesizes a linear relationship between the expected return of a security and the market return with a security-specific constant α and slope coefficient β:

$$(4)\ K_{it} = \alpha_i + \beta_i R_{mt}$$ [364]

A well known economic model is the capital asset pricing model (CAPM) of Sharpe (1964), Lintner (1965) and Mossin (1966). The CAPM is a one-period model that makes the economically motivated assumptions of perfectly competitive capital markets, unrestricted borrowing or lending at the risk-free rate, no transaction costs, mean-variance optimizing investors, and homogenous investor expectations. The model then shows that the risk premium on individual securities, i.e., their return over the risk free rate, is proportional to the risk premium on

---

ings from a finite variance distribution, converges to normality as the number of securities in the sample increases. In their simulation experiments Brown and Warner (1985) present strong evidence that if standard return-aggregation methods are used this convergence already happens in relatively small samples: tests are well specified in samples of only 5 shares, whereas optimal results are reported with 50 or more securities. This leads the authors to the conclusion that "non-normality of daily returns has no obvious impact on event study methodologies" (p. 25) and that there is in addition no obvious gain from the use of log-normally distributed security returns. MacKinlay (1997, p. 17) thus concludes that the use of simple returns and the joint-normality assumption are the (valid) standard in short-term event studies.

364 Note that the index model is a special case of the market model with $\alpha = 0$ and $\beta = 1$. For a discussion of the market model, see Fama (1976).

the market portfolio and the extent to which returns on the security and the market move together, which is measured with the securities "beta".[365] This leads to:

$$(5)\ K_{it} = R_{ft} + \beta_i (R_{mt} - R_{ft})$$

where R_{ft} is the risk-free rate of borrowing and lending. Like the market-model and indeed closely related to it,[366] the CAPM is a single-factor model relating the expected return of a security to a market factor and systematic risk. Other asset-pricing models, such as the Arbitrage Pricing Theory of Ross (1976) or the Three-Factor-Model of Fama and French (1993), instead explain the expected return on a security as a linear combination of multiple factors.

The potential advantage of the CAPM or other formal asset-pricing models is that more precise measures of expected returns can be calculated by imposing economically motivated restrictions in addition to those used in statistical models. However, theoretical arguments and vast empirical evidence cast serious doubt on the validity of the restrictions imposed by the CAPM.[367] Other formal (multifactor) asset-pricing models have the potential advantage over the CAPM of eliminating most biases introduced by the latter. But since these biases are also eliminated using statistical models and since the additional factors have little explanatory power (but increase the data need for a practical test), statistical models are considered preferable and, hence, dominate event studies.[368] For that reason, this study refrains from the use of a formal asset pricing model.

Evidence on the relative merits of the statistical models discussed is mainly based on the outcomes of the simulation experiments in the seminal papers of Brown and Warner (1980, 1985)[369] that have been confirmed in various studies

---

365 A derivation can be found in almost any contemporary graduate-level finance textbook, such as Franke and Hax (2004).

366 The identical notation of beta relative to (4) is justified because the formal representation of beta, the covariance of the security return with the market return over a given period divided by the variance of the market return, is identical to the OLS-estimator of beta in (4), see also the discussion below. Note that this implies that the market model can be viewed as a version of the CAPM, by interpreting α_i as an estimate of $R_{ft}(1-\beta_i)$. Also note that the original CAPM is an ex-ante model: the expected value of a share is determined by expected values of R_m and β. In practice, ex-post values are substituted as proxies.

367 See e.g., Fama and French (1996).

368 MacKinlay (1997). The literature review of Beitel (2002) also shows that for banking M&A event studies the vast majority of authors uses a statistical model – specifically the market model.

369 The later paper specifically considers the use of daily data and is, thus, more relevant in the present context.

thereafter.[370] A first finding is that all models, even the simple average return model, lead to well-specified and powerful test statistics: t-tests based on all three models (using a significance level of 5 percent and a sample of 50 securities) are well-specified. For the same significance level and number of securities, the average power across methods is approximately 80 percent (100 percent) for 1 percent (2 percent) induced abnormal performance.[371] Since average abnormal performance for both domestic and CBBM&A is usually found around 2 percent for bidders and significantly higher for targets[372] and given that the sample to be drawn will not be significantly smaller than samples in previous CBBM&A studies,[373] all statistical models should perform well in detecting abnormal returns.

Of further interest is the simulation evidence of Brown and Warner (1985) as well as the results of Klein and Rosenfeld (1987). The authors show that if events are clustered, i.e., securities' calendar-time event windows overlap and there is, hence, a high probability of individual security returns being cross-correlated, or in bull- or bear markets, the average return model is severely misspecified.[374] Results also indicate that the market model is slightly more powerful than the index model.

The preceding discussion yields two insights. First, event study results are surprisingly robust to the choice of an expected return model. As already discussed in section 3.3.1.2, the reason is that, given the short event windows, errors in calculating abnormal performance are unlikely to matter since daily expected returns are very close to zero across models. Second, as the market model is at least as good as all the discussed models and in some specific circumstances significantly better, it seems the best choice for event studies, which is also the conclusion of Brown and Warner (1985). Beitel (2002) shows that it is used in the vast majority of banking M&A studies. Thus, this study assumes joint normality of asset returns and that individual returns are determined according to

$$(6)\ R_{it} = \alpha_i + \beta_i R_{mt} + \varepsilon_{it}$$

370 For a summary of various methodological papers on event studies after Brown and Warner (1985), see Armitage (1995).

371 Brown and Warner (1985).

372 See e.g., the overview of Beitel (2002), p. 116.

373 See table 2.5 for an overview of sample sizes in previous CBBM&A studies.

374 This is not surprising since both circumstances are likely to increase the variance of the abnormal performance measure chosen and, ceteris paribus, the mean-adjusted model is likely to explain a smaller part of the variance than either the index- or market-model since it does not control for market movements or systemic risk.

where ε_{it}, the abnormal return, is a disturbance term, the other variables are defined as above and the usual Gauss-Markov conditions apply.[375]

In order to use (6) to calculate the sample abnormal returns, the slope coefficient (beta) and the intercept (alpha) is estimated for each security in the sample. This estimation is done for a period preceding the event window in order to avoid that the estimators used in the expected return model are influenced by the – potentially abnormal – returns around the event. To allow time series aggregation of the events which are dispersed in calendar time, time is indexed in event time τ. Define $\tau = 0$ as the event date, $\tau = t_1+1$ to $\tau = t_2$ as the event window[376] of length $L_2 = t_2 - t_1$ and $\tau = t_0+1$ to $\tau = t_1$ as the (preceding) estimation window of length $L_1 = t_1 - t_0$. Following Beitel et al. (2002), an estimation window of one trading year is chosen.[377] Then, under the above assumptions, OLS delivers the following consistent estimators:[378]

$$(7)\ \hat{\beta}_i = \frac{\sum_{\tau=t_0+1}^{t_1}(R_{i\tau} - \hat{\mu}_i)(R_{m\tau} - \hat{\mu}_m)}{\sum_{\tau=t_0+1}^{t_1}(R_{m\tau} - \hat{\mu}_m)^2}$$

$$(8)\ \hat{\alpha}_i = \hat{\mu}_i - \hat{\beta}_i \hat{\mu}_m$$

$$(9)\ \hat{\sigma}_{\varepsilon_i}^2 = \frac{1}{L_1 - 2}\sum_{\tau=t_0+1}^{t_1}(R_{i\tau} - \hat{\alpha}_i - \hat{\beta}_i R_{m\tau})^2$$

375 Therefore: $E[\varepsilon_{it}] = 0, E[\varepsilon_{it}^2] = \sigma_{\varepsilon_i}^2, E[\varepsilon_{it}\varepsilon_{is}] = 0 \forall t \neq s$ where E is the expected value operator.

376 As discussed in the preceding section, the concrete values are t_1=-21 and t_2=20 measured in days.

377 Therefore t_0=-273.

378 For a derivation, see e.g., Dougherty (2002), pp. 56. Several authors, e.g., Dimson (1979) and Scholes and Williams (1977) have noted that if the trading frequency of sample securities is different from the trading frequency of the chosen market index, OLS may deliver biased estimators. They instead propose adjusted estimation procedures. However, Brown and Warner (1985) show that these adjustments neither improve the specification nor the power of subsequent tests of abnormal performance. Therefore, the adjustments are not considered here.

where

$$(10)\ \hat{\mu}_i = \frac{1}{L_1} \sum_{\tau=t_0+1}^{t1} R_{i\tau}$$

$$(11)\ \hat{\mu}_m = \frac{1}{L_1} \sum_{\tau=t_0+1}^{t_1} R_{m\tau}$$

The question remains what data is used for estimating market returns. Here, the standard choice is a general market index of the home country of the bank in question. To enhance comparability of data across country, the Datastream total market index is chosen as a proxy.[379]

Thus, using (1), (4), (6) and (7) to (11), sample abnormal returns are arrived at as the disturbance terms of the market model calculated on an out-of-sample basis:[380]

$$(12)\ \hat{A}R_{i\tau} = R_{i\tau} - \hat{\alpha}_i - \hat{\beta}_i R_{m\tau}$$

Abnormal returns can now easily be calculated for bidders and targets. However, to assess the question whether transactions are value-generating on a net basis, the market-value-weighted average for deal *d* with bidder *b* and target *a* must be estimated. Following Huston and Ryngaert (1994) this is done according to:

$$(13)\ \hat{A}R_{d,\tau} = \frac{\hat{A}R_{b,\tau} \cdot MV_{b,t_1} + \hat{A}R_{a,\tau} \cdot MV_{a,t_1}}{MV_{b,t_1} + MV_{a,t_1}}$$

379 Total return values are used in order to account for dividend-effects. While the market-index is the norm in event studies, some authors have alternatively chosen an industry-specific index, see e.g., Cybo-Ottone and Murgia (2000) or Beitel et al (2004). However, here this could induce a simultaneity bias, since bidders in the sample are expected to be very large, listed banks, that hence could form a significant part of the relevant index. In addition, in the comparable study of Cybo-Ottone and Murgia (2000), the use of market- and industry-indices led to similar results. Therefore, this study refrains from the use of an industry-index.

380 This is also the reason why abnormal returns are sometimes referred to as prediction errors.

where the MVs are the respective market values of equity of bidder and target at the end of the estimation period.

5.2.1.3 Aggregation and Tests of Abnormal Returns

The most commonly used method of time series aggregation of sample abnormal returns is to add them up across any interval from τ_1 to τ_2 which lies in the event window. Thus cumulative abnormal returns (CAR*) are estimated according to:

$$(14)\ \hat{CAR}^{*}_{i,(\tau_1,\tau_1)} = \sum_{\tau=\tau_1}^{\tau_2} \hat{AR}_{i\tau}$$

In this event study, as usual, the goal is to find out whether a class of events is, on average, associated with changes in shareholder wealth. Therefore, the focus is on the mean of abnormal returns. For a sample of N securities and event time τ, this mean, the cross-sectional average abnormal return (AAR) is estimated using

$$(15)\ \hat{AAR}_{\tau} = \frac{1}{N}\sum_{i=1}^{N} \hat{AR}_{i\tau}$$

Obviously, to investigate the behavior of the cross-sectional means within the event window, both time-series and cross-sectional aggregation is necessary. This is done by simply summing cross-sectional means across a period within the event window. This leads to the CARs which are estimated by

$$(16)\ \hat{CAR}_{(\tau_1,\tau_2)} = \sum_{\tau=\tau_1}^{\tau_2} \hat{AAR}_{\tau}$$

Statistical significance of the CARs is tested with the Z-statistic proposed by Dodd and Warner (1983) that has become the standard test of significance in recent banking M&A event studies.[381] The Z-statistic is calculated as

$$(17)\ Z_1 = \sqrt{\frac{N}{\left|[\tau_1;\tau_2]\right|}}\sum_{\tau=\tau_1}^{\tau_2}\left(\frac{1}{N}\sum_{i=1}^{N}\frac{\hat{AR}_{i\tau}}{\hat{s}_{i\tau}}\right)$$

381 See e.g., Hudgins and Seifert (1996), DeLong (2001), Beitel et al. (2004).

where $|[\tau_1;\tau_2]|$ is the number of days in the sub-window and $s_{i\tau}$ is the adjusted sample standard deviation that is given by

$$(18)\ \hat{s}_{i\tau} = \sqrt{s_{i\tau}^2 \left(1 + \frac{1}{252} + \frac{(R_{m\tau} - \overline{R}_m)^2}{\sum_{k=-273}^{-21} (R_{mk} - \overline{R}_m)^2}\right)}$$

Here, R_{mk} is the return on the market index at day k in the estimation period and $\overline{R}_m$ is the average return on the market index in the estimation period. Note that this statistic standardizes estimated abnormal returns by the estimated adjusted sample standard deviation and, thus, controls for heteroscedasticity as a potential violation of the market model assumptions. Under the null hypothesis that abnormal returns in the specified sub-window are zero, the sum of standardized abnormal returns across time and securities (the term behind the square root in (17)) is asymptotically normally distributed with mean 0 and variance $\frac{|[\tau_1,\tau_2]|}{N}$. Thus, (17) is asymptotically unit normal under the null.

For testing the CARs of the joint bidder-target entity, following Houston and Ryngaert (1994), the standard deviation of the joint entity return is estimated according to:

$$(19)\ \hat{s}_{j\tau} = \left[\left(\frac{MV_{a,t_1}}{MV_{a,t_1} + MV_{b,t_1}}\right) \cdot \hat{s}_{a\tau}^2 + \left(\frac{MV_{b,t_1}}{MV_{a,t_1} + MV_{b,t_1}}\right) \cdot \hat{s}_{b\tau}^2 + 2 \cdot \left(\frac{MV_{a,t_1}}{MV_{a,t_1} + MV_{b,t_1}}\right) \cdot \left(\frac{MV_{b,t_1}}{MV_{a,t_1} + MV_{b,t_1}}\right) \cdot r_{d,(t_0+1,t_1)} \cdot \sqrt{s_{a,\tau}^2 \cdot s_{b,\tau}^2}\right]^{0,5}$$

where the MVs are defined as in (13) and r is the (sample) coefficient of correlation of bidder and target returns in the estimation period.

It has become standard in the event study literature to supplement a parametric test by a non-parametric one to enhance the perceived validity of the statistical inference.[382] In the banking M&A literature, many studies use a simple

382 Bowman (1983). Issues that can be addressed with non-parametric tests include e.g., event-induced variance and cross-correlation of errors due to event clustering (which is, however, not likely if small sub-windows of a few days are used), see Armitage (1995) for a more detailed treatment of these issues.

sign-test or at least indicate the observed proportion of positive abnormal returns.[383] This is done to judge the proportion of positive and negative abnormal returns against an assumed 50:50 split under the null hypothesis of no abnormal returns in the analyzed sub-window. Problematically, this assumes a symmetric return distribution, whereas abnormal returns, as discussed above, tend to be positively skewed and, hence, to be asymmetrically distributed. Accordingly, in their simulation experiments, Brown and Warner (1980) find that such tests suffer from serious misspecification.[384]

A simple adjustment of the sign-test, as proposed by Cowan (1992), leads to the generalized sign-test which addresses this misspecification. The adjustment is done via a comparison of the proportion of abnormal returns within the event window to the actually observed proportion in the estimation period that may well be asymmetric. Thus, the test statistic is given by

$$(20)\ Z_2 = \frac{W - N\hat{p}}{\sqrt{N\hat{p}(1-\hat{p})}}$$

where W is the number of estimated positive abnormal returns in the event window and p is the percentage of positive abnormal returns in the estimation window. Given that N is large and the percentage of positive abnormal returns in the estimation window is not too far away from 0.5, the normal approximation of the binomial distribution can be used and the test statistic is again unit normal under the null. All tests are two-sided.

5.2.2 Long-Term Event Study Methodology

This section, like the previous one, will discuss methodological selections for the choosen long-term event study approach within the basic event study building blocks.

5.2.2.1 Definition of Event and Event Window

Since the focus of the long-term study is on the behavior of returns after the deal has taken place and since in M&A the period between announcement of a deal

383 E.g., Waheed and Mathur (1995), Cybo-Ottone and Murgia (2000), Beitel et al. (2004).

384 The same is true for the also occasionally used Wilcoxon-test.

and its completion can be considerable, the event of interest is, as usual in the literature, redefined as the announcement of the legal deal closure in the financial press. Table 4.4 revealed that the typical post-event horizon in long-term event studies on banking M&A is about 3 years. Given the usual rule of thumb that full post-merger integration takes about three years[385], the same post-event window is chosen for this study. As in the short-term study, other sub-windows inside the main window will also be analyzed.

The discussion above identified the possible inclusion of confounding events as one key issue in studies that use long post-event windows. The literature tends to ignore this issue by assuming that there are no systematic confounding effects across large samples.[386] This seems a rather strong assumption. Therefore, two adjustments for confounding events are made: first, all deals where the market value of the target is less than 10% of the bidder market value are ignored. Second, of the remaining deals, monthly returns are only taken into account if the acquirer in question did not make another cross-border acquisition in the relevant period. As even this crude adjustment has the potential to strongly reduce the sample size and to induce a loss of valuable information, e.g., on the performance of multiple, more experienced bidders, results will be reported for the adjusted and the unadjusted sample.

5.2.2.2 Model, Aggregation and Tests of Long-Term Returns

The discussion in section 3.3.1.2 led to the insight that methodological issues with formal asset pricing models become more serious, as the time horizon under consideration increases. To bypass this problem, long-term abnormal returns are often calculated as the difference between the event firm's actual return and the return on a non-event-firm portfolio that is assumed to have similar return-determining characteristics.[387]

---

385 See Rhoades (1994), p. 8 and the cited literature.

386 From the long-term studies reviewed above, only Madura and Wiant (1994) explicitly address the issue, even though their adjustment is simply the exclusion of multiple bidders. Such an adjustment is in itself not without problems, see the discussion below.

387 Such "benchmarking" approaches are not per se superior to the use of formal asset-pricing models, especially as there is no consensus on what characteristics the return-benchmark should be matched. In fact, Fama (1998) notes that bad-model problems are unavoidable irrespective of the approach used. However, this is the most common approach in recent banking studies, see e.g., Bouwman (2004), Cagle and Nixon (2005) or Aggrawal et al. (2006).

Following Fama and French (1993), benchmark firms are usually matched to event firms in terms of size and book-to-market ratio,[388] but also on industry-relatedness[389] or other factors such as prior-1-year-bidder return[390] and are continuously adjusted for changes in these factors over time. Unfortunately, the multi-country setting of the study at hand makes such a matching prohibitively complicated. Therefore, following DeLong (2003), the relevant regional banking index is chosen as a benchmark.[391] Since the bidders in the sample will tend to be large and the relevant indices are value-weighted, there is some concern of a simultaneity bias. For this purpose, all tests are alternatively performed using the global banking total return index provided by Datastream.

Which regard to the concrete approach to measuring long-term abnormal returns, the above discussion indicated that the literature does currently not offer a standard approach, but rather a variety of methods that each have their strengths and weaknesses. To increase the reliability of results, this study employs three methods, which are all recommended in the literature. Concretely, this is a BHAR-approach that builds on Barber and Lyon (1997) and was refined by Cowan and Sergeant (2001), a wealth-relative approach developed by Jakobsen and Sørensen (2001), and a calendar-time-portfolio method that dates back to Jaffe (1974) and Mandelker (1974). The approaches are discussed in turn.

In the *BHAR-approach*, in order for the abnormal return measure to appropriately reflect investor experience, long-term abnormal returns of security i between period t_1 and t_2 are calculated as BHARs following Barber and Lyon (1997):

$$(21)\ BHAR_{i,t_1,t_2} = \prod_{t=t_1}^{t=t_2}(1+r_{i,t}) - \prod_{t=t_1}^{t_2}(1+r_{b,t})$$

388 Leshchinskii and Zollo (2005).

389 Bouwman (2004).

390 Aggrawal et al. (2006).

391 More concretely, the total return banking indices for Europe, North and South America, Asia, and Australia as provided by Datastream are used for bidders from the respective geographies. Since sample banks and banks in the index are always listed and listed banks tend to be larger than non-listed banks, use of this benchmark should also lead to a rough size-matching. Also, the new listing bias inherent in the use of an index as a benchmark as noted by Barber and Lyon (1997) should be limited as bank market entry is usually heavily regulated. Furthermore, the rebalancing bias as noted by Barber and Lyon (1997) is not an issue since the Datastream indices are value-weighted. Indices are converted into the currency of the bidder using daily exchange rates from Datastream if necessary.

whereby, $r_{i,t}$ is the actual return of security i in period t and $r_{b,t}$ is the corresponding benchmark return. As discussed above, the resulting measure suffers from a skewness problem. In addition, event clustering is a potential problem that may in turn lead to cross-sectional dependence of returns. This becomes even more relevant as all event firms are from the same or closely related industries.

To adjust for both problems the test procedure proposed by Cowan and Sergeant (2001) is used: first, abnormal returns are winsorized at three standard deviations thus reducing the skewness problem.[392] Then the average buy-and-hold abnormal returns (ABHARs) across all N securities between period t_1 and t_2 are calculated as

$$(22)\ ABHAR_{t_1,t_2} = \frac{1}{N}\sum_{i=1}^{N} BHAR_{i,t_1,t_2}$$

Given that returns are cross-sectionally dependent, a standard t-statistic would underestimate the variance of the abnormal returns and, thus, give too large t-values.[393] Instead a two-group difference of means test is used:

$$(23)\ Z_3 = \frac{\hat{ABHAR}}{\sqrt{\frac{\hat{\sigma}^2_{BHR-Firm}}{N} + \frac{\hat{\sigma}^2_{BHR-Benchmark}}{N}}}$$

whereby the denominator contains the estimated variance of the average buy-and-hold firm and benchmark returns. Under the null hypothesis that the means of the compounded firm returns and the compounded benchmark returns are equal, as-

392 Winsorization describes a procedure, in which all observations outside the winsorization limits are "drawn in" to these preset limits, thus reducing the number of outliers while keeping some of the information inherent in them, see e.g., Ruppert (1988).

393 To see this more formally, note that the standard deviation of the BHARs is given by $\sigma_{BHAR} = \sqrt{\frac{1}{N}\overline{\sigma}_i^2 + \frac{N-1}{N}\overline{\rho_{ij}\sigma_i\sigma_j}}$ whereby the first term in the square-root contains the average variance of the individual BHARs and the second term contains their average covariance which is positive if returns are (positively) cross-sectionally dependent.

suming the two populations to be independent, Z_3 is t-distributed with N-2 degrees of freedom. Obviously, the firm returns and the benchmark returns are not independent, causing the sample standard deviation to be overestimated. However cross-sectional dependence causes the sample standard deviation to be underestimated and so the two errors (partly) cancel each other out. The advantage of this procedure over alternative approaches such as the bootstrapping procedures proposed by Lyon et al. (1999) is that it is relatively straightforward and easy to implement, whereas it does not perform worse in terms of power and specification in simulation experiments.[394]

Arguably, the winsorization of returns is a crude method to adjust for skewness. Following Jakobsen and Sørensen (2001) a more sophisticated *wealth-relative approach*, which explicitly considers the distribution properties of long-term abnormal returns, is used in addition to the testing procedure as described above.[395] In a first step, firm- and benchmark buy-and-hold returns are transformed to wealth relatives which are, in turn, a log-normally distributed measure of abnormal returns. For the present study, for security *i* the wealth relative after *T* years is given by

$$(24)\; WR_{i,T} = \frac{\prod_{t=1}^{T}(1+r_{i,t})}{\prod_{t=1}^{T}(1+r_{b,t})}$$

if the initial wealth relative is set equal to one.[396] Next, the development of the wealth relative over time is modeled as a geometric Brownian motion:

$$(25)\; WR_{i,T} = W_{i,0} \cdot e^{((\mu_{i,T} - 0,5\sigma_T^2)T + \sigma_{i,T} Z_T)}$$

Here, $\mu_{i,T} = \alpha_{i,T} + 0,5\sigma_{i,T}^2$, $\alpha_{i,T}$ and $\sigma_{i,T}$ are constants that differ for different time horizons and that can be interpreted as the mean and the volatility compo-

394 Cowan and Sergeant (2001).

395 Jakobsen and Sørsensen (2001) apply the approach to the analysis of post-IPO performance but in a later contribution (Jakobsen and Voetmann, 2003) show that is also well-suited for post-M&A performance assessment.

396 The logarithm of the cross-sectional wealth relatives is tested for normality using the Jarque-Bera statistic to confirm the assumption of log-normality.

nent of the wealth relative and *dZt* represents a Wiener process. Since the wealth relative is normally distributed, its expected value at time horizon T in levels is given by:

$$(26)\ E(W_{i,T}) = e^{(\alpha_{i,T})T} \cdot e^{(0{,}5\sigma_{i,T}^2)T}$$

i.e., the expected value of the wealth relative depends on both the mean and the volatility component and the volatility parameter always contributes positively to the expected wealth relative. Next, it is tested whether the marginal parameter estimates of the mean component, i.e., the volatility-adjusted abnormal return, is equal to zero. The marginal parameter estimates are given by

$$(27)\ \hat{\alpha}_{i,T} = \frac{1}{NT}\sum_{i=1}^{N}\log(W_{i,T})$$

and

$$(28)\ \hat{\sigma}_{i,T} = \sqrt{\frac{1}{(N-1)T}\sum_{i=1}^{N}(\log(W_{i,T}) - \alpha_{i,T}T)^2}$$

For the (marginal) tests, a simple t-statistic is used that has N-1 degrees of freedom under the null hypothesis that the marginal mean component is equal to zero.

While the test procedure of Jakobsen and Sørsensen (2001) accounts for skewness more thoroughly then the Cowan and Sergeant (2001) approach, it does not take into account event clustering which is potentially a major issue in the sample. Therefore, as a third test procedure, a *calendar-time portfolio approach* that dates back to Jaffe (1974) and Mandelker (1974), is used that has been strongly recommended by Fama (1998).

For every calendar month between January 1985 and February 2006, a portfolio of firms is formed that have completed a cross-border transaction either in this or in the previous 36 months.[397] Firms enter and leave the portfolio as they enter and leave the 36-month post-merger window. The excess return for each security in this portfolio is calculated as the simple difference between the secu-

397 The number of months choosen here obviously depends on the length of the selected event window.

rity return and the benchmark return and excess returns are averaged across all firms in the portfolio. In this way, the effect of cross-correlation of returns across stocks is accounted for in the time-series variation of the monthly abnormal portfolio return. To further adjust for heteroscedasticity, following Mandelker (1974), the average portfolio abnormal returns are standardized by the estimated standard deviation of the abnormal portfolio return over the last 50 months.[398] The standardized average portfolio returns (SAPR) across all months in which portfolios are formed is then estimated according to:

$$(29)\ \hat{S}APR = \frac{1}{M}\sum_{t=X}^{Y}\hat{S}PR_{t+1} \cdot D_t$$

Whereby *X* and *Y* are the first and the last months for which standardized portfolio returns are available, SPR_t is the standardized portfolio return in month t, D_t is a term that is equal to 1 if a portfolio is formed for month t and 0 if not and *M* is the number of calendar months for which portfolios are formed, i.e., the sum of the D_t between months *X* and *Y*. The null hypothesis that SAPR is different from zero using a simple t-test that is approximately unit normal under the null. Again, all tests are two-sided.

5.2.3 Overall Assessment of Measurement Approach for Wealth Effects

In the discussion above, 7 potential issues of event study approaches were identified, whose relevance varied with the event window length under consideration, i.e., with the decision to analyze either short- or long-term abnormal returns. These were issues with regard to market efficiency, new information, confounding events, the model of normal returns, the method of return aggregation, event clustering, and sample selection. In the following, the robustness of the developed approach against these issues will be evaluated.

Market efficiency issues were highly relevant in short-term studies but not really addressable within such studies. This was precisely the reason why this study chose to test short- and long-term abnormal returns jointly, since long-term studies are implicit tests of market efficiency. Thus, this issue seems well covered.

398 Note that this implies that the first standardized value is available for March 1993.

With regard to the *new information issue*, this had low to medium relevancy for short-term studies. In the approach developed here, issues were addressed with an appropriate event definition plus additional press-search-based capturing of bidder and target specific leakage. While this approach certainly cannot address all possible leakage issues, it is at least more thorough than all previous efforts in this field known to the author. Since issues stemming from leakage or slow information dissemination are rather not an issue in long-term studies, this issue overall also seems well addressed.

Confounding events were shown above to be only an issue in long-term studies. Therefore, some adjustments to the long-term sample in the sense of restrictions to relatively large deals and deals in which the buyer did not previously perform CBBM&A were made. Admittedly, these adjustments were rather crude. However, they are again more thorough than those made in the previous literature and they have the potential to severely limit the sample size.

Bad model issues were shown above to be rather a small issue in short-term studies, that can be well handled with the use of the market model. In the long-term study, bad model problems were shown to be more of an issue. Moreover, the index-benchmarking approach developed here was shown to be less well-suited to address these than some previous efforts in the long-term literature, e.g., size- and book-to-market-matching, that could not be implemented due to data limitations. However, the developed approach was shown to be at least similar or better than the previous approaches used in the CBBM&A literature.

With regard to the *return aggregation method* and *event clustering*, potential issues in the short-term study were addressed with the use of the CAR measure, with its favorable statistical properties plus the use of the Dodd-Warner statistic and an additional non-parametric test statistic. The problem was more complex in the long-term literature where no standard aggregation method is available that reflects investor experience well and has favorable statistical properties. However, the joint use of a BHAR-approach (good capturing of investor experience, low to medium suitability to address skewness issues and cross-correlation), the wealth relative approach (good capturing of investor experience and skewness issues), and a calendar-time portfolio approach (high suitability with regard to skewness and cross-correlation issues) should be able to provide a thorough picture.

Finally, neither the short-, nor the long-term approach developed could address potential *sample selection biases* that stem from the listing requirements in event studies. However, such issues, if present, will be indicated by a comparison of concrete sample properties with the general properties of CBBM&A transactions identified.

Thus, overall, the developed methodology seems robust with regard to the identified issues in the analysis of short- and long-term abnormal returns.

5.3 Sample Selection Criteria and Data Sources

To identify deals, the Thompson SDC-Platinum, Bloomberg- and MergerMarket databases are used. Since Thompson SDC is the most comprehensive database of the three, it is also the main data source of the study. According to the CBBM&A definition developed in section 3.2.1, all deals are selected that satisfy the following six criteria simoultaneously:

1. One transaction partner is classified as a bank, the other as a bank, insurance or FSP. This condition satisfies the "broad" bank-merger definition developed above. The classification is based on a comparison of the relevant classifications in Thompson SDC and Bankscope. When neither source classifies the institution in question or in cases of doubt, a press search was conducted using Factiva.
2. The deal is announced and closed in the period 1985-2005. The restriction to closed deals will later allow the assessment of long-term returns. 1985 is the earliest available date in all selected databases. Since section 2.1 has shown only minimal transaction intensity in earlier years, the risk of omitting major transactions due to time restrictions should be low.
3. The headquarters of the target are not located in the same country as that of the ultimate parent of the acquirer. Thus, all deals satisfy the developed cross-border definition.
4. The bidder crosses a threshold of 50 percent of common equity in the target. This allows to capture only deals in which an effective change in control takes place.
5. Both partners are publicly traded during a period beginning 273 trading days before the event date and 20 days after it and total return information on bidder, target, and the relevant national market indices is available. This criterion guarantees that all deals can be analyzed at least with the short-term event study methodology developed in section 5.2.1. In addition, for the long-term event study, monthly total return data for a period up to 3 years after the deal closure is collected.[399]
6. The transaction volume is known. This guarantees that enough information about the deals is available.

---

399 However, availability of this data is not required for a deal to be selected for the sample.

5.4 Selection of Approach to Measure Determinants of Wealth Effects

The following sections first discuss methods for measuring determinant impact on wealth, i.e. techniques to determine, how a potential determinant affect the selected measures of transaction success. Then, methods to capture the identified potential determinants themselves are discussed.

5.4.1 Methods for Measuring Determinant Impact on Wealth

The maybe most traditional method to analyze the determinants of abnormal returns measured in event studies is what Hawawini and Swary (1990) call a dichotomization analysis.[400] In this type of analysis, the sample is separated into two non-overlapping sub-samples according to the identified determinants, for which a wealth effect is hypothesized. Then, the market reactions of the two sub-samples are compared and a standard mean difference test is performed to test if the difference is statistically different from zero. Such an analysis will also be carried out in this study. More concretely, following Hawawini and Swary (1990) and Beitel et al. (2004), for all determinants that are not binary and where, hence, such a comparison is trivial, the CARs for the thirty cases with the highest values for a variable will be compared with the thirty cases with the lowest values. The analysis is performed separately for bidders, targets, and the joint bidder-target entity.

Problematically, this approach does not account for the simultaneous impact of other possible determinants. Therefore, in addition, a multiple regression analysis, another common tool for the analysis of event study abnormal returns, is performed.[401] Thus, a linear relationship between CARs for bidders, targets and the joint entity, and a set of explanatory variables is assumed, according to the usual model:

$$(30)\, CAR_{(\tau_1,\tau_2)} = \delta_0 + \sum_{j=1}^{J} \delta_j X_j + \varepsilon$$

400 Hawawini and Swary (1990, p. 109). Examples of this type of analysis in CBBM&A studies can be found e.g., in Tourani-Rad and van Beek (1999) and Beitel et al. (2004).

401 Multiple regression analysis in CBBM&A studies is e.g. used by Waheed and Mathur (1995), Hudgins and Seifert (1996) and Beitel et al. (2004).

Where δ_0 is a regression constant, $X_j, j \in \{1,...,J\}$ is a vector of firm- and country-level explanatory variables, the $\delta_j, j \in \{1,...,J\}$ are coefficients for the independent variables and ε is a disturbance term.[402] Coefficients are estimated using Ordinary Least Squares (OLS), whereby heteroscedasticity is controlled for using White's (1980) method. Autocorrelation and multi-collinearity are tested for using the Durbin-Watson-statistic as well as tolerances and condition indices.[403] Also as usual, standard t-tests are performed to assess whether the estimated coefficients are statistically different from zero. In addition F-tests are performed to assess the joint fit of determinants and the adjusted R^2 ratio is calculated to indicate the overall model fit. Selection of determinants for inclusion in the model is performed with a standard inclusion/exclusion approach using partial F-tests.[404]

This approach also has its shortcomings as the assumption of a linear relationship between CARs and the identified determinants may be inadequate. However, again following Hawawini and Swary (1990) and Beitel et al. (2004), dichotomization and regression analysis together allow for a quite robust assessment of the determinants of wealth effects.

5.4.2 Choice of Variables to Capture Determinants

In the IM and the CF literature on possible determinants of banking M&A, *bidder size* is generally measured via the logarithm of an institution's total assets at book values.[405] The same proxy (BSIZE) is used here, using data from Bankscope.[406] Analogously, *relative target bidder size* (RELSIZE) is captured as the logarithm of total assets of the target divided by the logarithm of total assets of the bidder.

---

402 All regressors are assumed to be nonstochastic.

403 The analysis is carried out using the EViews 5.1 statistical software package.

404 See most graduate level econometrics textbooks, e.g., Schroeder et al. (1986), for t- and F-tests, partial F-tests and the R^2 measure.

405 See e.g., Tourani-Rad and van Beek (1999), Cornett et al. (2000), Focarelli and Pozzolo (2001), Piscitello (2003). Only one study, DeLong (2001) uses the market value of equity to proxy bidder size. This is deemed inadequate since market values also strongly reflect efficiency and growth prospects.

406 As usual in the abovementioned literature, total assets, like all accounting figures, are taken from the end of the year preceding the transaction and are converted to current USD using year end exchange rates from Datastream if necessary. In some instances where no values were available from Bankscope, figures were taken from Factiva.

Since bank-specific information on clients and their respective locations is not available, the *presence of home country clients in the host country* is usually proxied with the amount of home FDI into the host in the IM literature.[407] Since the same approach is chosen for the only event study that tests the impact of this factor, the work of Waheed and Mathur (1995), this study also uses the logarithm of the book value of home country outward FDI stocks in the host country in the year preceding the deal announcement as provided by the OECD as a proxy (CLIENT).[408]

Efficiency, whether absolute or relative, is captured with a variety of measures. It was noted above that the DE literature distinguished between the concepts of profit and cost efficiency. This is reflected in the use of profit-ratios well as cost-ratios in the OP literature. As in Beitel et al. (2004) this study also uses typical OP profit- and cost-efficiency measures, namely ROE and the cost-income ratio (CIR). This is not unproblematic, because of all the potential issues of OP measures discussed above, such as differences in capital structures that distort comparisons based on ROE, differences in the business that distort comparisons based on the CIR, differing accounting conventions in the different countries in the sample, potential for the (legal) manipulation of accounting ratios, etc. The choice is justified by the fact that both ratios are among the most robust OP measures for international comparisons[409] and are frequently used by practitioners. Values are again taken from Bankscope.

However, both CIR and ROE are inherently backward-looking measures. A common measure in the CF literature that combines efficiency with profitable future growth options is Tobin's Q, i.e., the relation of a firm's market value divided by its book value.[410] For the banking industry, this is equivalent to the much more common market-to-book ratio (MBR), also known as a bank's charter

---

407 See e.g., Brealy and Kaplanis (1996), Yamoro (1998), Wezel (2004). The only exception is Piscitello (2003) who uses the number of foreign affiliates.

408 The database used is "international direct investment by country volume 5, release 1." As usual in the literature (see again the studies cited above) current USD figures are used. Some studies further adjust the figure for banking FDI and/or for non-equity components of FDI, see e.g., Yamori (1998) or Buch (2000). Regrettably, the OECD databases do not permit this. However, since the dependent variable in this study, unlike in the aforementioned studies, is not itself an FDI flow or stock, this is most likely not a serious issue. The source also only provides information for deals with bidders from OECD countries. Since this should be the majority of deals, this is also not a serious issue.

409 See Vittas (1991).

410 Lang et al. (1989).

value.[411] Thus, relative efficiency is also measured via the MBR where book value of equity is taken from Bankscope and market values of equity are taken from DataStream.[412] Summarizing, *relative target efficiency* is measured via the target CIR divided by the bidder CIR (RELCOEF), the target ROE divided by the bidder ROE (RELPREF), and the target MBR divided by the bidder MBR (MBR). Target efficiency, in turn, is measured in a similar way with the corresponding target values for CIR (TCOEF), ROE (TPREF), and MBR (MBT).

Physical distance between bidder and target is proxied with the logarithm of the great circle distance between the capital cities of the bidder and the target country in thousand kilometers (DISTANCE). Data sources are the Trade Data Website of John D. Havemann and the great circle distance calculator of John A. Byers.[413]

Cultural distance between bidder and target is more difficult to measure. Since no information about bidder and target corporate cultures is available, reference is made to information about the cultural distance between bidder and target countries. Use is made of two proxies that are frequently used in the IM literature, namely a dummy variable that indicates whether bidder and target country share the same language (LANGUAGE) and whether both have a similar legal tradition (LAW).[414] As usual in the IM literature, legal systems are differentiated in systems of British, French, German, Scandinavian, and Socialist origin. Information on languages and legal tradition is again provided by the Trade Data Website of John D. Havemann and the Development Research Institute of the New York University.

Hofstede (1980) provides a more sophisticated measure of cultural distance. The so-called Hofstede measure indicates the distance between bidder and target country in the four cultural dimensions individualism, power-distance, uncertainty avoidance, and masculinity (CULTURE). Scores on each of these dimensions are provided by ITIM International.[415] Following its use in previous IM studies,[416] the Hofstede measure H for the combination of home country a and host country b is calculated as

---

411 Tobin's Q is usually measured as the sum of market value of equity and book value of debt divided by the sum of book value of equity plus book value of debt. This equals the market value of equity divided by book value of equity which is the MBR.

412 Market values are measured 21 days before the event day, i.e., on the last day of the estimation period for the normal return model parameters.

413 See the links below table 5.2. Last access on April 5th, 2006.

414 See e.g., Buch and DeLong (2004), Berger et al. (2004) for previous applications.

415 See the links below table 5.2. Last access on April 5th, 2006.

416 Grosse and Goldberg (1991), Fisher and Molyneux (1996).

$$(31)\ H_{a,b} = \frac{\sqrt{\sum_{c=1}^{4}(S_{a,c} - S_{b,c})^2}}{4}$$

whereby $S_{a,c}$ and $S_{b,c}$ are the scores of the home and the host country in cultural dimension c.

Functional differences between bidder and target captured with several variables. First, following e.g., DeLong (2001), this is the coefficient of correlation between bidder and target returns during the estimation period of the normal return model (CORREL). Higher correlations indicate higher similarities. Data is taken from Datastream. Second, a dummy variable is used to indicate deals between banks and nonbanks, notably FSPs and insurances (NONBANK). The classification into banks, FSPs, and Insurances is based on the relevant classifications in Thompson SDC Platinum and Bankscope.[417]

Unfortunately, the latter approach has its shortcomings. What is in practice known as an insurance or an asset manager tends to get classified correctly as an insurance or an FSP. However, institutions that would in practice rather be called investment banks, such as Morgan Grenfell or Bankers Trust or universal banks with a significant share of investment banking business such as Deutsche Bank, all get classified as (commercial) banks in the used databases. Thus, following Beitel et al. (2004) a bank's focus on the core commercial banking business is measured via the share of interest income on total operating income (FOC) as indicated by Bankscope. Then, the difference between bidder a and target b with regard to their focus on the banking business is calculated as

$$(32)\ BFOCUS_{a,b} = 1 - \frac{abs(FOC_a - FOC_b)}{\max(FOC_a, FOC_b)}$$ [418]

where abs is the absolute value operator and max is the maximum operator. Thus, higher values indicate a more similar focus.

Following Beitel et al. (2004), *previous bidder experience* with CBBM&A is measured with a dummy variable that indicates previous deals (PREBID). This is obviously a downward estimate of bidder deal experience since the sample selection criteria probably lead to the exclusion of some previous, most likely smaller

417 In case of doubt, Factiva was used for final classification.

418 This is a similar measurement method to that used for economic distance (see below) that was first used by DeYoung (1997).

deals with non-listed targets. The measure should, nonetheless, be indicative of previous bidder experience, especially as large deals are likely to require previous experience with such deals.

Measuring the *share of the acquisition price paid in cash* is straightforward as this relation (CASH) is provided by Thompson SDC Platinum. The last identified firm-specific factor was the bidder's *intention to pursue operational synergies or geographical diversification or functional diversification,* respectively. For that purpose, a press search using Factiva is performed that assesses all press articles related to the deal at the event date.[419] Based on a qualitative analysis of the relevant press announcements, it is then assessed if one or multiple of these motives drive the deal in question. Dummy variables then indicate whether the deal was driven by operational synergies (EFFIC), geographical diversification (MARKET) or functional diversification (ASSET).

The *IT sophistication of the bidder organization* is hard to measure on a firm level. Therefore, just as the presence of home country clients in the host country and physical as well as cultural distance, they are proxied with variables, that are frequently used to assess the impact of country-level IT sophistication,[420] namely the number of internet hosts per capita in a given home country and a given year (INET) and the natural logarithm of the annual level of national investments in telecommunications infrastructure per capita (TELCO).[421] Data is taken from the World Telecommunications/ICT Database provided by the International Telecommunications Union. However, the use of these proxies is not without issues. First, while the assumed relation between average country-level IT sophistication and firm-level IT sophistication may hold for the average firm, it seems more problematic for large multinational firms, which bidder organizations supposedly are. Second, even given that this relationship is sufficiently strong, it probably rather captures the availability of publicy available than of proprietary techno-

---

419 If no relevant articles on the event date could be found, earlier dates were also considered successively.

420 See e.g., the discussion in Bender (2002), pp. 59.

421 Internet hosts are computers in an economy that link directly to the Internet. The number is based on the country code in the host address and thus may not correspond with the actual physical location of the computer. To mitigate this problem, the statistic is based on national top-level domains (e.g., .de, .fr) and not on generic top-level domains (e.g., .com, .org), since the former a more likely to correspond with actual physical location. The national investments in telecommunications infrastructure is the expenditure associated with acquiring the ownership of telecommunication equipment or infrastructure, which includes supporting land, buildings and non-tangible assets such as software. It covers the acquisition of existing installations as well as additions to existing installations and is given in terms of current USD.

logical knowledge to the bidder, even though it is the latter, that is of major importance.[422]

Turning next to country- and industry-level determinants, the *size of the host market* is captured via the logarithm of the per capita gross domestic product (GDP) of the host country during the deal year as provided by World Market Monitor (MSIZE).[423] Arguably, this is a rough proxy for the market for banking services. Nevertheless, it is frequently used in the IM literature[424] and more bank-specific measures, such as the value of local deposits, are not easily available for all countries and years and are generally only relevant for specific institutions, e.g., pure commercial banks.

With regard to the *temperature of the equity market*, deals are regarded as occurring in a "hot phase" (HOTY), when they occur in one of the "hot" deal years 1999 to 2001. Following Berger et al. (2004), e*conomic distance* (ECSIM) between bidder country a and target country b, based on the per capita GDP (GDPCAP) in the home and the host country, is calculated as

$$(33)\quad ECSIM_{a,b} = 1 - \frac{abs(GDPCAP_a - GDPCAP_b)}{\max(GDPCAP_a, GDPCAP_b)}$$

Values for the per capita GDP are taken from World Market Monitor.[425]

To account for the *general economic openness of the host country*, the IM literature has frequently used the Index of Economic Freedom provided by the Heritage Foundation.[426] More concretely, following Wezel (2004), a sub-index is constructed by combining factors 5 (freedom with regard to capital flows and FDI) and 6 (freedom with regard to banking and finance) in the Index of Economic Freedom with an equal weighting (FREEDOM).[427]

As discussed above, the intensity of the bank regulation in the host country is measured with regard to the level of legal power assigned to the host country banking regulator (POWER) and the possibilities for private monitoring of host country banks (MONITOR). For both, reference is made to a recent study of Barth et al. (2005) that provides principal component indicators for these factors

---

422 Furthermore but less importantly, the database used only provides data until the year 2004.

423 Values are purchasing power parity adjusted at current prices.

424 E.g., Piscitello (2000), Berger et al. (2004), Buch and Lipponer (2004).

425 Again, values are purchasing power parity adjusted at current prices.

426 See e.g., Buch and DeLong (2003), Buch and Lipponer (2004), Wezel (2004).

427 Note that lower values indicate greater value in the Heritage Index.

that are based on a World Bank Survey.[428] High values indicate extensive power and possibilities.[429]

To account for specific geographic locations, i.e., *the host country being the US or the UK* (HOSTCA), *intra-EU deals* (EU) or those with *targets in Eastern Europe* (EAST) respectively, dummy variables are used that mark deals in which the target or bidder and target are from the respective regions.[430] Data on countries is provided by Thompson SDC Platinum, MergerMarket, and Bloomberg. Table 5.2 summarizes the measurement approach.

5.5 Summary

In this chapter, the findings on wealth effects and their determinants from the literature review were translated into testable hypotheses. Next, a set of event study methodologies for testing short- and long-term abnormal returns was selected. It was furthermore shown that the selected array of methods, together with the performed adaptations, is sufficiently robust against the identified pitfalls in the analysis of abnormal returns. With regard to analyzing the identified determinants of wealth effects, two types of analyses, dichotomization and regression analysis, were selected, that should, together, allow for a comprehensive analysis of the determinants of wealth effects. Finally, based on the previous literature, several proxies were selected to appropriately capture and represent the identified potential determinants of wealth effects.

---

428 The data underlying these indices was collected between late 1998 and early 2000. In this study, it is assumed that the regulatory environment changes slowly and that values are, therefore, indicative for the total 1985 to 2005 period. This assumption also underlies the abovementioned earlier application in a CBBM&A context.

429 Similar approaches have been used by Buch and Lipponer (2004) and Buch and DeLong (2004, 2005).

430 EU countries are Belgium, Germany, Luxembourg, France, Italy, the Netherlands, Denmark, Ireland, the UK, and Greece for the total sample period, Spain and Portugal since 1986, Austria, Finland, and Sweden since 1995 and Cyprus, the Czech Republic, Estonia, Hungary, Latvia, Lithuania, Malta, Poland, Slovakia, and Slovenia since 2004. Deals with targets in Eastern Europe are those were the target organization is located in the Czech Republic, the Slovak Republic, Slovenia or Poland.

Table 5.2: Measurement Approach for Determinants of Wealth Effects

Level of determinant	Determinant	Related M&A motive	Hypothesized impact	Proxy and Description	Data source	Expected Sign
Firm	1. Bidder size	Economies of scale	0/+	BSIZE is the logarithm of the total assets of the bidder at book value, converted to current USD using year-end exchange rates if necessary.	Bankscope, DataStream, Factiva	0/+
	2. Relative (target) size	Economies of scale, risk-shifting	0/+	RELSIZE is the logarithm of the total assets of the target at book values divided by the logarithm of the total assets of the bidder	Bankscope, Factiva	0/+
	3. Presence of existing (home country) clients in the host country	Economies of scale	+	CLIENT is the logarithm of the book value of outward FDI stocks of the home country into the host country in the year preceding the deal announcement in million current USD.	OECD	+
	4. Relative (target) efficiency	X-Efficiency	-/0	RELCOEF is the target CIR divided by the bidder CIR.	Bankscope	0/+
				RELPREF is the target return-on-equity (ROE) divided by the bidder ROE.	Bankscope	-/0
				MBR is the target MBR divided by the bidder MBR	Bankscope, DataStream	-/0
	5. Target efficiency		-/+	TCOEF is the target CIR.	Bankscope	-/+
				TPREF is the target ROE.	Bankscope	-/+
				MBT is the target MBR	Bankscope, DataStream	-/+
	6. Physical distance between bidder and target	Diversification	-/0	DISTANCE is the logarithm of the great circle distance between the capital cities of the home and the host country in 1000 kilometers.	Trade Data Website of John D. Havemann[1] and the great circle distance calculator of John A. Byers.[2]	-/0
	7. Social distance between bidder and target		-	LANGUAGE is a dummy variable that is equal to 1 if the primary languages in the home and host countries are identical.	Trade Data Website of John D. Havemann.[1]	+
				LAW is a dummy variable that is equal to 1 if the legal systems in the home and host countries are identical.	Development Research Institute of the New York University[3]	+

Table 5.2: Measurement Approach for Determinants of Wealth Effects (continued)

Level of determinant	Determinant	Related M&A motive	Hypothesized impact	Proxy and Description	Data source	Expected Sign
	8. Functional differences between bidder and target	Diversification, Economies of scope	-/0	CORREL is the coefficient of correlation of bidder and target returns in the estimation window.	DataStream	0/+
				NONBANK is a dummy variable that is equal to 1 if one of the transaction partners is not classified as a bank and 0 otherwise.	Thompson SDC Platinum, Bankscope, Factiva	-/0
				BANKFOCUS is an index that measures the differences in focus of the commercial banking business between bidder and target based on the share of interest income on total operating income. Higher values indicate greater similarity.	Bankscope	0/+
	9. Bidder M&A experience	All	0/+	PREBID is a dummy variable that is equal to 1 if there is a previous transaction in the sample with the same bidder	Thompson SDC Platinum, MergerMarket, Bloomberg	0/+
Firm	10. Share of the acquisition price paid in cash	Managerial utility maximization, Exploitation of private information	0/+	CASH is the percentage of the transaction value paid in cash.	Thompson SDC Platinum, Factiva	0/+
	11. Bidder intent to create operational synergies	All motives related to operational synergies	0/+	EFFIC is a dummy variable that is equal to 1 if the bidder strategy as published on the event day is classified as primarily "efficiency-seeking", i.e., seeking operational synergies.	Factiva	0/+
	12. Bidder intent to diversify geographically	All motives related to financial synergies	0/-	MARKET is a dummy variable that is equal to 1 if the bidder strategy as published on the event day is classified as primarily "market-seeking", i.e., geographically diversifying.	Factiva	0/-
	13. Bidder intent to diversify functionally		0/-	ASSET is a dummy variable that is equal to 1 if the bidder strategy as published on the event day is classified as primarily "asset-seeking", i.e., diversifying on a product-level.	Factiva	0/-

Table 5.2: Measurement Approach for Determinants of Wealth Effects (continued)

Level of deter-minant	Determinant	Related M&A motive	Hypothesized impact	Proxy and Description	Data source	Expected Sign
Firm	14. IT sophistication of bidder organization	Economies of scale, X-efficiency	+	INET is the number of internet hosts per capita in a given home country in a given year.	International Telecomunication Union World Telecomunication/ICT Database	+
				TELCO is the natural logarithm of the annual level of national investments in telecommunications equipment in current USD.	International Telecomunication Union World Telecomunication/ICT Database	+
Country/ Industry	15. Host market size	Economies of scale, X-Efficiency	+	MSIZE is the logarithm of the per capita GDP in the host country. Values are purchasing power parity adjusted to the USD at current prices.	World Market Monitor	+
	16. "Temperature" of equity market	Private Information	-	HOTY is a dummy variable that is equal to 1 if the event year is in the "hot" market phase 1999-2001.	Thompson SDC Platinum, MergerMarket, Bloomberg	-
	17. Economic distance between home and host country	All	-	ECSIM is an index of economic distance between home and host country, based on per capital GDP. Values are purchasing power parity adjusted to the USD at current prices.	World Market Monitor	+
	18. General economic openness of the host country		+	FREEDOM is an index of economic freedom in the host country, specifically with regard to banking, finance, capital flows and FDI. Following Wezel (2004), the index is constructed by combining factors 5 (capital flows & FDI) and 6 (banking and finance) in the annual index of economic freedom of the Heritage Foundation with an equal weighting. Lower values are associated with higher freedom.	Heritage Foundation	-

Table 5.2: Measurement Approach for Determinants of Wealth Effects (continued)

Level of deter-minant	Determinant	Related M&A motive	Hypothesized impact	Proxy and Description	Data source	Expected Sign
	19. Intensity of bank regulation in the host country		+	POWER is a principal component indicator that measures the legal power of the supervisory agency for banks in the host country. High values indicate extensive powers. See Barth et al. (2005) for a detailed list of the variables underlying the indicator.	Barth et al. (2005)[5]	+
				MONITOR is a principal component indicator that measures regulations that empowers private monitoring of banks in the host country. High values indicate extensive measures. See Barth et al. (2005) for a detailed list of variables underlying the indicator.	Barth et al. (2005)[5]	+
Country/ Industry	20. Host country is US or UK	All	+	HOSTCA is a dummy variable that is equal to 1 if the country of the target is either the UK or the US.	Thompson SDC Platinum, MergerMarket, Bloomberg	+
	21. Bidder and target are from the EU		0/+	EU is a dummy variable that is equal to 1 if both transaction partners are from the EU and 0 otherwise.	Thompson SDC Platinum, Merger Market Bloomberg	0/+
	22. Target is located in Eastern Europe		+	EAST is a dummy variable that is equal to 1 if the target is located in a country in Eastern Europe and 0 otherwise.	Thompson SDC Platinum, Merger Market Bloomberg	+

1 Available at http://www.macalester.edu/research/economics/Page/Haveman/Trade.Resources/TradeData.html.
2 Available at http://www.wcrl.ars.usda.gov/cec/moregen.htm.
3 Available at http://www.nyu.edu/fas/institute/dri/database.html.
4 Available at http://www.geert-hofstede.com/resources.shtml.
5 The original data, based on a World Bank survey, is available at http://www.worldbank.org/reaserach/projects/bank_regulation.htm.
6 Available at http://www.heritage.org/research/features/index/downloads.cfm.

6. New Empirical Evidence on Wealth Effects of Cross-Border Bank M&A

The chapter starts with a description of the sample in *section 6.1*. This serves to identify potential biases and limits of comparability to other studies. Since the sample is also found to be quite representative of the overall CBBM&A market, summary statistics on the identified determinants provide some new insights into what the typical, large cross-border bank deal looks like. *Section 6.2* continues with the analysis of the direction, size and benefactors of general wealth effects in CBBM&A by presenting results from the short- and long-term event study analyses. Furthermore, for the first time, detailed findings on the impact of "early" bidder- and/or target specific leakage is presented. *Section 6.3* presents the findings of the analysis of determinants of wealth effects. Separate results are given for the dichotomization and the multiple regression analysis. Results are summarized in *section 6.4*.

6.1 Sample Description

Figure 6.1 illustrates the impact of the sample selection criteria on sample size: in the databases identified above there were 3173 deals that satisfied sample selection criteria 1, 2, and 3, i.e., that were closed between 1985 and 2005, one transaction partner was a bank and the other an FI and the deals were cross-border. Of these 45 percent, 1427, did not lead to a change in control (criterion 4). Of the remaining 1749 deals more than 90 percent, 1586, did not feature listed bidders and targets which was a necessary condition to fulfill criterion 5. A further 34 deals were removed on which no information on deal size were available (criterion 6)[431] and another 33 deals had to be eliminated because either the listing history was not long enough to fully satisfy criterion 5[432] or deals were falsely classified by the databases in question.

---

431 Note that information on deal size was unavailable despite both parties being listed. A discussion with Datastream representatives could not exactly pinpoint the reasons for this, even though it seems possible, at least in some cases, that the relevant data was simply not correctly collected.

432 9 deals did not satisfy the required transaction history of 273 days but did have a relatively long pre-event price history of 100 days or more. Since estimating model parameters is still possible within such an estimation window, see Beitel (2002),

Figure 6.1: Impact of Selection Criteria on Sample Size

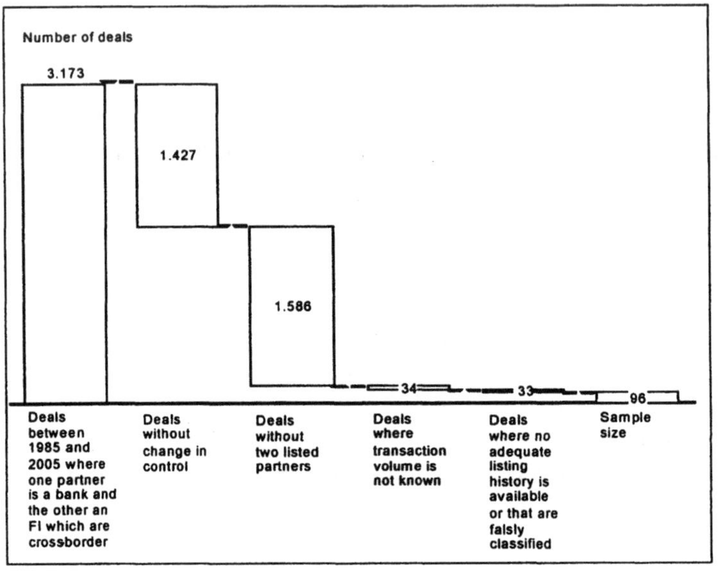

This led to a final sample size of 96 deals.[433] Thus, the sample selection criteria, especially the necessity for a change in control and two listed partners, indeed strongly reduce the sample size. Since some deals in the sample are too recent to have a sufficiently long post-event period, the sample size is further reduced in the long-term study, with the exact sample size being dependent on the length of the post-event window chosen. More concretely, sample size is reduced to 90 (12-month horizon), 81 (24-month horizon), or 78 (36-month horizon) deals, respectively. However, the relevant questions are if the selected sample reflects the properties of the overall market well enough to allow for general conclusion and how it compares to previously used samples in comparable studies. These are discussed in the following.

Table 6.1 gives an overview of sample properties. First, a rising transaction frequency until a downturn in 2002 is observable. Interestingly, roughly 50 percent of the captured deals fall into the "hot" market period 1999-2001, whereas there are no deals identified in some of the earlier years. The "hot" period also features a temporary increase in vertical deals.

---

these deals were also included. For the banks involved in these 9 deals, the average (median) number of trading days captured before the event date is 174 (191).

433 The full list is given in table A.4 in the appendix.

Table 6.1: Overview of Sample Properties

This table shows selected summary statistics for a sample of 96 cross-border bank mergers between 1985 and 2005 by event-year and for the full sample. Industry classification into banks, financial service providers (FSPs) and insurers is per SDC Platinum and Bankscope. For missing indications and in cases of doubt, classification is with reference to Factiva. In the years 1985-1987 and 1991 no deals satisfying the applied criteria could be found.

Year	# of deals	Average deal value (USD mn.)	# of horizontal deals	# of vertical deals ...involving FSPs	...involving Insurers
1988	3	392	3		
1989	4	499	4		
1990	1	35	1		
1992	1	15	1		
1993	1	502	1		
1994	2	264	2		
1995	5	788	4	1	
1996	5	657	4	1	
1997	7	1.670	5	1	1
1998	7	1.627	6	1	
1999	15	1.883	13		2
2000	13	3.222	6	6	1
2001	15	1.834	12	2	1
2002	4	4.153	2	2	
2003	3	884	1	2	
2004	8	4.718	7	1	
2005	2	9.276	1	1	
Full sample	**96**	**2.164**	**73**	**18**	**5**

Parallel to the rising deal frequency, average deal size rises. The data also captures the recovery of the market in 2004 with again an increase in deal frequency and size.[434] Thus, overall, in terms of deal frequency and size, the sample seems representative for the overall markets trends reviewed in section 2.1.

Data availability makes a thorough comparison of sample properties with the prior CBBM&A studies difficult. The available information is, nevertheless, instructive as table 6.2, which provides selected sample properties relative to prior studies, shows.

Despite the restrictivity of the applied criteria, the sample still almost doubles the size of the previously largest sample in terms of deal-pairs.[435] The median percentage of common equity acquired by the bidder is 95 percent, indicating that bidders usually take full control of the target, probably after acquiring the maximum percentage of target shares that does not trigger mandatory public disclosure. With an average deal size of USD 2,2 billion and average bidder (target) size in terms of total assets of USD 301 (28) billion, the sample features extremely large bidders and smaller but still large targets and is, thus, more comparable to the European than to the US-centric studies.[436] This is probably because of the smaller average size of US banks and the increase in bidder size due to the joint-listing requirement in this study. Relative to the full samples of the European studies,[437] targets are of a comparable size but bidders are much larger which is in line with the findings of Berger et al. (2000), who describe bidders in CBBM&A as extremely large. Indeed, the full list of bidder names reads like a Who's Who in global banking.[438]

Geographically, the sample contains bidders and targets from 41 countries. A more detailed view of deal frequency by home country and host country is given in table 6.3 (p. 174). The observed geographical patterns very closely reflect the global patterns discussed above: bidders are predominantly European with the UK, Germany, the Netherlands, France, Belgium, and Spain being especially active acquirers. Next to a few Canadian and Asian bidders, other home countries are relatively unimportant. With regard to host countries, the sample is more equally split between Europe and the US with the US being the single most im-

434 Note that the 2005 data is insofar incomplete, as that there might be deals which were announced but not closed in this year. Note also that total deal value in 2005 is strongly driven by the large Unicredito/HVB-deal.

435 Since Vander Vennet (2002) is a DE study, it more than doubles it with regard to the next larges event study, Beitel et al. (2004).

436 Note that the median sample size is even smaller and the comparison of average bidder and target size does not fully account for the size relations in actual deals. See further below for a more thorough discussion of relative size.

437 As indicated above, the European studies do not provide separate results for cross-border sub-samples.

438 See table A.4 in the appendix.

Table 6.2: Selected Sample Properties Relative to Prior Studies

This table shows selected summary statistics for a sample of 96 cross-border bank mergers between 1985 and 2005 relative to selected prior studies. For this study, deal-level data is from SDC Platinum whereas asset values are year-end values from the year preceding the event as given by Bankscope. Asset values are converted to USD at year-end spot rates from Datastream.

		Selected Prior Studies									
Property	This Study	WM (1995)	HS (1996)[1]	B (1997)	GM (1998)	TB (1999)	CM (2000)	BM (2002)	VV (2002)	ADS (2002)	BSW (2004)
Regional focus	International	US	US	International	US	Europe	Europe	Canada	Europe	International	Europe[2]
Period covered	1985-2005	1963-1989	1968-1989	1977-1987	1963-1996	1989-1996	1988-1997	1998-2001	1990-2001	1985-1998	1985-2000
# of bidders/targets/ joint entities	96/96/96	80/n.a/n.a.	88/n.a./n.a.	90/46/35	135/na/na	26/0/0[3]	13/14/13[3]	43[4]/na/na	62/62/62	214/12[6]/12	42/42/42[3]
Median % acquired by bidder	95	n.a.	40	n.a.	n.a.	n.a.	n.a.	n.a.	n.a.	n.a.	n.a.
Ø Deal volume (USD mn.)	2.164	n.a.	20[5]	n.a.	n.a.	n.a.	1.612[4]	n.a.	n.a.	n.a.	3.343[4]
Ø Assets (USD bn)		n.a.		n.a.	n.a.	n.a.		n.a.	n.a.	n.a.	
- Bidders	301		280[5]				106[4]				182[4]
- Targets	28		0,6[5]				24[4]				37[4]
- Targets in % of of bidders	9		2[5]				22[4]				20[4]

Legend: ADS = Amihud et al. (2002), B (1997) = Biswas et al. (1997), BM = Bessler and Murtagh (2002), BSW (2004) = Beitel et al. (2004), CM = Cybo-Ottone and Murgia (2000), GM = Gleason and Mathur (1998), HS = Hudgins and Seifert (1996), TB = Tourani-Rad and Van Beek (1999), VV = Vander Vennet (2002), WM = Waheed and Mathur (1995).

1 *Values for acquisitions of international targets by US financial firms.*
2 *European bidders and international targets.*
3 *Numbers for cross-border sub-sample.*
4 *Values for full sample (including domestic M&A).*
5 *Median Value.*
6 *The authors do not analyze wealth effects from a target perspective but note that they can only find 12 deals with jointly listed bidders and targets, implying that their sample includes 12 listed targets.*

Table 6.3: Sample Deal Frequency by Geography

This table shows the geographical distribution of a sample of 96 cross-border bank mergers between 1985 and 2005. Geographical distribution by deal value is almost identical.

		Continent of target																	
		Africa	Americas			Australasia			Europe										
Continent of bidder	Country/ Region	All	CDN	SA	US	JP	A	A/O	B	F	D	E	UK	NL	ROWE	ROEE	SCA	Sum	Sum Continent
Africa	All												1					1	1
Americas	CDN			1	7													8	14
	SA				3													3	
	US			1			1									1		3	
Australasia	JP												1					1	9
	A				1		4									1		6	
	A/O				1			1										2	
Europe	B				1					2				2	1	2		8	72
	F	1			1		2								1	2		7	
	D				2					1			3		1	2		9	
	E			5									1		2			8	
	UK	1		2	6		1	1		1					2			14	
	NL				2		1		1		1							5	
	ROWE				5					1	2		1			3		12	
	ROEE																	0	
	SCA															1	8	9	
	Sum	2	0	9	29	0	9	2	1	5	3	0	7	20	7	12	8	96	
	Sum Continent	2	38			11			45										

Legend: A = Asia, A/O = Australia/Oceania, B = Belgium, CDN = Canada, D = Germany, E = Spain, F = France, GB = United Kingdom, PL = Poland, ROEO = Rest of Eastern Europe, ROWE = Rest of Western Europe, SA = South America, SCA = Scandinavia, US = United States.

portant target country.[439] Table 6.3 also points to similar home-host hotspots as the general discussion above that all point to the importance of cultural similarity.

There are many Canadian and UK bidders acquiring US targets, Spanish bidders acquiring targets in South America and also pan-Scandinavian deals. Other than in the discussion above but also pointing to the role of cultural similarities is a small spade of intra-Asian deal activity. Otherwise, the geographical distribution of the sample well reflects the general CBBM&A trends discussed above.

Further interesting insights on the sample emerge from some summary statistics of the potential determinants of wealth creation. Table 6.4 gives an overview. For a more complete picture, summary statistics on some additional variables are reported. These factors, which are used for the calculation of other variables (e.g., bidder ROE) or which are non-logarithmic values that are easier to interpret, are shown in italics in table 6.4.[440] Since data limitations did not allow all variables to be captured for all deals, the number of available data points (N) is also indicated in the table.

Bidder characteristics are shown in panel A. As already indicated by table 6.2 above, bidders, with an average asset size of USD 300 bn, are very large. Furthermore, they are moderately cost-efficient (the average CIR is 63 percent), relatively profit-efficient (average ROE of 14 percent), and enjoy good growth perspectives (average MBR of 1.88). They are rather universal banks as only roughly half their operating income (53 percent) is related to interest payments and often already have previous large-scale CBBM&A experience: almost every second deal in the sample (46 percent) is performed by a bidder with a CBBM&A history. Furthermore, they strongly prefer to pay in cash (on average, 85 percent of the acquisition price is paid in cash which increases to 100 percent if median values are used).

---

439 In fact, the numbers for the US are more similar to those found in Amihud et al. (2002) than in Berger et al. (2004), which is not surprising since Amihud et al. (2002) also used event study methodology and thus also tends to include more (listed) US companies.

440 The following "new" variables are used: BSIZE* is the non-logarithmic bidder asset book value in USD bn, RELSIZE* is the non-logarithmic target asset book value divided by bidder asset book value, TSIZE is the target asset book value, BCOEF is the bidder CIR, BPREF is the bidder ROE, DISTANCE* is the non logarithmic great circle distance between home and host capital in 1000 km, FOCB is the share of interest income on total bidder operating income, and FOCT is the analogous value for the target. MBB is the bidder MBR. TELCO* is the non logarithmic total annual per capita investment in telecommunications equipment in the home country in USD. GDPCAPB is the purchasing power parity adjusted per capita GDP to the bidder country in the year of the bid. MSIZE* is the non-logarithmic size of the host market measured as the purchasing power adjusted per capita GDP.

Deals are rather performed in order to create operational synergies (as indicated in 44 percent of the cases) or geographical diversification (54 percent) than functional diversification (34 percent).[441]

Table 6.4: Summary Statistics on Determinants of Wealth Effects

This table shows selected summary statistics for potential determinants of wealth effects of a sample of 96 cross-border bank mergers between 1985 and 2005. BSIZE is the logarithm of the total assets of the bidder at book value, converted to current USD using year-end exchange rates if necessary. BSIZE* is the corresponding non-logarithmic value. CLIENT is the logarithm of the book value of outward FDI stocks of the home country into the host country in the year preceding the deal announcement in million current USD. BCOEF is the bidder CIR, BPREF is the bidder ROE, MBB is the bidder MBR, FOCB is the share of interest income on total income of the bidder, PREBID is a dummy variable that is equal to 1 if there is a previous transaction in the sample with the same bidder, CASH is the percentage of the transaction value paid in cash, EFFIC is a dummy variable that is equal to 1 if the bidder strategy as published on the event day is classified as primarily "efficiency-seeking", MARKET is a corresponding dummy variable for "market-seeking" strategies while ASSET indicates "asset-seeking" strategies. INET is the number of internet hosts per capita in a given home country in a given year, TELCO is the natural logarithm of the annual level of national investments in telecommunications equipment in current USD, TELCO* is the corresponding non logarithmic value, GDPCAPB is the ppp-adjusted GDP per capita in the bidder country. TSIZE is the target asset book value, TCOEF is the target CIR, TPREF is the target ROE, MBT is the target MBR, FOCT is the share of interest income on total income of the target, MSIZE is the logarithm of the total assets of the target at book value, converted to current USD using year-end exchange rates if necessary, MSIZE* is the corresponding non-logarithmic value, FREEDOM is an index of economic freedom in the host country, POWER is a principal component indicator that measures the legal power of the supervisory agency for banks in the host country, MONITOR is a principal component indicator that measures regulations that empower private monitoring of banks, HOSTCA is a dummy variable that is equal to 1 if the country of the target is either the UK or the US, EAST is a dummy variable that is equal to 1 if the target is located in a country in Eastern Europe. RELSIZE is the logarithm of the total assets of the target at book values divided by the logarithm of the total assets of the bidder, RELSIZE* is the corresponding non-logarithmic values, RELCOEF is the target CIR divided by the bidder CIR, RELPREF is the target ROE divided by the bidder ROE, MBR is the target MBR divided by the bidder MBR, DISTANCE is the logarithm of the great circle distance between the capital cities of the

441 Remember that a deal can be based each of the three motives. Thus, there are 8 possible motive combinations. There seems to be a certain preference for deals that exclusively diversify geographically (27 deals) or do so in combination with operating synergies (17). Meanwhile no bank cites all three motives and only few bidders diversity both geographically and functionally (8 deals) or cite none of the three motives (7). The others occur with a similar frequency (12 deals or 13 in the case of a combination of operating synergies and functional diversification).

home and the host country in 1000 kilometers, DISTANCE* is the corresponding non-logarithmic value, LANGUAGE is a dummy variable that is equal to 1 if the primary languages in the home and host countries are identical,, LAW is a dummy variable that is equal to 1 if the legal systems in the home and host countries are identical, CULTURE is the Hofstede measure between home and host country, CORREL is the coefficient of correlation of bidder and target returns in the estimation window, NONBANK is a dummy variable that is equal to 1 if one transaction partner is not classified as a bank, BANKFOCUS is an index measures measures the differences in focus of the commercial banking business between bidder and target, HOTY is a dummy variable that is equal to 1 if the event year is in the period 1999-2001, ECSIM is an index of economic distance between home and host country and EU is a dummy variable that is equal to 1 if the target is located in a country in Eastern Europe.

Variable	'N	Average	Median	Standard Deviation	Min	Max
Panel A: Bidder or home country specific variables						
BSIZE	95	12.10	12.28	1.22	7.40	14.05
*BSIZE**	95	301.17	215.08	265.82	1.63	1264.03
CLIENT	62	9.21	9.40	2.04	3.78	12.48
BCOEF	87	0.63	0.64	0.09	0.36	0.85
BPREF	87	0.14	0.14	0.05	0.03	0.33
MBB	91	1.88	1.70	1.02	0.41	7.13
FOCB	82	0.53	0.57	0.15	0.00	0.75
PREBID	96	0.46	0.00	0.50	0.00	1.00
CASH	96	0.85	1.00	0.34	0.00	1.00
EFFIC	96	0.44	0.00	0.50	0.00	1.00
MARKET	96	0.54	1.00	0.50	0.00	1.00
ASSET	96	0.34	0.00	0.48	0.00	1.00
INET	87	0.05	0.03	0.09	0.00	0.66
TELCO	84	4.87	4.87	0.42	3.72	5.74
TELCO*	84	141.52	130.70	59.65	41.15	311.39
GDPCAPB	96	22.95	23.73	5.86	7.54	39.90
Panel B: Target or host country specific variables						
TSIZE	96	27.97	5.93	73.78	0.00	635.32
TCOEF	65	0.65	0.63	0.22	0.26	1.98
TPREF	68	0.12	0.14	0.16	-0.81	0.55
MBT	89	1.36	1.33	0.62	0.20	2.72
FOCT	69	0.62	0.66	0.24	0.00	1.00
MSIZE	96	9.89	10.01	0.57	8.27	10.75
*MSIZE**	96	22.57	22.26	10.50	3.89	46.78
FREEDOM	91	2.14	2.00	0.55	1.00	3.50
POWER	87	0.38	0.59	0.93	-2.95	1.14
MONITOR	87	0.68	0.97	0.53	0.43	1.46
HOSTCA	96	0.38	0.00	0.49	0.00	1.00
EAST	96	0.11	0.00	0.32	0.00	1.00

Table 6.4: Summary Statistics on Determinants of Wealth Effects (continued)

Variable	N	Average	Median	Standard Deviation	Min	Max
Panel C: Relative bidder-target or home-host specific variables						
RELSIZE	95	0.71	0.72	0.19	-0.25	1.04
*RELSIZE**	95	0.14	0.03	0.27	0.00	1.76
RELCOEF	63	1.09	0.98	0.51	0.47	4.37
RELPREF	66	1.02	1.01	1.51	-7.38	4.27
MBR	86	0.88	0.80	0.53	0.07	2.69
DISTANCE	96	0.41	0.20	1.69	-8.30	2.94
DISTANCE*	96	3.59	1.22	4.01	0.00	18.84
LANGUAGE	96	0.34	0.00	0.48	0.00	1.00
LAW	96	0.54	1.00	0.50	0.00	1.00
CULTURE	96	9.74	7.91	5.70	0.01	23.81
CORREL	96	0.13	0.11	0.15	-0.19	0.71
NONBANK	96	0.25	0.00	0.44	0.00	1.00
BANKFOCUS	63	0.66	0.72	0.25	0.00	0.98
HOTY	96	0.45	0.00	0.50	0.00	1.00
ECSIM	96	0.68	0.73	0.23	0.18	1.00
EU	96	0.27	0.00	0.45	0.00	1.00

Given the geographical location of bidders discussed above, it is not surprising that they come from technologically relatively advanced countries – the average number of per capita internet hosts is in a similar order of magnitude as that of the UK in 2002 and the average per capita level of national investments in telecommunication equipment is roughly that of Belgium or Spain at the end of the last decade. Therefore, it is also not surprising that bidders come from relatively rich countries (average per capita GDP of USD 23,000).

Panel B indicates that, while targets are still large banks, they are also much smaller than bidders. Their average asset size of USD 28 bn is strongly driven by outliers, such as the giant Hypovereinsbank with an asset size of over USD 630 bn. Thus, the median value of about USD 6 bn paints a more realistic picture. Targets are on average about as cost-efficient as bidders (CIR of 65 percent) and slightly less profit-efficient (ROE of 12 percent). However, they are a much less homogenous group than bidders in terms of profit- and cost efficiency, including highly cost-efficient and profitable ones as well as loss-making turnaround cases. However, on average they still seem to enjoy growth opportunities (average MBR of 1.36). Targets also have a stronger retail-banking focus than bidders (average share of interest income on total operating income 62 percent) and likewise tend to be located in rather rich economies (an exception are the roughly 11 percent of deals with targets in Eastern Europe) with a similar per capita GDP to bidders, which is again not surprising given the geographical deal distribution discussed above. Likewise, the fact that these economies are rather open to FDI, grant banks many freedoms, have strict regulators and many possibilities for market-based monitoring is not surprising.[442] Not indicated in the table but also of interest is the target attitude to the deal. Interestingly, all deals are friendly. Probably, bidders refrain from deliberately adding the additional hurdle of a uncooperative target management to the already existing hurdles in CBBM&A.

Turning to variables that relate bidders to targets or host to home countries (panel C), it can be seen that large institutions tend to take over much smaller ones, indicated by an average (median) relative target size of 14 (3) percent. Bidders on average take over targets that are about as and even somewhat more profit-efficient, but that enjoy lower growth perspectives and are somewhat less cost-efficient. The average (median) bidder-target distance of 4000 (1000) km is not too far by modern travel standards but shows strong cross-sectional variation. Bidder and target countries do not necessarily share the same language, which is only the case in about a third of all deals, but are rather close in terms of economic distance, legal culture (which is identical in more than half of the deals), and also to an extent general culture.

The three indicators of functional bidder-target similarity are rather not in line, indicating that they indeed cover different aspects of similarity: while three quarters of deals are between banks, indicating a high degree of similarity between bidder and target, the coefficient of correlation, with an average value of 0.13, shows the returns of the merging partners to be rather uncorrelated. Finally, the indicator of revenue structure is also not conclusive and indicates neither very similar nor very dissimilar merger partners. As already indicated above, about a fourth of all deals happen within the EU[443] and almost half of all deals in the "hot" 1999 to 2001 deal years.

Correlation among variables is generally low, with some unsurprising exceptions:[444] obviously, the absolute and relative efficiency measures TCOEF and RELCOEF as well as RELPREF and TPREF correlate heavily. Also, unsurprisingly, larger bidders tend to have more previous acquisition experience, causing a positive correlation between BSIZE and PREBID. The remaining larger correlations are among country-level variables and are also not surprising: in line with findings of the (non-bank specific) IM literature, the amount of FDI from a given

442 The values indicate that the average host country is about as liberal with regard to FDI and banking freedoms as the US, hosts a regulator with a level of power somewhere between that held by regulators in the UK or Belgium and provides opportunities for market-based monitoring somewhere between those in Belgium and the US, respectively.

443 The difference to the larger number of intra-European deals obviously stems from deals between EU and non EU countries, e.g., acquisitions in Eastern Europe.

444 See table A.5 in the appendix for a detailed overview.

host country correlates positively with foreign market size, home and host country sharing a similar language, the degree of economic freedom in the host and, as a result of the above, the host being the UK or the US (correlation between CLIENT and MSIZE, LANGUAGE, FREEDOM and HOSTCA).[445]

Larger host markets also enjoy a high degree of economic freedom, have more opportunities and more market-based monitoring, receive M&A from countries that are economically similar, and are again, often the UK and the US (correlation between MSIZE and FREEDOM, MONITOR, ECSIM and HOSTCA). Countries with powerful regulators are rather the US and the UK than another country in the EU (correlation between POWER, HOSTCA and EU), and host countries with a high degree of economic freedom are often the UK and the US (correlation between FREEDOM and HOSTCA). Finally, since LANGUAGE, LAW and CULTURE are all proxies for social distance, they also correlate somewhat, just as INET and TELCO, the indicators of IT sophistication. Whether or not these few correlations cause multicollinearity issues in the regression analysis will have to be tested.

Finally, the amount of deal-clustering in the sample, i.e., deals sharing the same event window, is obviously dependent on the length of the event window chosen. If the event window covers only the event day itself, clustering is minimal, even though not completely absent, as there are two bidders in the sample that simultaneously acquire 2 targets at the same time.[446] If a 3-day (10-day) symmetric event window around the event data is chosen, clustering is still mostly absent with 5 (21) overlaps in the sample. However, if larger windows are chosen, e.g., a 20-day symmetric window or even the full 40-day window, the number of overlapping events increases to 39 (74), making cross-correlation of returns more likely. However, the majority of significant results in the previous literature, in line with the market efficiency hypothesis, are found in short 1- to 3-day windows, thus clustering should not be a serious issue.

6.2 New Evidence on Direction, Size and Benefactors of Wealth Effects

The following key sections discuss the results of the empirical tests on direction, size and benefactors of wealth effects from CBBM&A. First, a traditional short-

---

445 The same effect probably leads to a negative correlation between CLIENT and EAST, the indicator of the host country being located in the (smaller, still more "unfree") Eastern European region.

446 These are the simultanous acquistitons of Republic New York Corp. and Safra Republic Holdings by HSBC and of Banco Totta e Acores and Creditio Predial Portugues by Banco Santander, both in 1999.

term event study is performed and results for bidders, targets and the joint entity are discussed. Leakage effects are explicitely taken into account. Then, results from the long-term event study are given, whereby the results from the buy-and-hold, wealth-relative and calendar-time-portfolio approaches are discussed separately.

6.2.1 Results from Short-Term Event Study

Results of the short-term event study on bidder returns, in comparison to results of previous CBBM&A studies, are shown in table 6.5.

Table 6.5: Bidder Abnormal Returns in Comparison to Prior Studies

This table shows the results for an event study analyzing 96 banks and financial firms from 22 countries bidding for 96 corresponding target banks and financial firms in cross-border mergers between 1985 and 2005. Results are shown relative to findings of selected prior studies. Abnormal returns are calculated using the market model. Parameters were estimated using OLS in a period covering 252 trading days prior to the event window and total return data on ordinary common stocks and the corresponding national market indices. Tests for significance are two-sided and according to Dodd and Warner (1983) and Cowan (1992).

				CARs found in selected prior studies (%)								
Event window	**CAR in %**	**Z-Test**	**Sign-Test**	**WM (1995)**	**HS (1996)[1]**	**B (1997)**	**GM (1998)**	**TB (1999)[2]**	**CM (2000)[2]**	**BS (2001)[2]**	**ADS (2002)**	**BM (2002)**
[-20,0]	-0.51	-0.36	-0.50							-0.54		
[-4,0]	-0.62	-1.48	-1.54		-0.45							
[-1,0]	-0.67	-2.45**	-0.11	-0.51**	-0.05	0.13	-0.29*	-0.41		-0.62*		
{0}	-0.66	-3.69***	-2.57**					-0.32		-0.68		
[-1,1]	-1.07	-2.83***	-1.95*		-0.25		-0.32	-0.37		-0.85		-0.3
[-5,5]	-1.10	-1.88*	-1.75*			0.04		-0.19		-0.87		0.90***
[-10,1]	-1.04	-1.28	-0.11						2.00		-0.98***	
[-10,10]	-1.00	-0.74	-1.75*					0.08		-1.23		
[-20,20]	-0.72	-0.33	-1.34							-0.32		

Legend: ADS = Amihud et al. (2002), B (1997) = Biswas et al. (1997), BM = Bessler and Murtag (2002), BS (2001) = Beitel and Schiereck (2001), CM = Cybo-Ottone and Murgia (2000), GM = Gleason and Mathur (1998), HS = Hudgins and Seifert (1996), TB = Tourani Rad and van Beek (1999), VV = Vander Vennet (2002), WM = Waheed and Mathur (1995).

1 *Values for acquisitions of international targets by US financial firms.* 2 *Values for cross-border sub-sample.*

* *Significant at the 10 percent level.* ** *Significant at the 5 percent level.* *** *Significant at the 1 percent level.*

Bidder abnormal returns are around 0.5 to 1 percent negative in all selected windows and on the event day. This is a similar order of magnitude as found in prior research. However, other than in some prior studies, the negative returns are statistically significant on the event day and in the short windows including the days directly around it and become lower and insignificant as the window gets larger. Parametric and non-parametric tests are generally in line. The findings indicate that capital markets, on average, view CBBM&A as wealth-destroying for bidders, probably because bidders are seen as overpaying and/or sending unfavorable signals, e.g., of existing agency problems within their organizations. This is not in line with expectations, but with the domestic and especially interstate banking M&A literature discussed above. Therefore, this deviation from expectations is not a total surprise.

Turning to targets, table 6.6 shows very large, highly significant abnormal gains up to 20% in all selected windows.[447]

Table 6.6: Target Abnormal Returns in Comparison to Prior Studies

This table shows the results for an event study analyzing 96 banks and financial firms from 32 countries being acquired by 96 corresponding bidding banks and financial firms in cross-border mergers between 1985 and 2005 relative to findings of selected prior studies. Abnormal returns are calculated using the market model. Parameters were estimated using OLS in a period covering 252 trading days prior to the event window and total return data on ordinary common stocks and the corresponding national market indices. Tests for significance are two-sided and according to Dodd and Warner (1983) and Cowan (1992).

					CARs found in selected prior studies (%)		
Event window	**CAR in %**	**Z-Test**	**Sign-Test**	**HS (1996)[1]**	**B (1997)**	**CM (2000)[2]**	**BSW (2004)[2]**
[-20,0]	17.86	20.60***	7.74***				18.16***
[-4,0]	15.49	37.07***	6.72***	9.18***			
[-1,0]	13.56	53.16***	5.69***	7.53***	6.23**		
{0}	12.00	67.70***	4.67***				
[-1,1]	15.75	49.95***	6.31***	7.30***			15.15***
[-5,5]	17.71	28.89***	7.13***		8.77**		
[-10,1]	17.90	27.97***	7.54***			22.22***	
[-10,10]	17.54	20.92***	7.74***				
[-20,20]	20.74	16.81***	7.13***				19.68***

Legend: B = Biswas et al. (1997), BSW = Beitel et al. (2004), CM = Cybo-Ottone and Murgia (2000), HS = Hudgins and Seifert (1996).

1 Values for acquisitions of international targets by US financial firms. 2 Values for cross-border sub-sample.

**** Significant at the 1 percent level.*

447 Results were in fact significantly positive in all possible sub-windows within the main window.

Parametric and non-parametric results are fully in line. Findings are in accordance with expectations and the large majority of previous studies, whether cross-border or not. The magnitude of returns is interestingly roughly twice the size identified by the US-centric work of Hudgins and Seifert (1996) and, thus, more similar to the European studies of Cybo-Ottone and Murgia (2000) and Beitel et al. (2004), probably due to the discussed diverging sample properties of the US studies.[448]

Table 6.7: Joint Entity Abnormal Returns in Comparison to Prior Studies

This table shows the results for an event study analyzing the return of the combined bidder-target entity in 96 cross-border bank mergers between 1985 and 2005 relative to findings of selected prior studies. Abnormal returns are calculated using the market model. Parameters were estimated using OLS in a period covering 252 trading days prior to the event window and total return data on ordinary common stocks and the corresponding national market indices. Joint returns are calculated by weighting bidder- and target CAR by their market capitalization one 21 days before the event. Tests for significance are two-sided and according to Dodd and Warner (1983) and Cowan (1992).

				CARs found in selected prior studies (%)			
Event window	CAR in %	Z-Test	Sign-Test	B (1997)	CM (2000)	ADS (2002)	BSW (2004)[1]
[-20,0]	0.89	2.00**	3.30***				1.38**
[-4,0]	0.52	2.49**	1.45				
[-1,0]	0.40	3.50***	2.68***				
{0}	0.29	3.56***	1.65*				
[-1,1]	0.22	2.92***	0.83				0.78**
[-5,5]	0.28	1.33	0.83	3.20**			
[-10,1]	0.41	1.89*	2.48**		2.92	-1.27	
[-10,10]	0.39	1.56	1.04				
[-20,20]	0.84	1.55	1.24				1.60

Legend: ADS = Amihud et al. (2002), B = Biswas et al (1997) BSW = Beitel et al. (2004), CM = Cybo-Ottone and Murgia (2000).

1 *Values for cross-border sub-sample.*
* *Significant at the 10 percent level.*
** *Significant at the 5 percent level.*
*** *Significant at the 1 percent level.*

448 The international study of Biswas et al (1997), does not seem to fit into this picture. However, the authors report that more than half of their targets are from the US (p. 39).

Results for the combined entity given in table 6.7 are most interesting, since here previous evidence is scarcest. Findings show rather low but statistically significant positive abnormal returns. Again, parametric and non-parametric tests are broadly in line. There is, thus, evidence that markets view cross-border bank mergers as net wealth-creating activities, albeit only because target abnormal returns more than compensate for bidder losses.This finding, which is similar to that of Beitel (2004) and Biswas et al. (1997),[449] is again not in line with expectations. Most interestingly, it differs from the findings of Amihud et al (2002), which is certainly the most comparable CBBM&A study in terms of scope and research design. However, as discussed above, findings of the latter study might be distorted by small sample size.

With regard to bidder- and target-specific leakage, it turns out that leakage is indeed an issue for targets, with information about the target intending to merge being on average revealed 63 (median: 15) days before the event. Bidder leakage is less intense with information revealed on average 33 (median: 0) days before the event. To get more insight into the wealth implications of early information revelation, the sample is split into transactions where both new revelation dates fall within the original event window, which is true for roughly half of the sample (46 deals), and transactions where at least one transaction partner reveals information before the event window opens (50 deals). The "surprise" transactions are then compared to the "anticipated" transactions and differences are tested for significance using a mean-difference-test.

Results are shown in table 6.8. Panel A shows that the bidder results discussed above are similar to the results of the two sub-samples and that abnormal returns for surprise and anticipated bidders do not differ significantly. Wealth effects for bidders, thus, seem rather related to the characteristics of a specific deal than to the overall declared intent to merge across borders. Results for targets are shown in panel B. While again the results found above are generally similar to the findings for the sub-sample, surprise deals earn significantly higher abnormal returns than anticipated deals. Since there is no reason to assume that the samples systematically differ in other respects than in degree of leakage, this points to an underestimation of target gains in the original analysis.

---

449 The work of Biswas et al. (1997), however, is potentially biased from the inclusion of deals in which no controlling stake is acquired, see the discussion in footnote 246. This would also explain the unusually high level of positive abnormal returns in their study.

Table 6.8: Analysis of Leakage Effect

This table shows the results for comparing event-study abnormal returns of bidders, targets and the joint entities in 46 "surprise" cross-border bank mergers, where information about bidder or target alone intending to merge did not reach the market more than 20 days before the event date to a corresponding sample of 50 mergers where such information was leaked and which therefore were to a degree "anticipated". Abnormal returns are calculated using the market model. Parameters were estimated using OLS in a period covering 252 trading days prior to the event window and total return data on ordinary common stocks and the corresponding national market indices. Joint returns are calculated by weighting bidder- and target CAR by their market capitalization 21 days before the event. Tests for significance are two-sided and according to Dodd and Warner (1983) and Cowan (1992). The return-difference was tested for significance using a mean-difference test.

	Surprise deals			Anticipated deals			
Event window	CAR in %	Z-Test	Sign-Test	CAR in %	Z-Test	Sign-Test	Difference in %
Panel A: Bidders							
[-20,0]	-0.25	0.47	-1.06	-1.05	-1.31	-0.29	0.80
[-4,0]	-0.38	-0.31	-0.43	-1.13	-2.15**	-1.73*	0.75
[-1,0]	-0.77	-2.13**	-0.31	-0.46	-1.23	-0.29	-0.32
{0}	-0.72	-3.44***	-1.93*	-0.55	-1.52	-1.37	-0.17
[-1,1]	-1.12	-2.03**	-1.43	-0.97	-2.03**	-1.01	-0.15
[-5,5]	-0.65	-0.64	-0.68	-2.02	-2.39**	-1.73*	1.37
[-10,1]	-0.66	-0.09	-0.31	-1.83	-2.11**	-0.29	1.16
[-10,10]	-0.42	-0.33	-0.31	-2.23	-1.78*	-3.17***	1.81
[-20,20]	-0.10	-0.38	-0.43	-2.02	-1.12	-1.37	1.92
Panel B: Targets							
[-20,0]	24.18	21.21***	6.57***	10.08	7.23***	4.28***	14.10***
[-4,0]	21.07	39.02***	5.46***	8.60	12.06***	3.98***	12.48***
[-1,0]	20.06	59.17***	4.91***	5.54	13.74***	3.06***	14.52***
{0}	17.92	78.05***	4.91***	4.70	14.51***	1.53	13.22***
[-1,1]	23.21	54.29***	5.74***	6.56	14.36***	3.06***	16.65***
[-5,5]	25.03	30.96***	6.02***	8.69	8.80***	3.98***	16.35***
[-10,1]	24.27	28.56***	6.29***	10.05	10.10***	4.28***	14.21***
[-10,10]	25.17	22.45***	6.57***	8.13	6.34***	4.28***	17.04***
[-20,20]	28.60	17.50***	6.57***	11.06	5.70***	3.37***	17.53***
Panel C: Joint Entity							
[-20,0]	1.51	2.24**	2.28**	0.31	0.63	2.38**	1.20
[-4,0]	1.07	2.81***	1.69*	0.01	0.75	0.39	1.06*
[-1,0]	0.64	3.9***	2.58***	0.17	1.89*	1.24	0.47
{0}	0.53	3.6***	1.9**	0.07	1.52	0.39	0.46
[-1,1]	0.37	2.5***	0.05	0.09	1.40	0.67	0.27
[-5,5]	0.78	1.16	1.39	-0.17	-0.29	-0.18	0.95
[-10,1]	0.68	1.93*	1.69*	0.16	0.77	1.81*	0.52
[-10,10]	0.63	1.45	1.39	0.17	0.77	0.11	0.46
[-20,20]	1.43	1.57	1.69*	0.30	0.64	0.11	1.13

* *Significant at the 10% level.*
** *Significant at the 5% level.*
*** *Significant at the 1% level.*

Seemingly, a part of the target gains are already anticipated when the target declares its intention to merge. Panel C shows results for the joint entity. Returns are again higher for the surprise deals but at a much lower level and degree of significance than target returns. This is not surprising, since the target-effect is diluted by the effect for the on-average much larger bidder. There is, thus, evidence that the original joint entity returns are slightly underestimated. Thus, the results of the original analysis still hold but become more pronounced when information leakage is accounted for more thoroughly.

Thus, the analysis suggests that bidders on average destroy shareholder wealth on a small but statistically significant scale. Results may be related to perceived agency motives as deal drivers. Targets, as expected, strongly benefit from deals. Interestingly, the net effect from bidder losses and target gains is slightly but again statistically significantly positive. Thus, while the average deal is generally undesireable from the point of view of the bidding entity, it seems desireable from an overall economy point of view.

6.2.2 Results from Long-Term Event Study

Turning to the long-term analysis, table 6.9 shows the results from the BHAR-analysis. Results for the full sample are given in panel A. Average abnormal buy-and-hold returns are negative until 2 years after the acquisition, positive after the next half year and finally around zero after 3 years. Nevertheless, as expected, the hypothesis of zero abnormal returns in all displayed time windows cannot be rejected. If the global instead of the relevant regional banking index is used as a return benchmark, abnormal returns increase with the time horizons and finally reach approximately 14 percent after 3 years. Only the abnormal returns in the 3-year time window are weakly statistically significant. However, since bidders in the sample are predominantly European and European banks on average performed better than their non-European peers in the sample period, the observed increase in abnormal returns seems due to benchmark misspecification. If the noise-adjusted[450] instead of the full sample is used (panel B), abnormal returns relative to the regional index become more negative and reach approximately -11 percent after 3 years. Use of the global index again lifts the returns to their full-sample level. Independent of the choice of benchmark, none of the observed re-

450 Remember that the noise-adjusted sample includes only deals where the market value of the target is equal or larger than 10 percent of that of the bidder and where the bidder in question did not make another acquisition in the in the relevant period, see section 5.2.2.1.

turns is statistically significantly different from zero which is in line with expectations. Similar results are obtained if long-term abnormal returns are instead measured using wealth relatives.

Table 6.9: Long-Term Average Bidder Buy-and-Hold Abnormal Returns

This table shows the results for a long-term event study analyzing the long-term bidder average buy-and-hold returns (ABHAR) following the closure date of cross-border bank mergers. Abnormal returns are estimated using monthly bidder stock total returns and a banking total return index from the home-region of the bidder or a global banking index as a benchmark. Indices are taken from Datastream. Bidder returns are winsorized at 3 standard deviations and tested for significance using a two-groups test as laid out in the test procedure proposed by Cowan and Sergeant (2001). Tests for significance are two-sided. Tests are performed alternatively on the full sample and on a sub-sample that only includes bidders that acquired targets that had a equity market value of 10% or higher of the bidder and that did not make a cross-border acquisition in 3-year-window previous to the closure date. N indicates the number of bidders in the sample for the respective time-horizon.

Panel A: Full sample					
		Regional index benchmark		**Global index benchmark**	
Post-event months	**N**	**ABHAR (%)**	**t-test**	**ABHAR (%)**	**t-test**
6	92	-0.58	-0.20	0.51	0.18
12	90	-1.01	-0.24	2.04	0.52
18	87	-2.52	-0.52	2.09	0.42
24	81	-0.13	-0.02	5.82	0.90
30	79	2.15	0.27	11.42	1.62
36	78	0.03	0.00	13.77	1.74*
Panel B: Adjusted sample					
Post-event months	**N**	**ABHAR (%)**	**t-test**	**ABHAR (%)**	**t-test**
6	31	-3.76	-0.72	-1.90	0.37
12	30	-3.19	-0.39	3.65	0.48
18	29	-9.88	-0.95	0.71	0.07
24	23	-4.88	-0.32	10.89	0.74
30	23	-7.81	-0.44	11.19	0.75
36	23	-11.35	-0.56	14.39	0.89

* *Significant at the 10 percent level.*

Figure 6.2 shows the average wealth relatives of the full sample using the regional and the global index as a benchmark as well as the associated mean components.[451] Wealth relatives are initially weakly positive and even negative but start to increase after approximately 1.5 years if the regional index is used, while wealth relatives using the global index are always positive and increase strongly. However, much of this development is due to the upward bias of volatility, since, with the exception of returns relative to the global index after roughly 2.5 years, volatility-adjusted means are usually negative irrespective of the benchmark used. Results using the regional index are again more negative than global-index results, probably for the reasons discussed already above. Results for the adjusted sample are comparable.[452]

Figure 6.2: Wealth Relatives and Mean Components

The figure shows the results for a long-term event study analyzing the mean component of the bidder/benchmark wealth relatives following the closure date of a cross-border bank merger. Wealth relatives are the ratio of bidder stock price and a regional (global) banking index as provided by Datastream and with the initial wealth level normalized to one, averaged across securities. Wealth relatives are adjusted for volatility following the procedure laid out by Jakobsen and Sørsensen (2001) leading to marginal parameter estimates of the average wealth-relative mean component. Values are given in percentages.

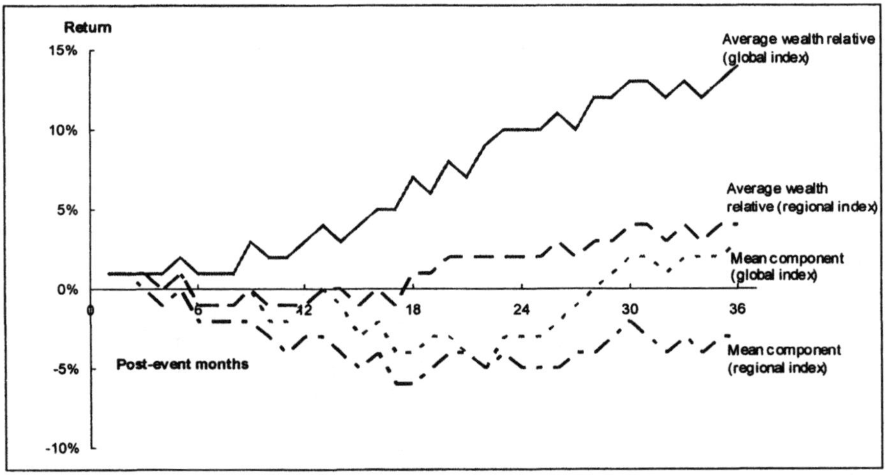

Source: Author

451 For better comparability, results are given as percentage values.
452 See figure A.1 in the appendix.

If mean components are tested for significance (table 6.10), results again show that, irrespective of adjustments of the benchmark used or changes in sample composition, the hypothesis that the measured abnormal returns are equal to zero cannot be rejected in all time windows.

Table 6.10: Marginal Long-Term Average Wealth Relative Mean Components

This table shows the results for a long-term event study analyzing the mean component of the bidder/benchmark wealth relatives following the closure date of a cross-border bank merger. Wealth relatives are the ratio of bidder stock price and a regional (global) banking index as provided by Datastream and with the initial wealth level normalized to one, averaged across securities. Wealth relatives are adjusted for volatility following the procedure laid out by Jakobsen and Sørsensen (2001) leading to marginal parameter estimates of the average wealth-relative mean component. Values are given as percentages. The marginal mean component is tested for significance using a simple two-sided t-test. Tests are performed alternatively on the full sample and on a sub-sample that only includes bidders that acquired targets that had a equity market value of 10% or higher of the bidder and that did not make a cross-border acquisition in 3-year-window previous to the closure date. N indicates the number of bidders in the sample for the respective time-horizon.

Panel A: Full sample					
		Regional index benchmark		**Global index benchmark**	
Post-event months	**N**	**Average wealth relative mean component (%)**	**t-test**	**Average wealth relative mean component (%)**	**t-test**
6	92	-2.44	-1.46	-1.01	-0.52
12	90	-3.11	-1.34	-0.96	-0.34
18	87	-5.77	-1.52	-4.32	-0.88
24	81	-4.52	-1.12	-3.17	-0.57
30	79	-2.19	-0.55	1.85	0.36
36	78	-2.71	-0.67	2.91	0.56
Panel B: Adjusted sample					
6	31	-4.95	-1.46	-3.81	-0.94
12	30	-5.95	-1.03	-2.60	-0.38
18	29	-14.49	-1.56	-9.31	-0.76
24	23	-9.62	-0.87	-4.96	-0.35
30	23	-11.83	-1.06	-5.30	-0.34
36	23	-11.54	-1.09	-1.71	-0.12

Finally, also the calendar-time-portfolio approach delivers consistent results (table 6.11). All measured average monthly returns are slightly positive. Again global-index based results are more positive and adjusted sample results are more negative. Also as above, with the exception of global-index returns in the full sample that are slightly significant at the 10 percent level, abnormal returns are not significantly different from zero. All results are consistent with expectations and the notion of efficient capital markets. Thus, the wealth effects found in the short-term study are indeed representative for the total wealth effects.

Table 6.11: Long-Term Average Calendar Time Portfolio Returns

This table shows the results for a long-term event study analyzing the average calendar time portfolio returns of bidder banks following a cross-border bank merger. Calendar time portfolios are constructed for each month between January 1985 and February 2006. In each calendar time portfolio, bidder stocks are included if the respective bidder closed a cross-border deal in one of the previous 3 years. Abnormal returns are then calculated as total returns on bidder stocks relative to a regional (global) banking index as provided by Datastream. Abnormal returns are averaged across firms in a portfolio and across portfolios. Abnormal returns are standardized and tested for significance following the procedure laid out be Mandelker (1975). Tests are performed alternatively on the full sample and on a sub-sample that only includes bidders that acquired targets that had a equity market value of 10% or higher of the bidder and that did not make a cross-border acquisition in 3-year-win-dow previous to the closure date. N indicates the number of bidders in the sample.

Sample	Benchmark	Average monthly unstandardized abnormal returns	t-test
Full	Regional Index	0.40	1.11
Full	Global Index	0.62	1.83*
Adjusted	Regional Index	0.03	0.28
Adjusted	Global Index	0.31	0.84

* *Significant at the 10 percent level.*

Results are, however, not in line with recent long term banking M&A studies. In addition to the possibility of chance results or measurement problems as discussed above, the differing results might be driven by the strongly diverging sample properties: the much larger size of the banks in the present sample potentially favors information dissemination with regard to the bidders, e.g., through broader analyst coverage, making a significant average market under- or overreaction less likely.[453]

453 If the detected long-term returns are added to the joint-entity returns, short-term returns sometimes lose significance but sometimes also gain significance, depending on the long-term horizon analyzed and the method of calculating long-term returns chosen without showing a systematic tendency. However, since long-term returns

6.3 New Evidence on Determinants of Wealth Effects

After the discussion of wealth effects of CBBM&A, the study now turns to the analysis of their potential determinants. First, a dichotomization analysis is performed. Then, the more complex regression approach is performed and discussed. Again, results are given separately for bidders, targets and the joint entity.

6.3.1 Results from Dichotomization Analysis

On the following pages, the results of the dichotomization analyses for bidders (table 6.12), targets (table 6.13), and the joint entities (table 6.14) are presented. The results per determinant are discussed in turn.

Results for *bidder size* indicate that net abnormal returns for large bidders are more negative than for small bidders. This is not in line with the expected positive impact of bidder size. However, expectations were formed based on the evidence presented in IM studies. The negative findings for bidder size are more in line with the theory put forward by some of the CF studies, namely of diseconomies of scale for larger banks.

The above results are supported by the findings on *relative (target) size.* Acquirers of larger targets are shown to have significantly higher negative abnormal losses than acquirers of smaller targets. However, differences between target and net abnormal returns are not significantly different from zero. Thus, findings are again not in line with expectations. Rather, findings support the notion of Hawawini and Swary (1990) that acquisitions of relatively large targets lead to scale diseconomies, and of Beitel et al. (2004), that relatively large targets require more complex and costly post-merger integration. However, the fact that results are only significant for bidders also supports the notion of Cornett and De (1991) that there are offsetting effects from relative target size.

With regard to the *presence of existing (home country) clients in the host country* results for bidders indicate that this factor does not make a difference for bidder results. However, targets located in countries with a strong presence of bidder home country clients enjoy abnormal gains that are twice as high as those located in countries with few home country clients. The resulting net effect is insignificant, but barely so (t-value of 1.14). Thus, results suggest that the presence of home country clients does, as expected, have a positive wealth effect but it is fully captured by the target and too small to be reflected in changes in net wealth.

---

are not systematically different from zero, the detected short-term returns alone best represent the total wealth effect of the deal.

Table 6.12: Dichotomization Analysis Results for Bidders

	Results for Top-Cases				Results for Bottom-Cases				
Variable	N	Average	Std. Dev.	CAR in [-1,1] (%)	N	Average	Std.Dev.	CAR in [-1,1] (%)	Difference Top-Bottom (%)
BSIZE	30	13.31	0.31	-2.29***	30	10.64	0.95	-1.87***	-0.43
RELSIZE	30	0.89	0.07	-1.75***	30	0.51	0.19	-0.21	-1.54**
CLIENT	30	10.88	0.92	-0.84	30	7.53	1.44	-0.87	0.03
RELCOEF	30	1.35	0.62	-1.43***	30	0.81	0.14	-0.66	-0.76
RELPREF	30	1.95	0.93	-0.94*	30	0.09	1.56	-1.46***	0.52
MBR	30	1.44	-0.45	-0.89	30	0.39	0.16	-1.20**	0.31
TCOEF	30	0.79	0.24	-1.60***	30	0.51	0.09	-0.92	-0.68
TPREF	30	0.21	0.08	-1.44***	30	0.02	0.18	-1.48***	0.04
MBT	30	2.07	0.31	-1.56***	30	0.69	0.23	-0.71*	-0.85
DISTANCE	30	2.11	0.31	-0.04	30	-1.31	1.57	-0.85	0.81
LANGUAGE	33	1.00	0.00	-0.65	63	0.00	0.00	-1.29***	0.65
LAW	52	1.00	0.00	-1.03**	44	0.00	0.00	-1.13**	0.10
CULTURE	30	17.04	3.02	-0.33	30	3.90	1.12	-1.14**	0.81
CORREL	30	0.31	0.13	-1.38***	30	-0.02	0.06	-0.50	-0.88
NONBANK	24	1.00	0.00	-0.32	72	0.00	0.00	-1.32***	1.00
BANKFOCUS	30	0.87	0.06	-0.96*	30	0.45	0.20	-2.04***	1.08
PREBID	44	1.00	0.00	-1.09***	52	0.00	0.00	-1.05*	-0.04
CASH	30	1.00	0.00	-0.44	30	0.51	0.45	-2.01***	1.56**
EFFIC	42	1.00	0.00	-1.05*	54	0.00	0.00	-1.09***	0.04
MARKET	52	1.00	0.00	-1.51***	44	0.00	0.00	-0.55	-0.96*
ASSET	33	1.00	0.00	-0.85	63	0.00	0.00	-1.19***	0.33
INET	30	0.10	0.13	-1.81***	30	0.01	0.00	-0.11	-1.70**
TELCO	30	5.29	0.25	-1.25**	30	4.45	0.28	-2.17***	0.92
MSIZE	30	10.45	0.11	-1.36***	30	9.17	0.03	-0.38	-0.98
HOTY	43	1.00	0.00	-2.00***	53	0.00	0.00	-0.32	-1.69***
ECSIM	30	0.92	0.05	-1.91***	30	0.38	0.09	-1.41**	-0.50
FREEDOM	30	2.73	0.29	-1.09	30	1.57	0.31	-2.24***	1.16*
POWER	30	1.14	0.00	-0.92	30	-0.66	0.84	-1.26***	0.34
MONITOR	30	1.15	0.24	-0.61	30	0.06	0.34	-1.55***	0.94
HOSTCA	36	1.00	0.00	-0.88*	60	0.00	0.00	-1.19***	0.31
EU	26	1.00	0.00	-1.60***	70	0.00	0.00	-0.87*	-0.73
EAST	11	1.00	0.00	-0.36	85	0.00	0.00	-1.16***	0.81

Table 6.13: Dichotomization Analysis Results for Targets

Variable	Results for Top-Cases				Results for Bottom-Cases				Difference Top-Bottom (%)
	N	Average	Std. Dev.	CAR in [-1,1] (%)	N	Average	Std. Dev.	CAR in [-1,1] (%)	
BSIZE	30	13.31	0.31	21.02***	30	10.64	0.95	20.15***	0.86
RELSIZE	30	0.89	0.07	16.68***	30	0.51	0.19	16.37***	0.32
CLIENT	30	10.88	0.92	22.92***	30	7.53	1.44	10.92***	12.01**
RELCOEF	30	1.35	0.62	15.10***	30	0.81	0.14	14.23***	0.87
RELPREF	30	1.95	0.93	14.59***	30	0.09	1.56	15.48***	-0.89
MBR	30	1.44	-0.45	14.50***	30	0.39	0.16	22.36***	-7.86
TCOEF	30	0.79	0.24	6.42***	30	0.51	0.09	24.92***	-18.50***
TPREF	30	0.21	0.08	14.20***	30	0.02	0.18	14.69***	-0.48
MBT	30	2.07	0.31	13.84***	30	0.69	0.23	18.58***	-4.74
DISTANCE	30	2.11	0.31	13.68***	30	-1.31	1.57	20.29***	-6.61
LANGUAGE	33	1.00	0.00	13.14***	63	0.00	0.00	17.12***	-3.98
LAW	52	1.00	0.00	17.20***	44	0.00	0.00	14.03***	3.17
CULTURE	30	17.04	3.02	14.47***	30	3.90	1.12	22.46***	-7.98
CORREL	30	0.31	0.13	13.39***	30	-0.02	0.06	19.84***	-6.46
NONBANK	24	1.00	0.00	21.19***	72	0.00	0.00	13.94***	7.26
BANKFOCUS	30	0.87	0.06	17.60***	30	0.45	0.20	11.85***	5.75
PREBID	44	1.00	0.00	17.76***	52	0.00	0.00	14.05***	3.71
CASH	30	1.00	0.00	19.25***	30	0.51	0.45	15.75***	3.50
EFFIC	42	1.00	0.00	19.70***	54	0.00	0.00	12.68***	7.03*
MARKET	52	1.00	0.00	14.41***	44	0.00	0.00	17.33***	-2.93
ASSET	33	1.00	0.00	17.90***	63	0.00	0.00	14.62***	3.27
INET	30	0.10	0.13	22.23***	30	0.01	0.00	6.54***	15.69***
TELCO	30	5.29	0.25	23.05***	30	4.45	0.28	14.22***	8.83
MSIZE	30	10.45	0.11	26.55***	30	9.17	0.03	2.84***	23.71***
HOTY	43	1.00	0.00	19.86***	53	0.00	0.00	12.42***	7.44*
ECSIM	30	0.92	0.05	20.37***	30	0.38	0.09	8.84***	11.53**
FREEDOM	30	2.73	0.29	7.53***	30	1.57	0.31	20.86***	-13.33**
POWER	30	1.14	0.00	25.88***	30	-0.66	0.84	14.92***	10.97*
MONITOR	30	1.15	0.24	15.94***	30	0.06	0.34	10.72***	5.22
HOSTCA	36	1.00	0.00	22.50***	60	0.00	0.00	11.70***	10.81***
EU	26	1.00	0.00	19.24***	70	0.00	0.00	14.45***	4.78
EAST	11	1.00	0.00	-0.76	85	0.00	0.00	17.89***	-18.65***

Table 6.14: Dichotomization Analysis Results for Joint Entities

Variable	Results for Top-Cases				Results for Bottom-Cases				Difference Top-Bottom (%)
	N	Average	Std. Dev.	CAR in [-1,1] (%)	N	Average	Std. Dev.	CAR in [-1,1] (%)	
BSIZE	30	13.31	0.31	-1.04	30	10.64	0.95	0.42**	-1.46**
RELSIZE	30	0.89	0.07	0.89***	30	0.51	0.19	0.39**	0.50
CLIENT	30	10.88	0.92	0.58***	30	7.53	1.44	-0.31	0.89
RELCOEF	30	1.35	0.62	-0.35	30	0.81	0.14	0.69***	-1.04*
RELPREF	30	1.95	0.93	0.58**	30	0.09	1.56	-0.55	1.14*
MBR	30	1.44	-0.45	0.82***	30	0.39	0.16	-0.02	0.84
TCOEF	30	0.79	0.24	-0.89	30	0.51	0.09	0.68***	-1.57**
TPREF	30	0.21	0.08	-0.24	30	0.02	0.18	-0.73	0.48
MBT	30	2.07	0.31	0.11	30	0.69	0.23	0.59*	-0.48
DISTANCE	30	2.11	0.31	0.77***	30	-1.31	1.57	0.34	0.43
LANGUAGE	33	1.00	0.00	0.75***	63	0.00	0.00	-0.05	0.81
LAW	52	1.00	0.00	0.64***	44	0.00	0.00	-0.26	0.90*
CULTURE	30	17.04	3.02	0.55***	30	3.90	1.12	0.26	0.29
CORREL	30	0.31	0.13	0.47**	30	-0.02	0.06	2.73***	-2.26
NONBANK	24	1.00	0.00	0.84***	72	0.00	0.00	0.02	0.82*
BANKFOCUS	30	0.87	0.06	0.57**	30	0.45	0.20	-1.01*	1.58**
PREBID	44	1.00	0.00	-0.18	52	0.00	0.00	0.57**	-0.75
CASH	30	1.00	0.00	0.72***	30	0.51	0.45	0.02	0.70
EFFIC	42	1.00	0.00	0.57***	54	0.00	0.00	-0.05	0.62
MARKET	52	1.00	0.00	0.10	44	0.00	0.00	0.37*	-0.28
ASSET	33	1.00	0.00	0.21*	63	0.00	0.00	0.23	-0.02
INET	30	0.10	0.13	-0.16	30	0.01	0.00	0.30	-0.46
TELCO	30	5.29	0.25	-0.05	30	4.45	0.28	-0.21	0.17
MSIZE	30	10.45	0.11	0.82***	30	9.17	0.03	-0.34	1.16*
HOTY	43	1.00	0.00	-0.63	53	0.00	0.00	0.92***	-1.55***
ECSIM	30	0.92	0.05	-0.17	30	0.38	0.09	-0.39	0.22
FREEDOM	30	2.73	0.29	-0.24	30	1.57	0.31	-0.76*	0.52
POWER	30	1.14	0.00	1.18***	30	-0.66	0.84	-0.32	1.50**
MONITOR	30	1.15	0.24	1.10***	30	0.06	0.34	-1.07**	2.17***
HOSTCA	36	1.00	0.00	1.02***	60	0.00	0.00	-0.25	1.27**
EU	26	1.00	0.00	-0.08	70	0.00	0.00	0.34**	-0.42
ÉAST	11	1.00	0.00	-0.41	85	0.00	0.00	0.31	-0.71

Relative (target) efficiency was measured with relative CIR and ROE as well as relative MBR. While the relative MBR does not seem to have a significant effect for either bidder, targets or the joint entity, this is not true for the relative CIR and ROE. The impact of these variables is not in line with the relative efficiency hypothesis that states that wealth creation should be higher, if relatively efficient bidders take over relatively inefficient targets. Quite to the contrary, results suggest that the net wealth effect is higher if targets are more cost-efficient[454] and profit-efficient than bidders.

While the relative efficiency results are not in line with the relative efficiency hypothesis, they fit with the target quality hypothesis that states that wealth creation should be higher if targets are relatively efficient ex-ante. The results for the factors that capture target quality, i.e., *target efficiency*, support the findings from the relative efficiency variables. Taking over targets that were already cost-efficient ex-ante increases bidder, target, and net wealth (even though only the latter two effects are significant). However, it seems to be only cost efficiency that makes a difference, as differences in target profit efficiency or MBR do not have a significant effect on shareholder wealth. A possible interpretation of this is that cost-cutting in newly acquired foreign bank is difficult.

Physical distance does not seem to have an impact on either bidder, target or net wealth. However, *social distance*, if measured with similarities in legal tradition, does make a difference. As expected, net wealth increases are significantly higher if bidder and target share the same legal tradition. However, differences in language or general culture as captured by the Hofstede index do not seem to play a role with regard to wealth effects.

Functional differences between bidders and targets were again measured with several proxies. Of these, the degree of correlation of bidder and target returns does not show an impact. Contrary to expectations, net wealth creation is also higher in bank-non-bank deals relative to bank-bank deals, indicating potential gains from diversification not found in previous studies. However, the BANKFOCUS variable, that measures the degree of similarity of two banks by their focus on lending and borrowing, tells a different story. It indicates that more wealth is created if the merging partners are more similar. Thus, possibly, while deals between investment and commercial banks (indicated by low values of BANKFOCUS) do not create net wealth, possibly because of strong cultural differences between the two types of banking, deals between banks and asset managers or insurances (which is what NONBANK captures) do, maybe because of the synergies associated with offering a broader spectrum of financial services and lower efficiency barriers due to more similar corporate cultures. Thus, the ef-

454 Remember that a higher CIR indicates less cost-efficiency.

fect measured here may rather be related to economies of scope of cultural distance than to diversification.

Previous bidder M&A experience is not found to have a significant impact while, as expected, bidder wealth increases with the *share of the acquisition price paid in cash.* The signaling and agency-effects, which are potentially behind this, are however not strong enough to also increase net wealth.

Also mostly in line with expectations is the market reaction to a bidder intent to create either *operational synergies* or *diversify geographically or functionally.* The market reacts positively to the announcement of an intent to create operational synergies, even though the effect is fully captured by the target and is not strong enough to significantly influence net wealth. Also as expected, an intent to diversify geographically is met with skepticism, leading to higher bidder losses. Again results are not strong enough to significantly influence net wealth. No significant reactions could be found upon an announcement to diversify functionally, probably due to the differing effects of functional diversification between commercial and investment banks, on the one hand, and banks and other FIs, on the other hand, that were found above.

With regard to the *IT sophistication of the bidder organization*, the hypothesis was that high sophistication increases shareholder wealth through a transaction cost effect that allows banks to grow larger and do so profitably. That effect was supposed to supersede any negative effects of IT advancements, especially a potential cost increase of the M&A solution versus a market solution, i.e., cross-border borrowing and lending, that is anyway, even inside the EU, severely regulated. While the TELCO variable, that measures IT sophistication with the investments in telecommunications equipment in the home country, does not support this theory, and in fact does not support any significant impact of this factor, the alternative variable, INET, shows a significant effect. For bidders, INET, that measures the number of internet hosts in the bidder country, has an unexpected significant negative effect while the effect for targets is, as expected, significantly positive. The two effects seem to cancel out, leading to an insignificant net effect. Maybe, "high tech" bidders are seen as rather wealth destroying when conducting CBBM&A because they forego a more efficient cross-border lending or borrowing alternative while targets of such bidders are seen as the benefactors of potential IT related efficiency increases. However, given the somewhat ambiguous nature of the two country-level proxies for firm-level factors discussed above this interpretation has to be tentative.[455]

455 The identified statistical relationsship could also point to a relationship between a tendency to overpay and bidders from large and highly developed countries during the "hot" deal period, like the US, Canada and Sweden (the countries with high

Turning to the identified country- and industry level determinants, the hypothesis of a significant positive effect of the *size of the host market* is supported. While bidders seem to lose more when acquiring in large host markets (albeit not significantly so), target gains are almost 10 times higher, leading to an also significantly positive net effect.

Also in line with expectations is the effect of the *equity market "temperature"*: In the "hot" market phase, bidders suffer higher losses while targets enjoy higher gains. However, wealth is not only redistributed from bidder to targets but net wealth is destroyed, as the figures for the joint entity indicate. Potentially, investors see such acquisitions as indicators of serious agency problems in the bidder organizations or of more such "frivolous" acquisitions coming up in the future.

Results for *economic distance between bidders and targets* are also unsurprising, as, in line with the hypothesis posed, low distance tends to increase wealth. Again, positive wealth effects are captured by targets and are not strong enough to influence net wealth.

With regard to the *general economic openness of the host country*, target results are as expected, indicating that higher freedom leads to higher wealth creation.[456] The opposite is true for bidders that seem to gain more from acquisitions in "unfree" countries, thus offsetting target gains. This may be due to higher possibilities for monopoly gains in unfree countries or the fact that some acquisitions in unfree countries[457] in the sample, especially in South America, happened after the recovery from banking crises, where many reforms were promised but had not yet been implemented.[458] Alternatively, bidders may bid generally higher in "free" countries, maybe due to a more competitive market for corporate control and thus more often tend to overbid. The insignificant effect on the joint entity is probably caused by offsetting bidder and target effects.

Results also support the notion that the regulatory environment in the host country plays a decisive role. As indicated in the previous literature, more *powerful regulators* and more *opportunities for market-based monitoring* increase net wealth and target wealth in the case of regulatory power.

INET values). However, note that table A.5 does not show significant correlations between INET and HOTYEAR (or any of the other factors used in this study) alone.

456 Remember that higher index values indicate more "unfree" countries.

457 Charap and Harm (2000) argue that dictatorships favor taxation via monopolies due to the administrative costs of taxing consumer surplus and, hence, have a tendency to allow monopolistic structures. This might also apply to other "unfree" systems and favor foreign bidders.

458 See Soussa (2004) on the characteristics of CBBM&A deals from developed into developing countries in the sample period.

Dropping indicators of individual country characteristics and using dummies for specific country combinations also delivers interesting results. *Acquisitions of targets in the US or the UK* leads to more positive target and net effects. Thus, the notion of country-specific comparative advantages of the US and the UK in importing financial CBBM&A is supported.[459] However, despite the efforts to harmonize regulatory environments and lower hurdles for cross-border capital flows and contrary to expectations, *intra-EU deals* do not turn out better or worse than non-EU deals for either bidders, targets or the joint entity.

Contrary to expectations, *targets located in Eastern Europe* gain significantly less than targets located elsewhere, while bidders and the joint entity do not exhibit wealth effects that differ significantly from deals, in which no target from Eastern Europe is involved. In fact, targets from Eastern Europe are the only group of targets that does not enjoy any significant gains and even suffers small losses (that are, however, not significantly different from zero). This is all the more surprising, as a look at the press documentation of these deals does not reveal that these were targets in distress. The reason behind this is probably that all Eastern European targets show significant leakage – often due to the fact that a majority stake in them was auctioned by the respective governments, making the fact that they were up for sale known long before the identity of the new owner was revealed. Consequently, the negative significance of this factor vanishes if the dichotomization analysis is performed on the leakage adjusted sample discussed below.[460]

To check whether leakage also biases other of the discussed factors, the above analysis was repeated on a leakage adjusted sample, whereby all deals that displayed bidder-, target-, or bidder- and target-leakage were eliminated if this leakage occurred more than 20 days before the event date. Detailed results are given in tables A.6 to A.8 in the appendix. Results for bidders indicate that the above results are overall robust with regard to leakage in the sense that most insignificant factors stay insignificant and many significant factors, namely MARKET, INET and HOTY, stay significant. Also, no factor shows an effect

459 Note, however, that the evidence for the UK is somewhat weak, as the sample only includes 7 deals in this country.

460 This issue already became apparent in the discussion of the Unicredito/Pekao deal discussed above. Unfortunately, the insignificant wealth effect with regard to this factor discussed below is mostly due to the fact that, once target leakage is adjusted for, only 2 deals with targets in Eastern Europe remain in the sample. Thus, even the adjusted sample does not allow for a thorough analysis of the effect that this factors has on target banks.

contrary to that described above. However, some factors gain or loose significance.[461] Results for targets and the joint entity show similar effects.[462]

As discussed above, dichotomization analysis is only one possible method of providing indications about the impact of determinants of abnormal returns and has some specific drawbacks, such as the inability to analyze the impact of several factors at the same time.[463] Thus, this study will now turn to a regression analysis in order to gain further insights into possible determinants of wealth effects.

6.3.2 Results from Regression Analysis

With regard to regression analysis results, results are not only discussed separately for bidders, targets and joint entities, but also for short- and long-term returns. Results are given in the following.

6.3.2.1 Regression of Short-Term Returns

Results for the regression analysis of bidder returns are given in table 6.15a. The analysis begins with a selection of factors that showed some relevancy in the dichotomization analysis and for which a set of one-factor regressions shows a

---

461 While RELSIZE, CASH and FREEDOM loose significance and no longer display a significant effect, RELPREF, NONBANK and BANKFOCUS become significant. However, note that, next to biases from leakage, results might be strongly driven by the relatively strong changes in sample size once adjustments are performed: The adjusted (sub)samples only contain 65 bidders, 53 targets and 46 joint entities and are in some cases further reduced by data availability with regard to the factor under consideration. This is also the reason why the number of top- and bottom-cases in the analysis is reduced relative to the unadjusted sample.

462 For targets, effects for TCOEF, INET and MSIZE are unchanged. CLIENT, ECSIM, POWER, HOSTCA and, as discussed above, EAST, loose significance whereas MBT does gain some. For the joint entity, effects for RELCOEF, RELPREF, TCOEF and HOTY are again unchanged, whereas MBR gains some significance and some factors, specifically BSIZE, LANGUAGE, NONBANK, BANKFOCUS, MSIZE, POWER, MONITOR and HOSTCA do loose some. Again, most insignificant factors stay insignificant and no factor shows a contradictory behaviour to that discussed above.

463 Note also that it has some similarity to singe-variable regressions, which have also been performed, see tables A.9, A.11 and A.12 in the appendix. Results have primarily been used to select a "starting point" for the inclusion/exclusion approach used for the multiple regression analysis. See also the discussion in the next section.

Table 6.15a: Multiple Regression Results for Bidders

This table shows the results for 6 multiple OLS-regression models run for the CAR of the bidders against different explanatory variables. Bidder CARs are calculated in a 3-day interval symmetric to the event day and were calculated using the market model. Parameters were estimated using OLS in a a period covering 252 trading days prior to the event window and total return data on ordinary common stocks and the corresponding national market indices. RELSIZE is the logarithm of the total assets of the target at book values divided by the logarithm of the total assets of the bidder, CASH is the percentage of the transaction value paid in cash, HOTY is a dummy variable that is equal to 1 if the event year is in the "hot" market phase 1999-2001, TCOEF is the target CIR, RELCOEF is the target CIR divided by the bidder CIR, MBT is the target MBR, LANGUAGE is a dummy variable that is equal to 1 if the primary languages in the home and host countries are identical., MARKET is a dummy variable that is equal to 1 if the bidder strategy as published on the event day is classified as primaiily "market-seeking", i.e., geographically diversifying. FREEDOM is an index of host country economic freedom, especially with regard to banking, finance, capital flows and FDI. EAST is a dummy variable that is equal to 1 if the target is located in a country in eastern Europe and 0 otherwise. Leakage-adjusted subsamples include only deals, were bidder-specific leakage did not occur more than 20 days before the event date.

Model		1	2	3	4	5	6
Sample		Regular	Regular	Regular	Regular	Regular	Leakage-Adjusted
N		95	63	62	61	60	39
Adj. R^2 (%)		11.11	29.28	30.71	44.77	44.20	30.29
F-Value		4.91***	7.42***	7.76***	7.95***	7.68***	3.36***
Con-stant		-0.007044 (-0.41)	0.05259 (5.25***)	0.048149 (4.84***)	0.010014 (0.70)	-0.001266 (-0.08)	0.013719 (0.53)
Coefficient (t-value)	RELSIZE	-0.020500 (-1.25)					
	CASH	0.021853 (2.06**)					
	HOTY	-0.017075 (-2.51**)	-0.020768 (-3.15***)	-0.022172 (-3.31***)	-0.024714 (-4.07***)	-0.025069 (-4.07***)	-0.023835 (-2.65**)
	TCOEF		-0.036016 (-2.76***)		-0.052949 (-4.19***)		-0.053009 (-1.54)
	RELCOEF			-0.016991 (-3.92***)		-0.023733 (-4.74***)	
	MBT		-0.015996 (-2.68***)	-0.015918 (-2.66***)	-0.015131 (-2.93***)	-0.013651 (-2.48**)	-0.012306 (-1.68)
	LANGUAGE				0.018032 (2.26**)	0.015263 (1.85*)	0.010815 (0.92)
	MARKET		-0.013967 (-1.92*)	-0.013473 (-1.89*)	-0.011681 (-1.81*)	-0.012691 (-1.97*)	-0.017154 (-1.94*)
	FREEDOM				0.020652 (3.47***)	0.021619 (3.62***)	0.019983 (2.92***)
	EAST				0.019516 (2.18**)	0.017034 (1.85*)	0.002471 (0.19)

* *Significant at the 10 percent level.*
** *Significant at the 5 percent level.*
*** *Significant at the 1 percent level.*

similar result.[464] Thus, the initial specification (model 1) tries to explain bidder CARs by the relative size of transaction partners, the amount of the acquisition price paid in cash, and the occurrence of the deal in the "hot" deal period. As expected, and just as in the dichotomization analysis, bidder abnormal returns increase with the share of the acquisition price paid in cash and decrease in the "hot" period. The relative size coefficient is, however, not significant. Also note, that the HOTYEAR and CASH variable interact in the sense that a high share of the acquisition price paid in cash (or analogously a low share paid in stock) has a more positive effect on bidder returns in "hot" years than in "cold" years, as an analysis of the interaction term in table 6.15b reveals. This is in line with the argument that investors see stock acquisitions in "hot" years as an indication of wealth-destroying agency issues on the bidder side.

The analysis of bidder abnormal returns as outlined in table 6.15a, model 1 can be improved with the application of the stepwise inclusion/exclusion approach, which leads to model 2.[465] While the effect of HOTY is unchanged, RELSIZE and CASH no longer turn up in the specification.[466] Instead, the target cost efficiency indicator (TCOEF), the target MBR (MBT), and the indicator of a geographically diversifying deal intent announced by the bidder around the event date (MARKET) turn out to have some explanatory power.The coefficient of the TCOEF variable is in line with expectations and the target quality hypothesis: the more cost-efficient the target is before the deal is announced, the more likely the deal is to cause positive abnormal bidder gains.[467]

However, the coefficient of the MBT variable tells a more differentiated story: while ex-ante cost efficiency generally increases bidder gains, high ex-ante growth perspectives decrease bidder gains. This is in line with the notion that target growth perspectives need to be sufficiently low in order for bidders to be able to increase them. Thus, in line with the literature review that found target quality

---

464 Results of the one-factor regressions are given in table A.9 in the appendix. It turns out that of the 6 factors identified as highly relevant in the dichotomization analysis only RELSIZE, CASH and HOTY are also significant in the one-factor analyses.

465 Note that not the whole sample is available for this analysis. This is caused by limited data availability with regard to the included determinants, see table 6.4 for a summary overview of data availability per determinant. Since the number of available cases is still more than 10 times larger than the number of regressors (5 times more cases is the rule of thumb in order for the regression to be well specified, see Schroeder et al., 1986), the drawn inferences seem nevertheless valid. This also applies to all of the regressions below.

466 The interaction variable CASH*HOTY is also not significant in any of the specifications.

467 Remember that TCOEF is the target CIR.

Table 6.15b: Analysis of Interaction between HOTY and CASH Variables

This table shows the results for a multiple OLS-regression run for the CAR of the bidders against different explanatory variables with a specific focus on the interaction between the variables HOTY and CASH. Bidder CARs are calculated in a 3-day interval symmetric to the event day and were calculated using the market model. Parameters were estimated using OLS in a a period covering 252 trading days prior to the event window and total return data on ordinary common stocks and the corresponding national market indices. HOTY is a dummy variable that is equal to 1 if the event year is in the "hot" market phase 1999-2001. CASHCENTER is the CASH variable, that equals the percentage of the transaction value paid in cash but is centered around its mean, which improves the analysis of interaction variables (see Jaccard and Turisi (2003)). HOTYCASHCENTER is the interaction variable between HOTY and CASH.

N		96
Adj. R^2 (%)		14.04
F-Value		6.17***
Constant		-0.003209 (-0.80)
Coefficient (t-value)	HOTY	-0.016396 (-2.50**)
	CASHCENTER[1]	0.007430 (0.60)
	HOTY* CASH-CENTER	0.040353 (2.05**)

** *Significant at the 5 percent level.*
*** *Significant at the 1 percent level.*

to be sometimes positively and sometimes negatively related to wealth creation, there seem to be two promising ways for bidders to increase wealth creation. One is to take over sufficiently cost-efficient targets which probably allows for further bidder-induced efficiency increases.[468] The other promising approach seems to be taking over targets that have low growth perspectives, but supposedly still untapped opportunities to create such perspectives, most likely through the means of bidder resources.[469] The results for the MARKET coefficient is again in line with an anticipated negative impact of diversification: bidder returns decrease if the bidder motivates the deal with a geographically diversifying intent.

468 An alternative interpretation is that synergy-driven mergers suffer less adverse consequences if the target is cost efficient.

469 An analysis of the interaction between TCOEF and MBT does not reveal significant results. Therefore, targets do not need to be both, cost-efficient and with low standalone growth perspectives.

Because of multicollinearity issues with TCOEF and RELCOEF, the two variables cannot be tested jointly.[470] Model 3, therefore, replaces TCOEF with RELCOEF. While the results for all other variables are comparable, RELCOEF is significant but does, as in the dichotomization analysis, not support the relative efficiency hypothesis. Again, results rather show that the more cost-inefficient the target is relative to the bidder, the lower bidder abnormal returns.

When country-specific variables are also considered, best results are obtained by an expansion of model (1) that leads to model (4). The two added country-specific variables with a significant impact are the index of economic freedom in the host country (FREEDOM) and the indicator of the target being located in Eastern Europe (EAST). EAST has the expected positive sign and supports the notion that market imperfections, which were supposedly present in these countries at the time of the acquisition, are seen as benefical to bidders. The positive sign of FREEDOM is somewhat surprising and contrary to expectations, even though it was also found in the dichotomization analysis. Results indicate that bidder returns decrease with the level of economic freedom in the host country, maybe through some loss of possibilities to extract monopoly rents[471] or again because there may be less bidder competition in unfree countries. Also, with the inclusion of the two country-variables, LANGUAGE, the indicator of a shared primary language between bidder and target country, turns significant. As expected, a similar language, and thus lower social distance, increases bidder wealth. The overall explanatory power of the model is moderate (adjusted R^2 of about 40 percent) but still much better than that of comparable models in previous studies.

Again, TCOEF can be replaced by RELCOEF (model 5) which leads to similar results. To check for potential biases due to information leakage, the final model is again estimated on the, unfortunately significantly smaller, bidder-leakage adjusted sample (model 6). Generally, results seem robust against leakage issues, even though the explanatory power of the model generally suffers and factors are less significant.[472]

---

470 Unless otherwise indicated, all displayed models do not show indications of multicollinearity, as measured by tolerance values, condition indices, or Durbin-Watson tests.

471 Remember that higher index values represent more "unfree" countries.

472 With regard to EAST, part of the problems is the discussed small number of bidders with targets in Eastern Europe that do not exhibit significant leakage. As in the models discussed above, use of RELCOEF instead of TCOEF leads to similar results.

With regard to target abnormal returns, the analysis is repeated with a set of factors that show some relevancy in both the dichotomization and a one-factor regression analysis.[473] This leads to an initial model specification (model 1 in table 6.16).

Here target abnormal returns are explained by the presence of home country clients in the host country market (CLIENT), target cost efficiency (TCOEF), the bidder announcement of an efficiency-increasing deal motive (EFFIC), the size of the host market (MSIZE), the degree of economic similarity of home and host country (ECSIM) and the level of economic freedom in the host country (FREEDOM). Additional factors are, whether the host country is the UK and the US (HOSTCA), the bidder-target correlation coefficient (CORREL), the "hot deal year" indicator (HOTY) and whether the target is located in Eastern Europe (EAST). However, besides some indications of collinearity issues in this specification, most probably because of the interaction of the country-level variables discussed above, the adjusted R^2 and the F-value indicate a poor model specification.

After applying the inclusion/exclusion procedure, model 2 is arrived at in which all of the above variables except MSIZE, CORREL, HOTY and EAST drop out and LANGUAGE drops in.[474] The model supports the hypothesis that acquisitions in large host markets create wealth as the coefficient of MSIZE is positively significant. Wealth creation, however, seems to be fully captured by the target as this proxy did not turn out significant in the bidder regressions. Assuming that the market for corporate control is competitive, this is not surprising since target market size is independent of bidder characteristics and related profits should, thus, be eroded by (potential) bidder competition. The negative and significant value of the coefficient of CORREL indicates that, contrary to expectations, wealth creation increases with functional bidder-target differences. Thus, either there is some value in functional diversification, that is, however, again fully captured by targets, or functionally diversifying bidders are seen as overpaying. However, since there was no sign of functional differences lowering bidder wealth above, the first interpretation seems somewhat more likely. Since HOTY is positively significant, targets gain in "hot" equity market phases. Thus, highly optimistic bidder expectations in boom phases and/or agency issues in bidder organizations benefit targets. The results for LANGUAGE indicate that contrary to bidders, targets gain less when bidder and target are closer in terms of

473 Results of the one-factor regressions are given in table A.10 in the appendix.

474 Note that there are more cases for analysis for this model than for the bidder models above. This is because all included determinants are available for all banks in the sample whereas in the above models some determinants, e.g. those that measure efficiency, were not.

Table 6.16: Multiple Regression Results for Targets

This table shows the results for 5 multiple OLS-regression models run for the CAR of the target against different explanatory variables. Target CARs are calculated in a 3-day interval symmetric to the event day and were calculated using the market model. Parameters were estimated using OLS in a a period covering 252 trading days prior to the event window and total return data on ordinary common stocks and the corresponding national market indices. CLIENT is the logarithm of the book value of outward FDI stocks of the home country into the host country in the year preceding the deal announcement in million current USD, TCOEF is is the target CIR, EFFIC is a dummy variable that is equal to 1 if the bidder strategy as published on the event day is classified as primarily "efficiency-seeking", i.e., seeking operational synergies, LANGUAGE is a dummy variable that is equal to 1 if the primary languages in the home and host countries are identical, MSIZE is the logarithm of the per capita GDP in the host country; values are purchasing power parity adjusted to the USD at current prices, ECSIM is an index of economic distance between home and host country, based on per capital GDP; values are purchasing power parity adjusted to the USD at current prices. FREEDOM is an index of economic freedom in the host country, specifically with regard to banking, finance, capital flows and FDI, HOSTCA is a dummy variable that is equal to 1 if the country of the target is either the UK or the US, CORREL is the coefficient of correlation of bidder and target returns in the estimation window, HOTY is a dummy variable that is equal to 1 if the event year is in the "hot" market phase 1999-2001 and EAST is a dummy variable that is equal to 1 if the target is located in a country in Eastern Europe and 0 otherwise; t-values are given in brackets. Leakage-adjusted subsamples include only deals, were target-specific leakage did not occur more than 20 days before the event date.

Model		1	2	3	4	5
Type of Sample		Regular	Regular	Regular	Leakage-Adjusted	Leakage Adjusted
N		38	96	96	53	36
Adj. R^2 (%)		9.63	26.10	22.60	17.54	23.02
F-Value		1.39	7.71***	7.93***	3.76***	3.62**
Constant		-3.093834	-1.678415	-1.958081	-1.833109	-1.911022
		(-1.92*)	(-4.93***)	(-4.81***)	(-4.21***)	(-2.31**)
Coefficient (t-value)	CLIENT	0.008225				0.054572
		(0.23)				(1.97*)
	TCOEF	-0.171505				
		(-0.66)				
	EFFIC	-0.025027				
		(-0.32)				
	LANGUAGE		-0.086450	-0.068804	-0.097830	-0.210634
			(-1.96*)	(-1.39)	(-1.56)	(-1.95*)
	MSIZE	0.350187	0.191022	0.217546	0.212231	0.183807
		(1.99*)	(5.16***)	(5.21***)	(4.42***)	(1.81*)
	ECSIM	-0.100290				
		(-0.28)				
	FREEDOM	0.040826				
		(0.44)				
	HOSTCA	-0.193726				
		(-1.01)				
	CORREL	-0.804572	-0.383418	-0.360762	-0.538833	-0.963832
		(-1.12)	(-2.08**)	(-2.36**)	(-1.79*)	(-1.86*)
	HOTY	0.096438	0.106883	0.080283	0.094680	
		(1.09)	(2.06**)	(1.73*)	(1.16)	
	EAST	-0.233400	-0.176530			
		(-1.70)	(-3.50***)			

* *Significant at the 10 percent level.*
** *Significant at the 5 percent level.*
*** *Significant at the 1 percent level.*

social distance. Maybe, target organizations that are socially close are less opaque to bidders, leading them to overpay (which in turn is benefical to targets) less often. EAST indicats that targets in Eastern Europe gain less. However, this has to be interpreted with care because of the issues with target leakage in Eastern Europe discussed above. Model 3 shows that all coefficients except LANGUAGE are robust to an exclusion of EAST.

Also, with the exception of HOTY and LANGUAGE that turn insignificant, the identified determinants are robust to target leakage issues, as a re-estimation of the model on the target-leakage adjusted sample shows (model 4).[475] This conclusion is supported when the inclusion/exclusion procedure is again performed on the leakage adjusted sample (model 5): HOTY drops out of the equation while CLIENT, already indicated as potentially important in the dichotomization and the single-variable regression analysis, drops in, suggesting that it is targets that benefit when bidders encounter their home country clients in the host country. Even though this is not surprising in the light of the findings on MSIZE,[476] results from model 5 have to be interpreted with caution due to the limited sample size.[477] Overall, it seems more difficult to explain target returns by the identified determinants than bidder returns, as indicated by the rather low explanatory power of model 2 (adjusted R^2 of around 20 percent).

Finally, with regard to the joint entity, model 1 in table 6.17 shows the initial model specification based on the results of the dichotomization analysis and the single-variable regressions.[478] Unsurprisingly, the model includes two factors that had a strong effect on either bidder or target returns, namely TCOEF, the target

475 Despite obvious leakage issues, EAST is not included in the model that is estimated on the target-leakage adjusted sample. This is, as already indicated above, because after target leakage adjustment, almost no deals with targets in Eastern Europe remain.

476 Like MSIZE, CLIENT is a characteristic of the host country so it could well be that competition among bidders will erode away their benefits from it and allocate it to targets.

477 This sample size reduction offsets some of the benefits from leakage adjustment. Together with the results from section 6.2.1, that indicate that leakage is only a serious issue with regard to target returns, this is also the reason why a re-estimation of the model on the leakage-adjusted sample using the inclusion/exclusion procedure is only performed for targets and not for bidders or the joint entity.

478 Single-variable regressions for the joint entity are given in table A.11 in the appendix. Note that MSIZE and MONITOR are left out of the initial specification because of some indications of multicollinearity issues. Alternative models with combinations of these variables do not lead to better results. Note also that there are more cases available for analysis than for bidders alone. This is again a result of the data availability of theincluded determinants.

Table 6.17: Multiple Regression Results for Joint Entities

This table shows the results for 4 multiple OLS-regression models run for the CAR of the joint entity against different explanatory variables. Joint entity CARs are calculated in a 3-day interval symmetric to the event day and were calculated using the market model. Parameters were estimated using OLS in a a period covering 252 trading days prior to the event window and total return data on ordinary common stocks and the corresponding national market indices. TCOEF is the target CIR, RELCOEF is the target CIR divided by the bidder CIR, HOTY is a dummy variable that is equal to 1 if the event year is in the "hot" market phase 1999-2001, HOSTCA is a dummy variable that is equal to 1 if the country of the target is either the UK or the US and INET is the number of internet hosts per capita in a given home country in a given year; t-values are given in brackets. Leakage-adjusted subsamples include only deals, were joint leakage did not occur more than 20 days before the event date.

Model		1	2	3	4
Type of Sample		Regular	Regular	Regular	Leakage-Adjusted
N		65	64	62	32
Adj. R^2 (%)		22.69	23.56	22.28	19.33
F-Value		7.26***	7.47***	6.83***	3.47**
Constant		0.042884 (4.91***)	0.053020 (5.14***)	0.038717 (5.24***)	0.069508 (2.54**)
Coefficient (t-value)	TCOEF	-0.58992 (-5.23***)	-0.062768 (-5.16***)		-0.091939 (-1.81*)
	RELCOEF			-0.023983 (-6.25***)	
	HOTY	-0.017135 (-2.53***)	-0.019632 (- 2.86***)	-0.017548 (-2.74***)	-0.019402 (-1.51)
	HOSTCA	0.011467 (1.47)			
	INET		-0.059906 (- 2.03**)	-0.054283 (-1.69*)	-0.047182 (-0.81)

* Significant at the 10 percent level
** Significant at the 5 percent level
*** Significant at the 1 percent level.

cost efficiency indicator, and HOTY, the "hot" deal phase indicator. The additional factor, HOSTCA, did not turn up in the final bidder or target model specifications but generally had a positive effect on targets and a non-negative effect on bidders.[479] Signs of the factors are also as expected: joint wealth increases with target cost efficiency and decreases if deals happen in "hot" deal phases.

Wealth also increases if targets are located in the US or the UK, even though the relevant coefficient is not significant. The inclusion/exclusion procedure leads to a similar model specification (model 2), albeit without HOSTCA and with INET, the indicator of the IT sophistication of the bidder, as an additional factor. TCOEF and HOTY show a similar behaviour as is model 1. Contrary to expectations but similar to the findings for bidders in the dichotomization analysis, INET has a negative sign, indicating that a high level of IT sophistication of the bidder decreases net wealth. One explanation may be that bidders that are highly sophisticated in that sense are seen as having a comparative advantage in cross-border lending (or borrowing) relative to M&A, leading to the reception of an M&A deal as the inferior solution. However, given the discussed above issues with interpreting INET (only) as a measure of bidder IT sophistication, this has to be a tentative interpretation.

Again, replacing TCOEF with RELCOEF (model 3) leads to similar results. Thus, results suggests that of the two value-creating bidder strategies identified above only one, namely taking over targets that are already cost-efficient, is also net wealth-creating. Also, interestingly, acquisitions in "hot" deal phases do not only redistribute wealth from bidders to targets but also destroy net wealth.[480] As indicated above, this is probably because investors perceive them as overpaying and suffering from agency problems. In the – again strongly reduced – non-leakage sample (model 4), coefficients keep their signs. However, HOTY turns (barely) insignificant, as does INET.[481]

6.3.2.2 Regression of Long-Term Returns

The above discussion on wealth effects found no evidence of average long-term abnormal stock returns to bidders following CBBM&A. It is nevertheless possible that certain deal characteristics do lead to abnormal long-term returns even if deals on average do not exhibit such abnormal performance. Therefore, in the following, long-term abnormal returns will be regressed on a set of potential de-

---

479 Note that again the number of available cases for the analysis is reduced by data restrictions with regard to the included determinants.

480 Deals in "hot years" decrease bidder value by roughly 2.5 percent and increase target value by 8 to 10 percent, which, since bidders are on average much larger than targets, translates into a net wealth decrease of roughly 2 percent.

481 Similar results (not shown here) are reached using RELCOEF.

terminants.[482] Due to the on average insignificant abnormal returns, results, however, have to be interpreted with care.

If individual results are driven by market under- or overreaction rather than by unrelated causes or chance, long-term abnormal returns should be related to announcement period abnormal returns.[483] To test this, long-term abnormal returns are regressed on announcement period abnormal returns in the 3-day event window symmetric to the original event date using OLS. Results for the 12, 24, and 36 month period for the full and the adjusted sample are given in table 6.18.[484] Interestingly, all relevant coefficients turn out to be insignificant. Therefore, as in Agrawal et al. (1992), the hypothesis of long-term abnormal returns as a consequence of market under- or overreaction is not supported.

Even though the above analysis thus suggests that there are, in general, no abnormal long-term returns following CBBM&A and that the existing abnormal returns are on average not related to announcement period abnormal returns, it might still be that some of the determinants discussed above can help to existing long-term abnormal returns. For that purpose, long-term abnormal returns are also regressed on the set of identified determinants. Results for 12-months BHARs are given in table 6.19.

Again using the stepwise inclusion/exclusion approach and the noise-unadjusted sample[485], model 1 is arrived at. Significant variables are BSIZE, that captures the size of the acquirer in terms of total assets, LANGUAGE, that indicates cultural similarity between bidder and target country in the sense of the same language being spoken, MARKET, the indicated geographically diversifying deal intent, and EU, the indicator of a deal inside the EU. The coefficient of BSIZE is positive, which is in line with either an initial market underreaction to the possibility of (revenue) scale economies or potential TBTF gains. However, since bidders are on average very large and relatively much larger than targets,

482 This approach is not uncommon in the literature, see e.g., Campa and Hernando (2005).

483 Agrawal et al. (1992).

484 Since the previously discussed evidence suggests that long-term abnormal returns are rather the exception than the rule and are, therefore, not of central importance to the research question posed, the following analysis only focuses on BHAR returns. Also, BHAR returns are more common in the previous literature. In fact, the author is not aware of a previous study that regresses non-BHAR abnormal return measures to potential determinants. Based on the above finding that the global index may not be the optimal benchmark for long-term returns, findings are furthermore restricted to returns relative to the relevant local index.

485 Remember that leakage-adjustment is not an issue in long-term studies, that are interested in ex-post returns. Here, adjustement for noise in the ex-post period becomes an issue.

Table 6.18: Results from Regression of Long- on Short-Term Abnormal Returns

This table shows the results of a regression of long-term bidder average buy-and-hold returns (ABHAR) following the closure date of cross-border bank mergers on announcement period abnormal returns of bidders. Long-term abnormal returns are estimated using monthly stock bidder stock total returns and a banking total return index from the home-region of the bidder or a global banking index as a benchmark. Indices are taken from Datastream. Bidder returns are winsorized at 3 standard deviations. Results are given alternatively for the full sample and on a sub-sample that only includes bidders that acquired targets that had a equity market value of 10% or higher of the bidder and that did not make a cross-border acquisition in 3-year-window previous to the closure date. N indicates the number of bidders in the sample for the respective time-horizon. Short-term abnormal returns are calculated using the market model. Parameters were estimated using OLS in a period covering 252 trading days prior to the event window and total return data on ordinary common stocks and the corresponding national market indices.

Panel A: Full sample				
Post-event months	**N**	**Adjusted R^2 (%)**	**Constant (t-value)**	**Coefficient of short-term return variable (t-value)**
12	90	-1.50	-0.008135 (-0.35)	0.178519 (0.28)
24	81	-1.17	0.001599 (0.04)	0.275989 (0.27)
36	78	-1.07	0.006366 (0.13)	0.546566 (0.43)
				Panel B: Adjusted sample
12	30	-3.04	-0.022502 (-0.38)	0.535767 (0.38)
24	23	-4.76	-0.047937 (-0.36)	0.045389 (0.02)
36	23	-4.74	-0.110558 (-0.80)	0.158432 (0.05)

the TBTF story sounds less plausible. There also seems to be an initial underreaction to cultural similarity, as the positive LANGUAGE coefficient indicates.

The positive coefficient of MARKET is especially interesting since short-term results for bidders indicated abnormal losses following the announcement of a geographically diversifying deal intent. In this context, results suggest that this initial reaction is partly an overreaction that is later corrected. Finally, EU enters with a negative sign, indicating a tendency of intra-EU deals to underperform in the long run.

Table 6.19: Multiple Regression Results for 12-Months Buy-and-Hold Abnormal Returns

This table shows the results for 3 multiple OLS-regression models run for the buy-and-hold abnor-mal returns of the bidders 12 months after the official closure of a cross-border bank merger against different explanatory variables. Results are given for all banks in the sample for which data on the the explanatory variables is available and a sample that is adjusted for "noise" in post-closure window. The latter contains only returns for bidders, that do not have other cross-border acquisitions in the selected period and acquire targets that are 10 percent of their own size or larger in terms of market value and for which data on the explanatory variables is available. BHARs are calculated following Cowan and Sergeant (2001) using regional banking indices as a benchmark and are winsorized at three standard deviations. BSIZE is the logarithm of the total assets of the bidder in million US-dollar. LANGUAGE is a dummy variable that is equal to 1 if the primary languages in the home and host countries are identical, CORREL is the coefficient of correlation of bidder and target returns in the estimation window, MARKET is a dummy variable that is equal to 1 if the bidder strategy as published on the event day is classified as primarily "market-seeking", i.e., geographically diversifying, POWER is a principal component indicator that measures the legal power of the supervisory agency for banks in the host country. High values indicate extensive powers, EU is is a dummy variable that is equal to 1 if both transaction partners are from the EU and 0 otherwise.

Model		1	2	3
Type of sample		Regular	Noise-Adjusted	Noise-Adjusted
N		89	30	27
Adj. R^2 (%)		14.89	32.47	38.43
F-Value		4.85***	4.48***	9.12***
Constant		-0.616252 (-2.38**)	-0.993291 (-2.13**)	-0.437100 (-3.11***)
Coefficient (t-value)	BSIZE	0.047750 (2.33**)	0.077912 (1.87*)	
	LANGUAGE	0.076140 (1.68*)	0.123536 (1.51)	
	CORREL			0.993120 (2.76**)
	MARKET	0.067362 (1.69*)	0.156280 (2.03*)	
	POWER			0.325937 (2.74**)
	EU	-0.122784 (-2.92***)	-0.316161 (-3.01***)	

* *Significant at the 10 percent level.*
** *Significant at the 5 percent level.*
*** *Significant at the 1 percent level.*

While testing the identified factors also on the adjusted long-term sample (model 2)[486] generally confirms the validity of model 1, results are not identical and somewhat inferior to the model that emerges if the inclusion/exclusion procedure is run on the adjusted sample (model 3). Here, only the coefficient of correlation between bidder and target stock returns (CORREL) and the regulatory power index (POWER) enter significantly and suggest long-term abnormal overperformance following deals with more similar deal partners and in countries with strong regulators. However, results for the adjusted sample again have to be interpreted with caution, since adjusting the sample reduces the sample size strongly.

Repeating the exercise for 24-months BHARs and the full sample (see model 1 in table 6.20) reveals long-term abnormal returns to be still positively related to BSIZE and negatively related to EU. Seemingly, under- and overreaction with regard to these factors is not corrected within the two years after the deal. Additionally, EFFIC, the indicator of an efficiency-enhancing deal motive, enters with a positive sign. CORREL and POWER no longer turn out to contribute significantly to the model and are therefore not included. The model also performs much worse in the adjusted sample (model 2), in which all determinants turn out insignificant (barely so in the case of BSIZE and EU). Usage of the inclusion/exclusion procedure on the adjusted sample leads to model 3, that again confirms the effects of BSIZE and EU, while it also indicates negative abnormal returns following long-distance mergers and positive abnormal returns following acquisitions in large markets. Again, results for the adjusted sample have to be interpreted with care, due to severe sample size limitations.

Finally, for 36-months BHAR, results for the full sample (table 6.21, model 1) are similar to 24-months BHARs.

Obviously, over- and underreaction to the included factors is quite persistent. Also again, the model performs less well in the adjusted sample (model 2). Here, model 3 is more suitable, but again includes additional variables such as DISTANCE, which show a similar effect to 24-months BHAR and CORREL, where the effect is similar to 12-months BHARs. POWER, again, does not contribute significantly and is not added to the model.

Thus overall, there seems to be some underreaction with regard to bidder size and overreaction with regard to intra-EU deals that persists for the 3-years post-event window analyzed here. However, generally the significant variables vary significantly with the time horizon under consideration and when results are noise-adjusted. Thus, overall, the evidence on determinants on long-term abnormal returns is very weak.

---

486 See section 5.2.2.1 for the "noise adjustment" methodology.

Table 6.20: Multiple Regression Results for 24-Months Buy-and-Hold Abnormal Returns

This table shows the results for 3 multiple OLS-regression models run for the buy-and-hold abnormal returns of the bidders 24 months after the official closure of a cross-border bank merger against different explanatory variables. Results are given for the full sample of deals on which data on the explanatory variables is available and a sample that is adjusted for "noise" in post-closure window and that contains only returns for bidders, that do not have other cross-border acquisitions in the selected period and acquire targets that are 10 percent of their own size or larger in terms of market value. BHARs are calculated following Cowan and Sergeant (2001) using regional banking indices as a benchmark and are winsorized at three standard deviations. BSIZE is the logarithm of the total assets of the bidder at book value, converted to current USD using year-end exchange rates if necessary, DISTANCE is the logarithm of the great circle distance between the capital cities of the home and the host country in 1000 kilometers, EFFIC is a dummy variable that is equal to 1 if the bidder strategy as published on the event day is classified as primarily "efficiency-seeking", i.e., seeking operational synergies, MSIZE is the logarithm of the per capita GDP in the host country. Values are purchasing power parity adjusted to the USD at current prices, EU is a dummy variable that is equal to 1 if both transaction partners are from the EU and 0 otherwise.

Model		1	2	3
Type of sample		Regular	Noise-Adjusted	Noise- Adjusted
N		80	23	23
Adj. R^2 (%)		13.41	21.66	34.03
F-Value		5.08***	3.03*	3.84**
Constant		-0.570038 (-1.62)	-1.926288 (1.24)	-4.890259 (-2.18**)
Coefficient (t-value)	BSIZE	0.047036 (1.67*)	0.165970 (1.49)	0.146183 (1.98*)
	DISTANCE			-0.083957 (-3.42***)
	EFFIC	0.123795 (1.82*)	0.174223 (0.72)	
	MSIZE			0.336756 (1.76*)
	EU	-0.216967 (-3.23***)	-0.367540 (-1.70)	-0.521613 (-3.00***)

* *Significant at the 10 percent level.*
** *Significant at the 5 percent level.*
*** *Significant at the 1 percent level.*

Table 6.21: Multiple Regression Results for 36-Months Buy-and-Hold Abnormal Returns

This table shows the results for 3 multiple OLS-regression models run for the buy-and-hold abnormal returns of the bidders 36 months after the official closure of a cross-border bank merger against different explanatory variables. Results are given for the full sample of deals on which deals on the explanatory variables is available and a sample that is adjusted for "noise" in post-closure window and that contains only returns for bidders, that do not have other cross-border acquisitions in the selected period and acquire targets that are 10 percent of their own size or larger in terms of market value. BHARs are calculated following Cowan and Sergeant (2001) using regional banking indices as a benchmark and are winsorized at three standard deviations. BSIZE is the logarithm of the total assets of the bidder at book value, converted to current USD using year-end exchange rates if necessary, DISTANCE is the logarithm of the great circle distance between the capital cities of the home and the host country in 1000 kilometers, CORREL is the coefficient of correlation of bidder and target returns in the estimation window, EFFIC is a dummy variable that is equal to 1 if the bidder strategy as published on the event day is classified as primarily "efficiency-seeking", i.e., seeking operational synergies, EU is a dummy variable that is equal to 1 if both transaction partners are from the EU and 0 otherwise.

Model			1	2	3
Type of sample			Regular	Noise-Adjusted	Noise-Adjusted
N			77	23	23
Adj. R^2 (%)			13.87	22.55	39.56
F-Value			5.08***	3.13**	4.60***
Constant			-0.783181 (-2.07)	-1.945537 (-1.75*)	-2.016176 (-3.08***)
	Coefficient (t-value)	BSIZE	0.062683 (2.06**)	0.164250 (1.61)	0.166646 (3.01***)
		DISTANCE			-0.087459 (-3.62***)
		CORREL			1.249875 (1.80*)
		EFFIC	0.181575 (2.21**)	0.167603 (0.67)	
		EU	-0.235849 (-2.58**)	-0.501353 (-2.34**)	-0.708444 (-4.39***)

* *Significant at the 10 percent level.*
** *Significant at the 5 percent level.*
*** *Significant at the 1 percent level.*

6.4 Summary

At the beginning of this chapter, it was shown that the applied sample selection criteria, especially the "change in control" and the "joint listing" requirements, significantly reduced the number of deals available for analysis. Nevertheless, the data set was still shown to be the largest such sample in terms of joint bidder-target entities and also well representative for the overall CBBM&A market. With regard to results, CBBM&A were found to be overall wealth creating activities, albeit only because target gains more than compensated for bidder losses. Since no long-term abnormal returns could be found, these results seem to well reflect the total wealth effects stemming from such deals.

With regard to the determinants of wealth effects, an overview of the key findings, relative to that of selected prior studies is given in table 6.22.[487] Highlighted in the table are those findings that are supported by both the dichotomization and the regression analysis as here the available empirical evidence is most reliable. Those findings are discussed first.

Both the dichotomization and the regression analysis supported a positive effect of the *presence of home country (bidder) clients in the host country*. This was in line with expectations and the previous indications by the IM literature. Interestingly, results also show that wealth benefits accrue fully to targets but are not strong enough to influence the net effect. This is probably because the presence of host country clients is a host country or, respectively, a target characteristic,[488] and competition among bidders may distribute all potential wealth effects that are related to this factor to targets. Conflicting earlier CF evidence is probably explained by a much more narrow geographical scope and lack of a target wealth perspective in this earlier contribution.

The effect of *relative target efficiency*, independently how it was measured and whether analyzed by the dichotomization or the regression anlysis, was also not in line with the previous literature, that indicated positive wealth effects if more efficient bidders take over less efficient targets. Instead, results indicated that taking over relatively more efficient targets create bidder and net wealth.

---

487 Due to the large number of reviewed studies, the table restricts itself to comparisons to some representative earlier studies. A more detailed comparison is provided in table A.3 in the appendix. Also given in the appendix is a more detailed overview of the outcomes of both the dichotomization and the regression analyses, see table A.12.

488 Remember that the true factor of interest is the number of home country clients in the host that can be served via the target.

Table 6.22: Determinants of Wealth Effects in Comparison to Prior Studies

Determinant	Findings in the previous literature and expected impact in this study[1]	Findings in this study[2]
Bidder size	*CF evidence:* no significant impact on bidders (Hawawini and Swary, 1990; Tourani-Rad and van Beek, 1999). *IM evidence:* indications for positive impact (Ursacki and Vertinsky, 1992; Focarelli and Pozzolo, 2001). *Expected impact:* positive.	Not fully in line with expectations but generally supportive of the previous CF literature, no significant impact is found. However, tentative evidence of a net negative impact is found that seems to be offset in the long term.
Relative target size	*CF evidence:* some support that takeover of relatively larger targets creates bidder and net wealth (DeLong, 2001) but mostly no significant impact (Vander Vennet, 2003; Beitel et al., 2004). *Expected impact:* positive.	Not in line with expectation and in contrast to previous studies, there is evidence that taking over larger targets reduces bidder wealth. Evidence is, however, tentative.
Presence of home country clients in the host country	*CF evidence:* only one study with unexplained negative impact on bidders (Waheed and Mathur, 1992). *IM evidence:* indications for positive impact (Yamori, 1998; Wezel, 2004). *Expected impact:* positive.	In line with expectations and previous IM studies, there is evidence that this factors creates wealth for targets. Differing results from previous CF study probably explained by broader geographical scope in inclusion of target and net perspective.
Relative (target) efficiency	*CF evidence:* relatively higher bidder profit efficiency increases bidder and net wealth (Vander Vennet, 2003; Beitel et al., 2004). *Expected impact:* negative.	Not in line with expectations and in contrast to previous studies, taking over more efficient targets seems to create bidder and net wealth. See the findings on target efficiency below.
Target efficiency	*CF evidence:* conflicting. Supports that either low (DeLong, 2001) or high (Beitel et al., 2004) target efficiency creates wealth. *Expected impact:* positive or negative	More differentiated than expected or in the literature: both high and low target efficiency can increase wealth since taking over targets with low standalone growth perspective is wealth creating for bidders, as is taking over targets with high ex-ante cost efficiency for all involved parties.
Physical distance between bidder and target	*CF evidence:* mixed with rather negative impact in the interstate literature (Cornett et al., 2003) but no obvious impact in the cross-border literature (Hudgins and Seifert, 1996). *IM evidence:* indications for a negative impact (Buch and DeLong, 2003, 2004, 2005). *Expected impact:*negative.	Not in line with expectations but supportive of the CF cross-border literature, no immediate impact of this factor is found. However, some indications of negative long-term returns following large-distance deals, that fit with the IM evidence.
Social distance between bidder and target	*CF evidence:* not relevant (Kiymaz, 2004). *IM evidence:* indications for a negative impact, (Buch and DeLong 2003, 2004, 2005). *Expected impact:* negative.	In line with expectations and previous IM studies. Evidence that factor is indeed wealth destroying from a bidder and net perspective.
Functional differences between bidder and target	*CF evidence:* drawbacks of diversification either offset (Cybo-Ottone and Murgia, 2000) or outweighted (DeLong, 2001) benefits of diversification. *Expected impact:* negative.	More differentiated results than expected and in previous studies: net wealth effects of diversification depends on type of merger partner (negative for I-banks, positive for insurers/FSPs).
Bidder M&A experience	*CF evidence:* either no (Waheed and Mathur, 1995) or sometimes even negative (Gleason and Mathur, 1998) impact found, possibly due to agency-effects. *IM evidence:* indications of a positive impact due to experience effects (Ursacki and Vertinsky, 1992). *Expected impact:* positive.	Contrary to expectations but in line with most previous CF studies, no significant impact is found.

Determinant	Findings in the previous literature and expected impact in this study[1]	Findings in this study[2]
Share of acquisition price paid in cash	*CF evidence:* mixed evidence with some studies supporting positive (Cornett et al., 2003) and some neutral (DeLong, 2001) bidder impact. *Expected impact::* positive.	In line with expectations and previous studies positive impact on bidder wealth found. Evidence, however, is only tentative.
Bidder strategy	No previous evidence.[3] *Expected impact:* positive for synergy creating strategies and negative for diversifying strategies.	In line with expectations, indications of a negative impact of geographically diversifying deals and positive impact of synergy creating deals found.
IT sophistication of the bidder	No previous evidence.[4] *Expected impact:* positive.	Contrary to expectations, some indications that bidder IT sophistication lowers bidder and increases target wealth.
Host market size	*CF evidence:* negative impact (Gleason and Mathur, 1998). *IM evidence:* Indications of a positive impact (Yamori, 1998; Focarelli and Pozzolo, 2005). *Expected impact:* positive.	In line with expectations and supportive of IM study findings. First direct evidence that factor is wealth creating for targets and net.
Temperature of equity market	*CF evidence:* negative impact, probably due to agency effects (Beitel, 2002). *Expected impact:* negative.	In line with expectations and previous evidence, results strongly supportive of negative effect for bidder and net. However, targets rather gain in "hot" markets.
Economic distance between home and host country	*CF evidence:* Not relevant (Kiymaz, 2004). *IM evidence:* indications of a negative impact (Berger et al. 2004). *Expected impact:* negative.	In line with expectations and supportive of IM study findings. Tentative evidence that factor indeed decreases (target) wealth.
General economic openness of the host country	*IM evidence:* indications of positive impact (Buch and Lipponer, 2004). *Expected impact:* positive.	Contrary to expectations and previous IM study findings, indications that while factor increases target wealth, it also lowers bidder wealth.
Intensity of bank regulation in the host country	*IM evidence:* indications of a positive impact of a powerful bank regulator and a high degree of bank transparency in the host country (Buch and Lipponer 2004, Buch and DeLong, 2005). *Expected impact:* positive.	In line with expectations and previous IM studies. First direct evidence that factor is wealth creating for all involved parties.
Host country is US or UK	*IM evidence:* indications of a positive impact (Berger et al., 2004). *Expected impact:* positive.	In line with expectations and IM study findings. First tentative evidence that factor is wealth creating for targets and net.
Bidder and target are from the EU	*IM evidence:* mostly indications that factor rather decreases than increases wealth (Berger et al. 2004, Buch and Lipponer, 2004). *Expected impact::* positive.	Mostly not in line with expectations or previous studies, rather no impact of factor found. However, some indications of negative long-term abnormal returns following intra-EU deals.
Targets are from Eastern Europe	*IM evidence:* Indications for a positive impact of factor (Buch and DeLong, 2003, Wezel, 2004). *Expected impact:* positive.	In line with expectations and previous IM study findings. First direct evidence that factor is wealth creating for bidders but not for targets.

1 In brackets: Exemplary previous studies from the CF and IM literature. For a more detailed overview of previous results, see table A.3 in the appendix.

2 For a more detailed overview of results, see table A.3 in the appendix.

3 The previous literature did analyze the effect of synergy creating mergers versus geographically and functionally diversifying ones, see the above results on efficiency-related factors, physical distance and functional bidder-target differences. The impact of the declared long-term strategy followed with a deal has, to the knowledge of the author, not been analyzed previously.

4 Previous studies have, however, analyzed the general impact of IT on bank efficiency, see the literature discussed in section 2.2.2.

This links directly to results with regard to *target efficiency*. Here, some earlier studies indicated that taking over inefficient targets creates wealth while others showed wealth creation to be related to the acquisition of relatively efficient targets. Consequently, either a significant positive or a significant negative effect was expected. However, results hint at a more differentiated story that incorporates both views. First, there was strong evidence that bidder, target and net wealth increase when bidders take over targets that were already relatively cost efficient ex-ante. This supports the positive role of high target efficiency and is also in line with the findings from the OP and DE literature, that cost-efficiency increases in CBBM&A usually do not realize. However, there were also indications from the regression analysis that taking over targets with low standalone growth perspectives (but that supposedly show some improvement potential) is an alternative, wealth-creating strategy for bidders.

Previous studies have extensively covered the question on the effect of diversification, either geographical or functional. Results from these contributions and also the corresponding findings of this study have been discussed in the context of the determinants "geographical distance" and "functional bidder-target differences". However, to the knowledge of the author, there is no previous evidence on the impact of the *long-term bidder strategy* as declared by the bidder at the time of deal announcement. As discussed above, these announcements were grouped into strategies that intend to create operational synergies on the one hand or functionally or geographically diversifying strategies on the other hand.[489] In line with expectations, the analysis showed a negative impact of deals with an intent to diversify geographically and a positive impact of deals with an intent to create operational synergies. The announcement of a functionally diversifying strategy was not found to significantly influence wealth.

Country- and industry-specific characteristics were also shown to have a significant impact on shareholder wealth. Thus, again both the dichotomization and the regression analysis showed target and net wealth gains to be related to target *market size*. This is in contrast to previous findings from the CF literature, which, however, did not take into account a target and a net perspective and used a smaller, geographically more restriced sample. Therefore findings are the first applicable evidence that supports the expectations from the IM literature that market size is strongly positively related to shareholder wealth.

In line with expectations and the previous literature, strong evidence of a significant negative effect on bidder and net wealth of deals conducted in *"hot" deal phases* were found. Results support the notion that deals are (also) driven by

489 As discussed above, bidders could also pursue multiple of these strategies at the same time.

agency issues within the bidder organization which is partly seen through by shareholders, resulting in increases in target but decreases in bidder and net wealth.

Surprisingly and contrary to both expectations and findings from previous IM studies, the general *economic openness of the host country* was found to have a negative effect on bidder wealth, even though, as expected, target wealth was found to increase with economic freedom in the host country. Possibly, this points to a relationship between restrictions in economic freedom and the possibility for monopoly gains for bidders or reflects the fact that deregulation in some of the "unfree" countries in the sample followed shortly after the respective deals and might have already been anticipated.

Findings on the remaining factors are less strong since here, if they were found to have a significant impact at all, these findings were supported only by the dichotomization or the regression analysis.

With regard to firm-level factors the hypothesized positive effect of *bidder size* was only partly supported. Findings were, however, in line with the reviewed CF literature. More concretely, the dichotomization analysis indicated a negative net effect in the short-term, which hinted at potential scale diseconomies associated with this factor. However, the long-term analysis provided (weak) evidence that this effect is partly an overreaction, that is corrected in the long-term, where bidder size tends to be followed by long-term abnormal gains.[490]

The hypothesized positive effect of *relative (target) size* was also not supported. Results from the dichotomization analysis were in contrast to findings from the previous literature in that they indicated a negative effect on bidders. This is in line with higher integration hurdles for larger targets but also with partly offsetting effects of bidder size. Regression results were, however, not significant.

The hypothesized negative effect of *physical distance* between bidder and target could only partly be supported. While no such effect was found in either the dichotomization or the regression analysis, which was in contrast to the reviewed IM literature but in line with the mostly insignificant results from CBBM&A event studies, there are some weak signs of long-term negative returns following long-distance deals. Thus, the market possibly underreacts to large bidder-target physical distance.

---

490 One explanation for the long term abnormal returns might be that banking industry insiders, who strongly believe in size as a deceisive driver for wealth generation, see e.g. The Economist (2006a), are right but that this insight has not yet reached the broader market. However, since average long-term abnormal returns are insignificant, this is only a tentative interpretation.

Social distance played a somewhat more important role: The dichotomization analysis supported the hypothesized negative effect of mergers between countries with different legal systems while the regression analysis also supported the notion that at least bidders create less wealth when they acquire targets in countries where a different primary language is spoken. Targets in turn rather benefitted from the latter deals, maybe because social distance increases target "opacity" for the bidder, thus making overbidding more likely. Just as with physical distance, there were indications of market underreaction to this factor. Results are thus in line with the insights of the IM literature. The diverging results from the only other CF study that tested this factor, the work of Kiymaz (2004), may stem from the fact that the latter only concentrates on the US.

Based on the literature review, a negative impact of *functional bidder-target differences* was expected. This hypothesis could only be partly supported. The dichotomization analysis indicated that while deals between banks and investment banks rather decrease wealth, deals between banks and insurers or FSPs increase wealth, maybe because of differences in corporate cultures. The regression analysis furthermore showed a beneficial effect of diversification if measured by the coefficient of correlation of stock returns, that was, however, corrected in the long run.

Contrary to expectations but in line with most previous CF studies, *previous bidder M&A experience* was not found to have a significant impact. There were some signs that the *share of the acquisition price paid in cash* had such an impact but only in the dichotomization analysis. This was in line with previous expectations and the previous CF literature. However, results were only tentative.

The study also made a first attempt to analyze the impact of *bidder IT sophistication* on wealth creation. Surprisingly, the expected positive effect found in other service-intensive industries could only be supported for targets while "high tech" bidders and indeed also the joint bidder-target entity in such deals seem to loose wealth. Thus, the facts rather support the notion of cost-increases of CBBM&A relative to a market solution, i.e., cross-border borrowing and lending or similar activities. However, due to some ambiguity in the choosen country-level proxies for bidder IT sophistication, results are tentative and need to be validated using firm-level data that was unavailable for this study.

With regard to other factors on the country-level, for which, at best, only one of the two sorts of analysis showed results, a negative effect of *economic bidder target distance* on wealth, mostly due to low market demand and insufficient factors endowments in the less developed country, was expected. The study found indeed some evidence that economic distance lowers target wealth, even though results are only based on the dichotomization analysis.[491]

Again in line with expectations and previous IM studies, the analysis delivered the first available evidence that the *intensity of banking regulation* in the host country in the form of "powerful" regulators and a transparent banking sector with ample opportunities for market based monitoring increase target and net wealth, even though results are again only based on the dichotomization analysis.

Finally, interesting evidence was also gained with respect to the wealth effects in specific geographic locations. First, in line with expectations, the study provided tentative evidence that deals with *targets from the US and the UK* have higher target and net wealth effects. However, results were only based on the dichotomization analysis and are somewhat weaker with regard to the UK due to limited sample size. Second, despite intense efforts to harmonize European Financial markets, *intra-EU deals* were not found to create more wealth than other deals. In fact, no significant impact of this factor was found, which is at least more positive than a majority of previous IM studies, that even found a negative impact. Third, taking over *targets from Eastern Europe* was found to be wealth creating for bidders, which is again the first evidence that the respective findings from the IM literature are indeed also applicable to wealth effects.

Overall, evidence on the impact of the presence of home country clients in the host country, target and relative target efficiency, bidder strategy, host market size, temperature of the equity market and the general economic openness of the host country were strongest in the sense that they were supported by both regression and dichotomization analysis. Bidders gain most wealth, when they do not follow a strategy of geographical diversification, acquire in rather unfree economies and "cold" market phases. Targets in turn gain most, when they are located in large, free economies, in which bidder clients are already present and during "hot" market phases. Most net wealth is generally created when targets are ex-ante cost-efficient – and, surprisingly, especially when they are also relatively more cost-efficient than bidders – and during "cold" market phases.

The study has also addressed previous gaps in the literature. More specifically, it took into account a larger set of potential determinants than all previous studies and analyzed their effects on bidders, targets and joint entities. Thus, it could also reconcile some previously conflicting views on certain determinants, on to which the IM literature attributed a different effect than the CF literature.

491 The fact that results differ from those of Kiymaz (2004) may again stem from the fact that the latter only concentrates on the US or from his use of a somewhat less sophisticated measure of economic distance, the correlation in country GDP development.

Examples are the effects of home country clients in the host country or the size of the host market of the target. It was found that these factors indeed have an impact on wealth effects, just as the IM literature had previously found, but this wealth effect was found to be only relevant for targets. This explained why the CF literature, that primarily focused on bidders, had previously declared these factors as irrelevant. Other IM factors, like the economic openness of the target economy, could for the first time shown to have an impact on wealth effects.

7. Conclusion and Outlook

The primary questions to be answered in this study concerned the wealth effects of CBBM&A and their determinants. Furthermore, answers to these questions were expected to shed some light on the alleged paradox of CBBM&A, namely the observation that these deals strongly grew in importance despite evidence that they are not shareholder wealth creating for bidders.

With regard to the question on general wealth effects, the literature review made transparent that there was a lack of comprehensive empirical evidence on the subject. What was lacking concretely was evidence based on a large, global sample that also considers the net wealth perspectives and long-term wealth effects. Unfortunately, the only methodology that was shown to be well suited for this task, event studies, only allowed to analyze a small fraction of the theoretically relevant CBBM&A deals. Nevertheless, a sample was collected that was shown to be by far the largest to date in terms of jointly listed bidder-target entities. Furthermore, the sample did well reflect the properties, including the geographical distribution, of the worldwide CBBM&A market. On this sample, several analyses on wealth effects for all involved entities, including the usage of multiple, rather sophisticated long-term methods, were performed. The selected methodology was also shown to be robust to potential pitfalls in the analysis of abnormal returns.

The analyses themselves delivered some interesting results. First, bidders on average destroy shareholder wealth and while these losses are relatively small in the 1 percent range, they are still statistically significant. Thus, together with the presented evidence for the growing importance of CBBM&A in various dimensions, the CBBM&A merger paradox seems to be real. One of the most likely explanations for this is the prevalence of agency problems in the bidder organization, namely managers that execute deals in order to maximize their own utility. While data availability prohibited a more thorough analysis of agency motives as deal drivers, the results with regard to deals in "hot" market phases, that also relate to agency motives, strongly support this conclusion.

Results for targets were less surprising. As expected and in line with the clear majority of previous banking M&A studies, targets strongly benefit from deals. More interesting were the insights on the net wealth effect that results from bidder losses and target gains. Here the study provided the first reliable evidence so far that CBBM&A are indeed wealth value-creating corporate activities because target gains more than compensate for bidder losses. In that sense, CBBM&A are generally successful. However, the size of these net gains, 0.5 to 1 percent abnormal return, is quite small and, in a sense, only underlines the fundamental CBBM&A paradox: bidder management usually spends a significant amount of time and resources on transactions, that make their targets on average barely rich enough, to compensate for their own shareholders losses.

The described effects seem very robust in the sense that they only get more pronounced after a thorough accounting for information leakage and they are on average not distorted by offsetting long-term share price reactions. In fact, no average long-term abnormal returns in the three years that follow after a CBBM&A deal could be found, which is in itself a reassuring proof of market efficiency, which was questioned by some earlier studies on long-term wealth effects of banking M&A. This may be related to the fact that the large, well known institutions involved in CBBM&A make long-term abnormal returns less likely, and/or to methodological issues in the previous literature.

Further interesting insights were generated on the second research question after the determinants of wealth effects. Here the literature review had revealed three primary gaps in the previous literature, besides the obvious problem that a lack of an adequate sample that allows for an analysis of CBBM&A wealth effects also prohibits an adequate analysis of wealth effects. This was firstly the fact that no previous studies had considered the full range of identified potential determinants nor their potential interactions. Secondly, there was sometimes conflicting evidence on the impact of a specific factor from the CF literature on the one hand and the IM literature on the other hand, without any effort to reconcile the opposing views. Thirdly, the IM literature had identified a set of potentially relevant factors, whose impact on shareholder wealth had not yet been tested directly. Again, these gaps in the literature have been addressed and, again, many new interesting insights were gathered.

One was that, while many of the "usual suspects" from the CF literature like firm size, efficiency or functional relatedness, also determine wealth effects in CBBM&A, there are indications that the underlying dynamics are somewhat different in a cross-border context. For example, other than in domestic deals, wealth creation is higher if targets are relatively smaller, have their costs well under control and are FSPs or insurances but not investment banks. This probably reflects the special difficulties in integrating corporate entities across national and cultural borders.

Another interesting insight, this time with regard to the factors on which IM and CF studies drew conflicting conclusions, is that testing the notions of the IM literature in a CF context with a differentiated view of wealth effects on bidders, targets and the joint-entity, can often solve the conflict. Furthermore, it can increase the understanding of the underlying mechanisms beyond the level attainable by either the CF or the IM literature alone. Thus, this study could, for example, support the notion of the IM literature that the presence of home country clients in the host country increases shareholder wealth, as does the acquisition of targets in large host markets. Since wealth benefits from these deals seem to accrue exclusively to targets, probably due to bidder competition, it is unsurprising that the relevant previous CF studies did not notice them, since they took a bidder-only perspective. However, it also questions the prescriptive IM literature, that frequently declares "following the client" or "growing into large markets" as successful bidder strategies.

However, despite these dangers of using IM study findings uncritically to generate advice for practicioners, a final interesting insight is that this literature provides a rich set of theories and empirical findings, that can enhance our understanding of corporate finance issues in a cross-border context. This became obvious in the analysis of determinants like social or economic distance (negative wealth effects on bidders and targets), economic openness of an economy (positive wealth effects on bidders and negative ones on targets) or the characteristics of the regulatory environment (positive wealth effects on the joint entity), that turned out to have relevancy, but had so far not been considered by the CF literature.

The answers to the posed research questions also point to interesting directions for future research. First, future research should further investigate the agency mechanisms that supposedly drive deals. Especially worthwhile will be analyses that show if and how corporate governance mechanisms can help to mitigate these issues. Second, drawing on both the CF and the IM literature to identify relevant determinants of wealth effects also seems a worthwhile approach in other research on M&A wealth effects, e.g. in studies on the effects of M&A in different industries. Finally, given the analysis of leakage effects in this study, future event study research is called upon to address potential leakage problems more thoroughly. The strong effect that leakage was shown to have especially on target wealth effects, together with the often somewhat arbitrary selection of event dates in the standard M&A databases, requires at the minimum a high level of transparency with regard to event day selection criteria and thorough cross-checks with the available press-databases. Also, notice that in the leakage-adjusted regressions analyses for bidders, targets and the joint entities, many of the identified determinants loose significance. While it is unfortunately unclear, if this is primarily due to small sample size, that is strongly further reduced by leakage adjustment or due to the confounding effects of leakage, the latter hypothesis can at least not be rejected. Thus, the leakage issue also requires a careful interpretation of analyses of determinants of wealth effects. Ideally, future event study results should also be explicitly tested for robustness with regard to leakage.

Findings also suggest practical advice for decision makers. Bidder managers that want to increase shareholder value and their shareholders should invest enough time in target selection and look for partners that have their costs well under control, lack own growth perspectives and come from a culturally similar background. Furthermore, while exploitation of market imperfections in the host economy may work, "jumping on the roaring M&A train", i.e., acquiring when everybody else does or acquiring purely for the sake of geographical diversification usually does not. Somewhat weaker evidence also suggested that choosing relatively smaller targets and paying in cash rather than in stock are worthwhile strategies for bidders.

Target shareholders can on average rest assured that deals will make them significantly richer. That is especially true for shareholders of banks in large markets, where bidders meet many of their home country clients, when bidders are – in a cultural sense – obvious foreigners, and during merger waves.

In addition, the presented evidence is also of interest to policy makers and the wider public. As some rather recent prominent examples have shown, policy makers, especially in Europe, sometimes resist CBBM&A on the grounds of some greater public good that needs to be defended from greedy "barbarians at the gate." Ironically, evidence shows that such deals are in fact very good news for targets and also increase net wealth, which is the relevant indicator from an economy-level perspective. Moreover, even though not explicitly tested in this study, the literature review presented evidence that CBBM&A is generally accompanied by at least wealth-neutral and often wealth-positive effects for other stakeholders, including regulators, customers, and employees. Therefore, CBBM&A even seem to be socially desirable activities in the sense of Quasi-Pareto-Optimality that policy makers and their electorate should rather endorse than oppose. Thus, if anywhere, there seem to be barbarians behind the gates, trying to hold them closed against foreign do-gooders.

References

ABRAHAM, J.-P., VAN DIJCKE, P., 2002. European financial cross-border consolidation: at the crossroads in Europe? By exception, evolution or revolution? SUERF Study No. 22. Vienna: Société Universitaire Européenne de Recherches Financières.

ACHARYA, S., DREYFUS, J., 1989. Optimal bank reorganization policies and the pricing of federal deposit insurance. Journal of Finance 44, 1313-1332.

ACHLEITNER, A. K., 1999. Handbuch Investment Banking. Wiesbaden: Gabler.

AFX NEWS, 2004. SCH's Botin rules out a merger with equals in Europe. July 20th, 2004.

AGGARWAL, R., AKHIGBE, A., MCNULTY, J. E., 2006. Do shareholders benefit from bank mergers when there are underlying efficiency gains? Forthcoming in: Journal of Financial Services Review.

AKERLOF, G. A., 1970. The market for lemons: qualitative uncertainty and the market mechanism. Quarterly Journal of Economics 84, 488-500.

AKHIGBE, A., MADURA, J., 2004. Bank acquisitions of security firms: the early evidence. Applied Financial Economics 14, 485-496.

ALIBER, R. Z., 1976. Towards a theory of international banking. Economic Review, Federal Reserve Bank of San Franscisco (Spring), 5-8.

ALLEN, L., CEBENOYAN, A. S., 1991. Bank acquisitions and ownership structure: theory and evidence. Journal of Banking and Finance 15, 425-448.

ALLEN, F., SANTOMERO, A. M., 1998. The theory of financial intermediation. Journal of Banking and Finance 21, 1461-1485.

ALLEN, F., SANTOMERO, A. M., 2001. What do financial intermedaries do? Journal of Banking and Finance 25, 271-294.

ALTUNBAS, Y., IBÁÑEZ, D. M., 2004. Mergers and acquisitions and bank performance in Europe. The role of strategic similarities. European Central Bank Working Paper No. 398, Frankfurt: European Central Bank. Forthcoming in: Journal of Economics and Business.

ALTUNBAS, Y., MOLYNEUX, P., THORNTON, J., 1997. Big bank mergers in Europe: an analysis of the cost implications. Economica 64, 317-329.

AMEL, D., BARNES, C., PANETTA, F, SAELLO, C., 2004. Consolidation and efficiency in the financial sector: a review of the international evidence. Journal of Banking and Finance 28, 2493-2519.

AMIHUD, Y., DELONG, G., SAUNDERS, A., 2002. The effects of cross-border bank mergers on bank risk and value. Journal of International Money and Finance 21, 857-877.

APPELDOORN, B., HORN, L., 2004. Levelling the playing field for whom? The European Takeover Directive and the European marketisation project. Working Paper presented at the Deutsche Vereinigung für Politische Wissenschaft (Sektion Politik und Ökonomie) annual conference, December 3th-4th , Cologne.

ARMITAGE, S., 1995. Event study methods and evidence on their performance. Journal of Economic Surveys 8, 25-52.

ARNOLD, G., 2005. Handbook of corporate finance. Harlow et al.: Prentice Hall.

AYADI, R., PUJALS, G., 2005. Banking mergers and acquisitions in the EU: Overview, assessment and prospects. SUERF Study 2005/3. Vienna: Société Universitaire Européenne de Recherches Financières.

BALL, R., BROWN, P., 1968. An empirical evaluation of accounting income numbers. Journal of Accounting Research (Autumn), 159-178.

BALL, C. A., TSCHOEGL, A. E., 1982. The decision to establish a foreign bank branch or subsidiary: an application of binary classification procedures. Journal of Financial and Quantitative Analysis 17, 411-424.

BALTENSPERGER, E., 1980. Alternative approaches to the theory of the banking firm. Journal of Monetary Economics 6, 1-37.

BALTENSPERGER, E., 1989. The economic theory of banking regulation. In: Furubotn, E. and Richter, R. (eds.): The economics and law of banking regulation. Occasional Paper 2. Saarbrücken: University of the Saarland.

BANNERJEE, A., COOPERMAN, E., 1998. Returns to targets and acquirers: evidence for bank mergers in the 90s. Working Paper. Denver: University of Colorado.

BARADWAJ, B. G., DUBOFSKY, D. A., FRASER, D. R., 1991. Bidder returns in interstate and intrastate acquisitions. Journal of Financial Services Research 5, 261-273.

BARADWAJ, B. G., FRASER, D. R., FURTADO, E. P.-H., 1990. Hostile bank takeover offers: analysis and implications. Journal of Banking and Finance 14, 1229-1242.

BARBER, B AND LYON, J., 1997. Detecting long-run abnormal stock returns: the empirical power and specification of test statistics. Journal of Financial Economics 43, 341-372.

BARTH, J. R., CAPRIO, G., LEVINE, R., 2001. The regulation and supervision of banks around the world. Policy Research Working Paper 2588. Washington: The World Bank.

BARTH, J., CAPRIO, G., LEVINE, R., 2005. The microeconomic effects of different approaches to bank supervision, Working Paper. Providence: Brown University.

BASLE COMMITTEE ON BANKING SUPERVISION, 2006. International convergence of capital measurement and capital standards. A revised framework. Comprehensive version. Basle: BIS.

BECHER, D. A. 2000. The valuation effects of bank mergers. Journal of Corporate Finance 6, 189-214.

BEITEL, P., 2002. Akquisitionen und Zusammenschlüsse europäischer Banken. Wertsteigerung durch M&A-Transaktionen. Wiesbaden: Deutscher Universitäts Verlag.

BEITEL, P., SCHIERECK, D., 2001. Value creation at the ongoing consolidation of the European banking market. Working Paper presented at the 10th International Conference on Banking and Finance, Rome, December 5th-7th, 2001.

BEITEL, P., SCHIERECK, D., WAHRENBURG, M., 2004. Explaining M&A success in European banks. European Financial Management 10, 109-139.

BENDER, C. 2002. Changing firm boundaries in a new information and communication environment. Evidence from the manufacturing and music Industry. Dissertation. University of Münster.

BEN SALEM, A., 2006. The patterns of cross-border banking activity in European countries. Working Paper. University of Lyon.

BENSTON, G., 1976. A transaction cost approach to the theory of financial intermediation. Journal of Finance 31, 215-231.

BENSTON, G., HUNTER, W, WALL, L., 1990. Potential diversification and bank acquisition prices. Working Paper of the Federal Reserve Bank of Atlanta No. 90-11. Georgia: Federal Reserve Bank of Atlanta.

BERGER, A. N., 1998. The efficiency effects of bank mergers and acquisition: a preliminary look at the 1990s data. In: Amihud, Y. and Miller, G. (eds.): Bank mergers & acquisitions, London et al.: Kluwer Academic Publishers, 79-111.

BERGER, A. N., 2003. The economic effects of technological progress: evidence from the banking industry. Journal of Money, Credit and Banking 35, 141-176.

BERGER, A. N., DAI, Q., ONGENA, S., SMITH, D. C., 2003. To what extent will the banking industry be globalized? A study of bank nationality and reach in 20 European nations. Journal of Banking and Finance 27, 383-415.

BERGER, A. N., DELONG, G., DEYOUNG, R., BUCH, C., 2004. Exporting financial institutions management via foreign direct investment mergers and acquisitions. Journal of International Money and Finance 23, 333-366.

BERGER, A. N., DEMSETZ, R. S., STRAHAN, P. E., 1999. The consolidation of the financial services industry: causes, consequences, and implications for the future, in: Journal of Banking and Finance 23, 134-194.

BERGER, A. N., DEYOUNG, R., 2001. The effects of geographic expansion on bank efficiency. Journal of Financial Services Research 19, 163-184.

BERGER, A. N., DEYOUNG, R., GENAY, H., UDELL, G. F., 2000. Globalization of financial institutions: evidence from cross-border banking performance. Brookings-Wharton Papers on Financial Services, 23-158.

BERGER, A. N., HUMPHREY, D., 1997. Efficiency of financial institutions: international survey and directions for future research. European Journal of Operational Research 98, 175-212.

BERGER, A. N., MESTER, L., 1997. Inside the black box: what explains differences in the efficiencies of financial institutions? Journal of Banking and Finance 21, 895-947.

BERTIN, W. J., GHATANFARI, F., TORABZADEH, K. M., 1989. Failed bank acquisitions and successful bidders' returns. Financial Management (Summer), 93-100.

BESSLER, W., MURTAGH, J. P., 2002. The stock market reaction to cross-border acquisitions of financial services firms: an analysis of Canadian banks. Journal of International Financial Markets, Institutions & Money 12, 419-440.

BHATTACHARYA, S. BOOT, A, THAKOR A.V., 1998. The economics of bank regulation. Journal of Money, Credit & Banking 30, 745-770.

BHATTACHARYA, S., THAKOR, A. V., 1993. Contemporary banking theory. Journal of Financial Intermediation 3, 2-50.

BISWAS, R., FRASER, D. R., MAHAJAN, A., 1997. The international market for corporate control: evidence from acquisitions of financial firms. Global Finance Journal 8, 33-54.

BITTLINGMEYER, G., HAZLETT, T. W., 2000. DOS Kapital: Has antitrust action against Microsoft created value in the computer industry? Journal of Financial Economics 55, 329-359.

BJÖRKMAN, I., VAARA, E., 2006. Nordea Markets: socio-cultural integration challenges. In: Risberg, A. (ed.): Mergers and Acquisitions. A critical reader. London and New York: Routledge, 231-240.

BLACK, F., SCHOLES, M., 1976. The pricing of options and corporate liabilities. Journal of Political Economy 81, 637-654.

BLISS, R. T., ROSEN, R. J., 2001. CEO compensation and bank mergers. Journal of Financial Economics 61, 107-138.

BOHL, M. T., HAVRYLCHYK, O., SCHIERECK, D., 2004. Foreign acquisitions and industry wealth effects of privatisation: evidence from the Polish

banking industry. Working Paper 10/2004. Oestrich-Winkel: European Business School.
BOUWMAN, C. H. S., 2004. The governance of banks: how do bank capital and monitoring impact post-acquisition risk-taking and performance? Working Paper, presented at the Financial Management Association 2004 Annual Meeting, New Orleans, October 6-9th, 2004.
BOWMAN, R., 1983. Understanding and conducting event studies. Journal of Business Finance & Accounting 10, 561-584.
BREALY, R. A., KAPLANIS, E. C., 1996. The determination of foreign bank location. Journal of International Money and Finance 15, 577-597.
BREWER, E. I., JACKSON, W. E. I., JAGTIANI, J. A., NGUYEN, T., 2000. The price of bank mergers in the 1990s. Federal Reserve Bank of Chicago Economic Perspectives (1st Quarter), 2-23.
BRICKLEY, J. A., JAMES, C. M., 1987. The takeover market, corporate board composition, and ownership structure: the case of banking. Journal of Law and Economics 30, 161-180.
BRIMMER, A. F., DAHL, F. R., 1975. Growth of American international banking: implications for public policy. Journal of Finance 15, 577-597.
BROWN, J., WARNER, J., 1980. Measuring security price performance. Journal of Financial Economics 8, 205-258.
BROWN, J. WARNER, J., 1985. Using daily stock returns – the case of event studies. Journal of Financial Economics 14, 3-31.
BRUCKNER, B., O'SHEA, J., 2002. Mergers in European banking: a managerial perspective. CoBAR Working Paper No. 2002-01. Vienna: Business University Vienna.
BRUNER, R., 2002. Does M&A pay? A survey of evidence for the decision maker. Journal of Applied Corporate Finance 12, 48-68.
BUCH, C. M., 2000. Why do banks go abroad? – Evidence from German data. Financial Markets, Institutions & Instruments 9, 33-67.
BUCH, C. M., 2005. Distance and international banking. Review of International Economics 13, 787-804.
BUCH, C. M., DELONG, G., 2003. Determinants of cross-border bank mergers: is Europe different? In: Herrmann, H., Lipsey, R. (eds.): Foreign direct investment in the real and financial sector of industrial countries. Frankfurt, New York: Springer.
BUCH, C. M., DELONG, G., 2004. Cross-border bank mergers: What lures the rare animal? Journal of Banking and Finance 28, 2077-2102.
BUCH, C. M., DELONG, G., 2005. Cross-border bank mergers: Regulatory arbitrage or good business? Working Paper presented at the International Con-

ference on Competition, Stability and Integration in European Banking, Brussels, May 23rd-24th, 2005.

BUCH, C. M., LIPPONER, A. 2004. FDI versus cross-border financial services: The globalization of German banks. Deutsche Bundesbank Discussion Paper Series 1: Studies of the Economic Research Center No. 05/2004. Frankfurt: Deutsche Bundesbank.

BUDZEIKA, G., 1991. Determinants of the growth of foreign banking assets in the United States. Federal Reserve Bank of New York Research Paper No. 9112. New York: Federal Reserve Bank of New York.

BUSINESS WEEK, 2004. Bargain-sniffing in the States; European banks are shopping once again aggressively for American acquisitions. February 23rd, 2004.

BUSINESS WEEK ONLINE, 2005. Way up down under. Available at http://www.businessweek.com/magazine/content/05_41/b3954170.htm. Access at 15.03.2006.

BÜSCHGEN, H., BÖRNER, C., 2003. Bankbetriebslehre. 4th edition. Stuttgart: Lucius & Lucius.

CAGLE, J., NIXON, T. D., 2005. Long-term bank performance following financial institution mergers/acquisitions in the 1990s. Working Paper presented at the Financial Management Associations 2005 Annual Meeting, Chicago, October 12-15th, 2005.

CALOMIRIS, C., KARCESKI, J., 1998. Is the bank merger wave of the 1990s efficient? Lessons from nine case studies. Washington: AEI Press.

CAMPA, J. M., HERNANDO, I., 2005. M&A performance in the European financial industry. Working Paper presented at the 11th Dubrovnik Economic Conference, Dubrovnik, June 29th-July 2nd, 2005.

CANALS, J., 1997. Universal banking. Oxford: Oxford University Press.

CARUSO, A., PALMUCCI, F., 2005. Measuring value creation in bank mergers and acquisitions. Working Paper. Bologna: University of Bologna.

CAVES, R., 1989. Mergers, takeovers and economic efficiency: foresight vs. hindsight. International Journal of Industrial Organization 7, 151-174.

CHAN, Y.-S., GREENBAUM, S., THAKOR, A., 1992. Is fairly priced deposit insurance possible? Journal of Finance 47, 227-245.

CHARAP, J., HARM, C., 2000. Institutionalized corruption and the kleptocratic state. In: Menard, C. (ed.): Institutions, contracts and organizations: perspectives from New Institutional Economics. Cheltenham and Northhampton: Edward Elgar, 188-208.

CHO, K. R., 1986. Determinants of international banks. Management International Review 26, 10-23.

CLARKE, G., CULL, R., MARTINEZ PERIA, M. S., SANCHEZ, S. M., 2003. Foreign bank entry: experience, implications for developing economies, and agenda for future research. World Bank Observer 18, 25-59.

COASE, R. H., 1937. The nature of the firm. Economica 4, 386-405.

COELLI, T., PRASADA RAO, D., BATTESE, G., 1998. An introduction to efficiency and productivity analysis, Boston et. al.: Kluwer Academic Publishers.

CORNETT, M. M., DE, S., 1991. Common stock returns in corporate takeover bids: Evidence from interstate bank mergers. Journal of Banking and Finance 15, 273-295.

CORNETT, M. M., HOVAKIMIAN, G., PALIA, D., TEHRANIAN, H., 2003. The impact of the manager-shareholder conflict on acquiring bank returns. Journal of Banking and Finance 27, 103-131.

CORNETT, M. M., TEHRANIAN, H., 1992. Changes in corporate performance associated with bank acquisitions. Journal of Financial Economics 31, 211-234.

COWAN, A. R., 1992. Nonparametric event study tests. Review of Quantitative Finance and Accounting 2, 343-358.

COWAN, A. R., SERGEANT, A., 2001. Interacting biases, non-normal return distributions and the performance of tests for long-horizon event studies. Journal of Banking and Finance 25, 741-765.

CYBO-OTTONE, A., MURGIA, M., 2000. Mergers and shareholder wealth in European banking. Journal of Banking and Finance 24, 831-859.

CYREE, K. B., DEGENARRO, P., 1999. A generalized method for detecting abnormal returns and changes in systematic risk. Working Paper. Tennessee: University of Tennessee.

DALBORG, H. 1999. Shareholder value in banking. Working Paper presented at the May 1999 session of the Institut International d'Etudes Bancaire, Paris, May 15-17th, 1999.

DAMODARAN, A., 2001. Corporate finance. Theory and practice. 2nd edition. New York et al.: John Wiley & Sons.

DA SILVA, J. A. S. V., DIZ, M. C. R., 2005. Mergers and acquisitions in the Portuguese banking industry: is there a process of value creation? Working Paper. Evora: University of Evora.

DE, S., DUPLICHAN, D., 1987. Effects of interstate bank mergers on shareholder wealth: theory and evidence. Geld, Banken, Versicherungen 2, 751-773.

DE CARMOY, H., 1990. Global banking strategy. Cambridge: Basil Blackwell.

DE COSSIO, F., TRIFTS, J. W., SCANLON, K.P., 1988. Bank equity returns: the difference between intrastate and interstate bank mergers. Proceedings of the 29th annual conference on bank structure an and competition. Federal Reserve Bank of Chicago, 591-600. Chicago: Federal Reserve Bank of Chicago.

DEGRYSE, H., ONGENA, S., 2004. The impact of technology and regulation on the geographical scope of banking. Oxford Review of Economic Policy 20, 571-590.

DELONG, G., 2001. Stockholder gains from focusing versus diversifying bank mergers. Journal of Financial Economics 59, 221-252.

DELONG, G., 2003. Does long-term performance of mergers match market expectations? Evidence from the US banking industry. Financial Management (Summer), 132-164.

DERMINE, J., 2002. European banking: past, present and future. Working Paper presented at the Second ECB Central Banking Conference, Frankfurt, October 24-25th, 2002.

DESAI, A. S., STOVER, R. D., 1985. Bank holding company acquisitions, stockholder returns and regulatory uncertainty. Journal of Financial Research 8, 145-156.

DEWATRIPOINT, M., TIROLE, J., 1994. The prudential regulation of banks. Cambridge: MIT Press.

DEYOUNG, R., 1997. Bank mergers, X-efficiency and the market for corporate control. Managerial Finance 23, 32-47.

DIAMOND, D., 1984. Financial intermediation and delegated monitoring. Review of Economic Studies 51, 393-414.

DIAMOND, D., DYBVIG, P., 1983. Bank runs, deposit insurance, and liquidity. Journal of Political Economy 91, 401-419.

DIMSON, E., 1979. Risk measurement when shares are subject to infrequent trading. Journal of Financial Economics 7 (June), 197-226.

DI SALVO, R., MAZZILIS, M., GUIDI, A. 2002. Are Italian mutual banks efficient? Evidence from two different cost frontier techniques. SUERF Studies No. 15/2003, 7-42. Vienna: Société Universitaire Européenne de Recherches Financières.

DITTMANN, I., ULBRICHT, N., 2004. Timing and wealth effects of German dual class stock unifications. Forthcoming in European Financial Management.

DODD, P., WARNER, J., 1983. On corporate governance: a study of proxy contests. Journal of Financial Economics 11, 401-438.

DONGES, J., FREYTAG, A., 2001. Allgemeine Wirtschaftspolitik. Stuttgart: Lucius & Lucius.

DOUGHERTY, C., 2002. Introduction to econometrics. 2nd edition. Oxford: Oxford University Press.

DOW JONES INTERNATIONAL NEWS, 1998. Italy's Unicredito CEO: Mediobanca stake strategic. October 20th, 1998.

DOW JONES INTERNATIONAL NEWS, 1999. Unicredito, Allianz say in final talks for Poland's Pekao. April 23th, 1999.

DOWD, K., 1992. Is banking a natural monopoly? Kyklos 45, 379-392.

DUBOFSKY, D. A., FRASER, D. R., 1985. Bank mergers and acquiring bank stockholders' returns. Working Paper presented at the Eastern Finance Association meeting, Williamsburg, April 1st, 1985.

DUBOFSKY, D. A., FRASER, D. R., 1989. Regulatory change and the market for bank control. In: Gup, B. E. (ed.): Bank mergers. Norwell: Kluwer Academic Publishers, 121-139.

DUNNING, J. H. 1977. Trade, location of economic activity and MNE: a search for an eclectic approach. In: Ohlin, B., Hesselborn, P. O., Wijkman, P. M. (eds.): The international allocation of economic activity, London: McMillian, 395-418.

DUNNING, J. H., 1992. Multinational enterprises and the global economy. Workingham: Addison-Wesley Publishers Ltd.

DUNNING, J. H., 2000. The eclectic paradigm as an envelope for economic and business theories of MNE acticity. International Business Review 9, 163-190.

DUURSMA, D. 1999. Fusionskontrolle bei Banken: Europäische und nationale Regelungen. Vienna: Bank-Verlag.

EDEN, L., 2003. A critical reflection and some conclusions on OLI. In: Cantwell, J. and Narula, R. (eds.): International business and the eclectic paradigm: developing the OLI framework, New York: Routledge, 277-297.

EISENFÜHR, F., WEBER, M. 1999. Rationales Entscheiden. 3rd edition. Berlin et al.: Springer.

ERHARDT, O., KOERSTEIN, R., 2001. Der Einfluß der Benchmarkwahl auf das Ergebnis langfristiger Ereignisstudien. OR Spektrum 21, 445-475.

EUROPEAN CENTRAL BANK, 2000. Mergers and acquisitions involving the EU banking industry – facts and implications. Frankfurt: European Central Bank.

EUROPEAN COMMISSION, 2006. FASP Evaluation. Part I: Process and implementation. Brussels: European Commission.

FABIANA PENAS, M., UNAL, H., 2004. Gains in bank mergers: evidence from the bond markets. Journal of Financial Economics 74, 149-179.

FAMA, E. F., 1976. Foundations of Finance. New York: Basic Books.

FAMA, E. F., 1998. Market efficiency, long-term returns, and behavioral finance. Journal of Financial Economics 49, 283-306.

FAMA, E. F., FISHER, M., JENSEN, M., ROLL, R., 1969. The adjustment of stock prices to new information. International Economic Review (February), 1-21.

FAMA, E. F. AND FRENCH, K., 1993. Common risk factors in the returns on stocks and bonds, in: Journal of Financial Economics 33, 3-56.

FAMA, E. F. AND FRENCH, K., 1996. Multifactor explanations of asset pricing anomalies. Journal of Finance 51, 55-84.

FINANCIAL TIMES, 1999. BCP drops Champalimaud bids. November 19th, 1999.

FISHER, A., MOLYNEUX, P., 1996. A note on the determinants of foreign bank activity in London between 1980 and 1989. Applied Financial Economics 6, 271-277.

FOCARELLI, D., POZZOLO, A. F., 2001. The patterns of cross-border bank mergers and shareholdings in OECD countries. Journal of Banking and Finance 25, 2305-2337.

FOCARELLI, D., POZZOLO, A. F., 2005. Where do banks expand abroad? An empirical analysis. Journal of Business 78, 2435-2464.

FRAME, W. S., LASTRAPES, W. D., 1998. Abnormal returns in the acquisition market: the case of bank holding companies, 1990-1993. Journal of Financial Services Research 14, 145-163.

FRANKE, G., HAX, H., 2004. Finanzwirtschaft des Unternehmens und Kapitalmarkt. 5th edition. Berlin and Heidelberg: Springer.

FREIXAS, X., ROCHET, J.-C., 1998. Microeconomics of banking. Cambridge et al.: MIT Press.

FREIXAS, X., SANTOMERO, A. M., 2003. An overall perspective on banking regulation. UPF Economics and Business Working Paper No. 664. Barcelona: University Pompeu Fabra.

FROOT, K. A., STEIN, J. C., 1991. Exchange rates and foreign direct investment: an imperfect capital markets approach. Quarterly Journal of Economics 106, 1191-1217.

FROOT, K. A., STEIN, J.C., 1998. Risk-management, capital budgeting, and capital structure policy for financial institutions. Journal of Financial Economics 47, 55-82.

GALAI, D., MASULIS, R., 1975. The option pricing model and the risk factor of stock. Journal of Financial Economics 3, 53-81.

GALINDO, A., MICCO, A., SERRA, C., 2003. Better the devil that you know: evidence on entry costs faced by foreign banks. IADB Bank Working Paper 477. Washington: Inter-American Development Bank.

GLEASON, K. C., MATHUR, I., 1998. Wealth effects of international acquisitions by US banks. Financial Markets, Institutions & Instruments 7, 54-69.

GOLDBERG, L. G., GROSSE, R., 1994. Location choice of foreign banks in the United States. Journal of Economics and Business 46, 367-379.

GOLDBERG, L. G., JOHNSON, D., 1990. The determinants of US banking activity abroad. Journal of International Money and Finance 9, 123-137.

GOLDBERG, L. G., SAUNDERS, A., 1980. The causes of U.S. bank expansion overseas. Journal of Money, Credit and Banking 12, 630-643.

GORT, M., 1969. An economic disturbance theory of mergers. Quarterly Journal of Economics 83, 624-642.

GORTON, G., WINTON, A., 2002. Financial intermediation. NBER Working Paper 8928. Cambridge: National Bureau of Economic Research.

GRANT, R., 1998. Contemporary strategy analysis. Concepts, techniques, applications. Cambridge: Basil Blackwell.

GRAY, J. M., GRAY, P. H., 1981. The multinational bank: a financial MNC? Journal of Banking and Finance 5, 33-63.

GREENBAUM, S. I., THAKOR, A. V., 1995. Contemporary financial intermediation. Fort Worth: The Dryden Press.

GRINBLATT, M., TITMAN, S., 1998. Financial markets and corporate strategy. Boston et al.: McGraw Hill.

GROSSE, R., GOLDBERG, L. G., 1991. Foreign bank activity in the United States: an analysis by country of origin. Journal of Banking and Finance 15, 1093-1112.

GROUP OF TEN, 2001. Report on consolidation in the financial sector. Basle: BIS.

GRUBEL, H., 1977. A theory of multinational banking. Banca Nazionale del Lavoro Quarterly Review 30, 345-363.

HALEY, C., SCHALL, L., 1973. The theory of financial decisions. New York: McGraw-Hill.

HANNAN, T. W., WOLKEN, J. D., 1989. Returns to bidders and targets in the acquisition process: evidence from the banking industry. Journal of Financial Services Research 3, 5-16.

HARM, C. 2002. Bank management between shareholders and regulators. SUERF Study No. 21. Vienna: Société Universitaire Européenne de Recherches Financières.

HARTMANN-WENDELS, T., PFINGSTEN, A., WEBER, M., 2004. Bankbetriebslehre. 3rd edition. Berlin et al.: Springer.

HAWAWINI, G., SWARY, I., 1990. Mergers and acquisitions in the U.S. banking industry. Evidence from the capital markets. Amsterdam et al.: North-Holland.

HÄRLE, P., 2005. Negotiating better cross-border banking mergers in Europe. McKinsey Quartely Web Edition. Available at http://www.mckinseyquarterly.com/article_page.aspx?ar=1704&L2=10. Access at 20.06.2006.

HEINEMANN, F., JOPP, M., 2002. The benefits of a working European retail market for financial services. Europa Union Verlag: Bonn.

HELLGREN, B., LÖWSTEDT, J., TIENARI, J., VAARA, E., WERR, A., 2003. Agents of homogenization: on the role of management consultants in mergers. Working Paper presented at the 17th Nordic Conference on Business Studies, Reykjavik, August 14-16th, 2003.

HELLWIG, M. F. 1994. Banking and finance at the end of the twentieth century. WWZ Discussion Paper No. 9426. Basel: University of Basel.

HELLWIG, M. F., 1997. Unternehmensfinanzierung, Unternehmenskontrolle und Ressourcenallokation: Was leistet das Finanzsystem. In: Gahlen, H., Hesse, H., Nauss, J. (eds.): Finanzmärkte. Tübingen: J. C. B. Mohr, 211-243.

HIGGINS, R., SCHALL, L. 1975. Corporate bankruptcy and conglomerate merger. Journal of Finance 30, 93-113.

HOFSTEDE, G., 1980. Culture's consequences: international differences in work-related values. Beverly Hills: Sage Publications.

HOUSTON, J. F., JAMES, C. M., MARCUS, D., 1997. Capital market frictions and the role of internal capital markets in banking. Journal of Financial Economics 46, 135-164.

HOUSTON, J. F., JAMES, C. M., RYNGAERT, M. D., 2000. Where do merger gains come from? Bank mergers from the perspective of insiders and outsiders. Journal of Financial Economics 60, 285-331.

HOUSTON, J. F., RYNGAERT, M . D., 1994. The overall gains from large bank mergers. Journal of Banking and Finance 18, 1155-1176.

HOUSTON, J. F., RYNGAERT, M., 1997. Equity issuance and adverse selection: a direct test using conditional stock offers. Journal of Finance 52, 197-219.

HUDGINS, S. C., SEIFERT, B., 1996. Stockholder returns and international acquisitions of financial firms: an emphasis on banking. Journal of Financial Services Research 10, 163-180.

HUGHES J., MESTER, L., 1993. A quality and risk adjusted cost function for banks: Evidence on the "too big to fail doctrine". Journal of Productivity Analysis 4, 293-315.

HUIZINGA, H., NICODÈME, G., 2002. Deposit insurance and international bank deposits. European Commission Economic Paper No. 164. Brussels: European Commission.

HULTMANN, C. W., MCGEE, L. R., 1989. Factors affecting the foreign banking presence in the US. Journal of Banking and Finance 13, 383-396.

JACCARD, J., TURRISI, R., 2003. Interaction Effects in Multiple Regression. 2nd edition. Thousands Oaks: Sage Publications.

JAFFE, J., 1974. Special information and insider trading. Journal of Business 47, 410-428.

JAKOBSEN, J., SØRENSEN, O., 2001. Decomposing and testing long-term returns: An application on Danish IPOs. European Financial Management 7, 393-417.

JAKOBSEN, J., VOETMANN, T., 2003. Post-acquisition performance in the short and long run. Evidence from the Copenhagen Stock Exchange 1993-1997. The European Journal of Finance 9, 323-342.

JAMES, C. M., WIER, P., 1987A. An analysis of FDIC failed bank auctions. Journal of Monetary Economics 20, 141-153.

JAMES, C. M., WIER, P., 1987B. Returns to acquirers and competition in the acquisition market: the case of banking. Journal of Political Economy 95, 355-370.

JENSEN, M. C., 1984. Takeovers. Folklore and science. Harvard Business Review 62, 109-121.

JENSEN, M. C., 1986. Agency costs of free cash flow, corporate finance, and takeovers. American Economic Review 76, 323-329.

JENSEN, M. C., MECKLING, W., 1976. Managerial behaviour, agency costs and ownership structure. Journal of Financial Economics 3, 305-360.

JENSEN, M.C., RUBACK, R. S., 1983. The market for corporate control. Journal of Financial Economics 11, 5-50.

JENTZSCH, N., 2003. The regulation of financial privacy: the United States versus Europe. ECRI Research Report No. 5. Brussels: European Credit Research Institute.

JONES, G., 1990. Banks as multinationals. In: Jones, G. (ed.): Banks as multinationals. New York: Routledge.

KAENE, F. R., TEHRANIAN, H., 1989. New Hampshire bank mergers: the returns to acquiring bank shareholders. In: Gup, B. (ed.): Bank mergers. Norwell: Kluwer Academic Publishers, 141-156.

KANE, E. J., 1995. Three paradigms for the role of capitalization requirements in insured financial institutions. Journal of Banking and Finance 19, 431-459.

KANE, E. J., 2000. Incentives for banking megamergers: what motives might central-bank economists infer from event study evidence? Journal of Money, Credit, and Banking 32, 6671-699.

KAPLAN, S., 1989. Management buyouts: evidence on taxes as a source of value. Journal of Finance 44, 611-632.

KERLER, P., 2000. Mergers & Acquisitions und Shareholder Value. Bern: Haupt.

KINDLEBERGER, C. P., 1969. American business abroad: six lectures on direct investment: New Heaven: Yale University Press.

KIYMAZ, H., 2004. Cross-border acquisitions of US financial institutions: impact of macroeconomic factors. Journal of Banking and Finance 28, 1413-1439.

KLEIN, A. AND ROSENFELD, J., 1987. The influence of market conditions on event study residuals. Journal of Financial and Quantitative Analysis 22, 345-351.

KOTHARI, S., WARNER, J., 2004. The econometrics of event studies. Working Paper. Hanover: Dartmouth University. Forthcoming in: Eckbo, E. (ed.): Handbook of Corporate Finance.

KOTZEN, J., NEENAN, C., ROOS, A., STELTER, D., 2003. Winning through mergers in lean times. Boston Consulting Group Research Report. Boston: Boston Consulting Group.

KWG, 2005. In: Bankrecht. 33th edition, 1999. Munich: C. H. Beck.

KROSZNER, R. S., STRAHAN, P. E., 2005. Regulation and deregulation of the U.S. banking industry: causes, consequences, and implications for the future. Forthcoming in Rose, N. (ed.): Economics of Regulation, NBER Conference Volume.

KUMBHAKAR, S., KNOX-LOVELL, C., 2000. Stochastic Frontier Analysis. Cambridge: Cambridge University Press

KUTSCHKER, M., SCHMIDT, S., 2005. Internationales Mangement. 4th edition. Munich, Vienna: Oldenbourg Verlag.

KÜRSTEN, W., 2000. "Shareholder Value" – Grundelemente und Schieflagen einer polit-ökonomischen Diskussion aus finanzierungstheoretischer Sicht. Zeitschrift für Betriebswirtschaft 70, 359-381.

KWAN, S. H., EISENBEIS, R., 1999. Mergers of publicy traded banking organizations revisted. Federal Bank of Atlanta Economic Review 84, 26-37.

LANG, L., STULZ, R., WALKLING, R., 1989. Managerial performance, Tobin's Q, and the gains from successful tender offers. Journal of Financial Economics 24, 137-154.

LESHCHINKSKII, D., ZOLLO, M. 2005. Can firms learn to acquire? The impact of post-acquisition decisions and learning on long-term abnormal returns. Working Paper. Philadelphia: University of Pennsylvania.

LEVY, H., SARNAT, M., 1970. Diversification, portfolio analysis and the uneasy case for conglomerate mergers. Journal of Finance 25, 795-802.

LEWELLEN, W., 1971. A pure financial rationale for the conglomerate merger. Journal of Finance 26, 521-537.

LINTNER, J., 1965. The valuation of risky assets and the selection of risky investments in stock portfolios and capital budgets. Review of Economics and Statistics 47, 13-37.

LOBUE, M., 1984. Categorical bank acquisitions. Journal of Bank Research 14, 274-282.

LOUGHRAN, T., VIJH, A. M., 1997. Do long-term shareholders benefit from corporate acquisitions? Journal of Finance 52, 1765-1790.

LYON, J., BARBER, B., TSAI, C., 1999. Improved methods of tests of long-horizon abnormal stock returns. Journal of Finance 54, 165-201.

MACKINLAY, A., 1997. Event studies in economics and finance. Journal of Economic Literature 35, 13-39.

MADURA, J., WIANT, K. J., 1994. Long-term valuation effects of bank acquisitions. Journal of Banking and Finance 18, 1135-1154.

MANDELKER, G., 1974. Risk and return: the case of merging firms. Journal of Financial Economics 1, 303-335.

MANNE, H. G., 1965. Mergers and the market for corporate control. Journal of Political Economy 73, 110-120.

MAQUIERA, C., MEGGINSON W., NAIL, L., 1998. Wealth creation versus wealth redistribution in pure stock-for-stock mergers. Journal of Financial Economics 48, 3-33.

MARCH, J., 1994. A primer on decision making. New York: The Free Press.

MARCUS, A., 1984. Deregulation and bank financial policy. Journal of Banking and Finance 8, 557-565.

MARKUSEN, J. R., VENABLES, A. J., 1996. The increased importance of direct investment in North Atlantic economic relationships: a convergence hypothesis. In: Canzoneri, M. B., Ethier, W. J., Grilli, V.: The new transatlantic economy. Cambridge: Cambridge University Press, 169-189.

MCKINSEY, 2005. EU banking M&A – recent trends. Amsterdam: McKinsey & Company, Inc.

MCWILLIAMS, A., SIEGEL, D., 1997. Event studies in management research: theoretical and empirical issues. Academy of Management Journal 40, 626-657.

MERGERMARKET, 2006. EC eyes new rules to ease M&A deals in the financial sector. September 13th, 2006.

MILLER, S. R., PARKHE, A., 1998. Patterns in the expansion of U.S. banks' foreign operations. Journal of International Business Studies 29, 359-390.

MITCHELL, M. L., STAFFORD, E., 2000. Managerial decisions and long-term stock price performance. Journal of Business 73, 287-329.

MOELLER, S. B., SCHLINGEMANN, F. P., 2005. Global diversification and bidder gains: A comparison between domestic and cross-border acquisitions. Journal of Banking and Finance 29, 533-564.

MORCK, R., SHLEIFER, A. AND VISHNY, R., 1990. Do managerial objectives drive bad acquisitions? Journal of Finance 45, 31-48.

MOSER, G., POINTNER, W. SCHARLER, J., 2005. Financial globalization, capital account liberalization and international consumption risk-sharing. Focus on European Economic Integration No. 1/05, Vienna: Austrian National Bank.

MOSSIN, J., 1966. Equilibrium in a capital asset market. Econometrica, October 1966.

MUßHOFF, J., SCHIERECK, D., 2005. Erfolgreiche Bankakquisitionen in Europa – Das Beispiel Unicredit und Pekao. Working Paper Nr. 09/2005. Oestrich-Winkel: European Business School.

NEELY, W. P., 1987. Banking acquisitions: acquirer and target shareholder returns. Financial management 16, 66-74.

NEUE ZÜRCHER ZEITUNG, 1999. Unicredito/Allfinanz-Erfolg in Polen. April 24th, 1999.

NIGH, D., CHO, K. R., KRISHNAN, S., 1986. The role of location-related factors in U.S. banking involvement abroad: an empirical examination. Journal of International Business Studies 17, 59-72.

O'HARA, M., SHAW, W., 1990. Deposit insurance and wealth effects: the value of being "too big to fail". Journal of Finance 45, 1587-1600.

PALIA, D. 1993. The managerial, regulatory, and financial determinants of bank merger premiums. Journal of Industrial Economics 41, 91-102.

PEEK, J., ROSENGREEN, E. S., KASIRYE, F., 1999. The poor performance of foreign bank subsidiaries: were the problems acquired or created? Journal of Banking and Finance 23, 579-604.

PETERSON, P., 1989. Event studies: a review of issues and methodologies. Quarterly Journal of Business and Economics 28, 36-66.

PETTWAY, R. H., TRIFTS, J. W., 1985. Do banks overbid when acquiring failed banks? Financial Management 14, 5-15.

PILOFF, S. J., 1996. Performance changes and shareholder wealth creation associated with mergers of publicly traded banking institutions. Journal of Money, Credit, and Banking 28, 294-310.

PILOFF, S. J., SANTOMERO, A. A., 1998. The value effects of bank mergers and acquisitions. In: Amihud, Y., Miller, G. (eds.), Bank Mergers & Acquisitions, Boston et al.: Kluwer.

PISCITELLO, L., 2003. The recent globalization of the Italian banking sector. An interpretation based on the eclectic paradigm. In: Cantwell, J. and Narula,

R. (eds.): International business and the eclectic paradigm: Developing the OLI-framework, London: Routledge, 252-275.

PORTER, M., 1998. Competitive Advantage – Creating and sustaining superior performance: with a new introduction. New York: The Free Press.

RAMANATHAN, R., 2003. Introduction to data envelopment analysis. Thousand Oaks: Sage Publications.

RAPPAPORT, A., 1998. Creating shareholder value. A guide for managers and investors. New York: The Free Press.

RAVENSCRAFT, D., SCHERER, F., 1987. Mergers, sell-offs and economic efficiency. The Brookings Institution: Washington.

RESTI, A., 2000. Do bank acquisitions increase shareholders' wealth? A comparison between market-based and accounting-based performance indicators for some Italian banks. Working Paper. Bergamo: University of Bergamo.

REUTERS NEWS, 1999A. Italy's Unicredito in final phase for Pekao buy. April 23rd, 1999.

REUTERS NEWS, 1999B. Unicredito buys largest Polish bank Pekao. June 23rd, 1999.

RHOADES, S., 1994. A summary of merger performance studies in banking, 1980-1993, and an assessment of the "operating performance" and the "event study" methodologies, Staff Study No. 167, Board of Governors of the US Federal Reserve System. Washington: Board of Governors of the US Federal Reserce System

RHODES-KROPF, M., VISWANATHAN, S., 2004. Market valuation and merger waves. Journal of Finance 59, 2685-2718.

ROLL, R., 1986. The hubris hypothesis of corporate takeovers. Journal of Business 59, 197-216.

ROSS, S. A., 1976. The arbitrage theory of capital asset pricing. Journal of Economic Theory 13, 341-360.

RUGMAN, A. M., 1980. Internalization as a general theory of foreign direct investment: a re-appraisal of the literature. Weltwirtschaftliches Archive 116, 365-379.

RUGMAN, A. M., VERBEKE, A., 1993. Multinational banking strategies in the Pacific. In: Sletmo, G. K., Boyed, G. (eds.): Pacific service enterprise and pacific cooperation. Boulder: Westview Press.

RUPPERT, D., 1988. Trimming and winsorization. In: Kotz, S., Johnson, N. L. (eds.) Encyclopedia of Statistical Sciences 9, New York: John Wiley & Sons, 348-353.

SABI, M., 1988. An application of the theory of foreign direct investment to multinational banking in LDCS. Journal of International Business Studies, Fall 1988, pp. 433-447.

SAGARI, S. B., 1992. United States foreign direct investment in the banking industry, Transnational Corporations 1, 93-123

SANTOMERO, A. 1984. Modeling the banking firm. Journal of Money, Credit and Banking 16, 576-602.

SANTOMERO, A. 1985. Financial risk management: the whys and hows. Financial Markets, Institutions and Intruments 4, 1-14.

SCHÄFER, H., 1971. Zum Begriff des Bankbetriebes. Göppingen: Poeschl.

SCHIERECK, D., STRAUSS, M. 2000. Zum Ankündigungseffekt großer Bankfusionen. Mergers and Acquisitions 11/2000, 421-425.

SCHIERENBECK, H., HÖLSCHER, R., 1998. Bank Assurance. 4th edition. Stuttgart: Schäffer Poeschl.

SCHMITTMANN, S., PENZEL, H., GEHRKE, N. 1996. Integration des Shareholder Value in die Gesamtbanksteuerung. Die Bank (without number), 648-653.

SCHOLES, M. AND WILLIAMS, J., 1977. Estimating betas from nonsynchronous data. Journal of Financial Economics 5, 309-328.

SCHREYÖGG, G., 1993. Unternehmenskultur zwischen Globalisierung und Regionalisierung. In: Haller, M., Bleicher, K., Pleitner, H., Wunderer, R., Zünd, A. (eds.): Globalisierung der Wirtschaft. Einwirkung auf die Betriebswirtschaftslehre. St. Gallen: Paul Haupt, 149-170.

SCHROEDER, L. D., SJOQUIST, D. L., STEPHAN, P. E., 1986. Understanding regression analysis: An introductory guide. Thousands Oaks: Sage Publications.

SCHUSTER, L., 2000. Shareholder value management in banks. New York: Macmillian.

SEIDEL, G. R., 1995. Kritische Erfolgsfaktoren bei Unternehmensübernahmen: Eine Analyse der US-Bankbranche. Wiesbaden: Gabler.

SETH, R., NOELLE, D. E., MOHANTY, S. K., 1998. Do banks follow their customers abroad? Financial Markets, Institutions and Instruments 7, 1-25.

SHARPE, W., 1964. Capital asset prices: a theory of market equilibrium. Journal of Finance 19, 425-424.

SIEMS, T. F., 1996. Bank mergers and shareholder wealth: Evidence from the 1995s megamerger deals. Financial Industry Studies of the Federal Reserve Bank of Dallas, 1-12.

SLAGER, A. 2004. Banking across borders. ERIM Ph.D series in management research 41, Rotterdam: Erasmus Research Institute of Management.

SLAGER, A., 2005. Internationalization of Banks: Strategic Patterns and Performance. SUERF Studies No. 4/2005. Vienna: Société Universitaire Européenne de Recherches Financières.

SMITH, C. W., 1995. Corporate risk management: theory and practice. Journal of Derivatives 2, 21-30.

SMITH, C. W., STULZ, R. 1985. The determinants of firms hedging policies. Journal of Financial and Quantitative Analysis 20, 391-406.

SOUSSA, F., 2004. A note on banking FDI in emerging markets: literature review and evidence from M&A data. Bank of England Working Paper submitted to the BIS Working Group on Foreign Direct Investment in the Financial Sector of Emerging Market Economies.

SPICHER, T., 1997. Kapitalmarkt, unvollständige Verträge und Finanzintermediäre. Lohmar and Cologne: Josef Eul.

STANLEY, T. O., ROGER, C., MCMANIS, B., 1993. The effects of foreign ownership of US banks on the availability of loanable funds to small businesses. Journal of Small Business Management 31, 51-66.

SUBRAHMANYAM, V., RANGAN, N., ROSENSTEIN, S., 1997. The role of outside directors in bank acquisitions. Financial Management 26, 23-26.

SUSHKA, M. E., BENDECK, Y., 1988. Bank acquisitions and stockholder wealth. Journal of Banking and Finance 12, 551-562.

THE BANKER, 2002. SCH is a banking behemoth built by Emilio Botin, but can his personality sustain the bank's momentum? May 2nd, 2002.

THE ECONOMIST, 2005. An Italian comedy, October 1st, 2005.

THE ECONOMIST, 2006A. The limits to size. Special report on international banking, May 18th, 2006.

THE ECONOMIST, 2006B. Hail Santesa. September 2nd, 2006.

THE ECONOMIST, 2006C. Ready or not. September 9th, 2006.

TOURANI RAD, A., VAN BEEK, L., 1999. Market valuation of European bank mergers. European Management Journal 17, 532-540.

TOYNE, M. F., TRIPP, J. D., 1998. Interstate bank mergers and their impact on shareholder returns: evidence from the 1990s. Quarterly Journal of Business and Economics 37, 48-58.

TRAUTWEIN, F., 1990. Merger motives and merger prescriptions. Strategic Management Journal 2, 283-295.

TRIFTS, J. W., SCANLON, K. P., 1987. Interstate bank mergers: the early evidence. Journal of Financial Research 10, 305-311.

TSCHOEGL, A. E., 2003. Who owns the major US subsidiaries of foreign banks? A note, Working Paper No. 03/11, Philadelphia: University of Pennsylvania.

UNCTAD, 2000. World investment report: cross-border mergers and acquisitions. New York: United Nations.

UNCTAD, 2005. World investment report: transnational corporations and the internationalization of R&D. New York: United Nations.

URSACKI, T., VERTINSKY, I., 1992. Choice of entry timing and scale by foreign banks in Japan and Korea. Journal of Banking and Finance 16, 405-421.

UYEMURA, D. G., KANTOR, G. C., PETIT, J.M., 1996. EVA for banks: value creation, risk management and profitability measurement. Journal of Applied Corporate Finance 9, 94-105.

VANDER VENNET, R., 1996. The effect of mergers and acquisitions on the efficiency and profitability of EC credit institutions. Journal of Banking and Finance 20, 1531-1558.

VANDER VENNET, R., 2003. Cross-border mergers in European banking and bank efficiency. In: Herrmann, H., Lipsey, R. (eds.), Foreign direct investment in the real and financial sector of industrial economies. Frankfurt, New York: Springer, 295-321.

VITTAS, D., 1991. Measuring commercial bank efficiency, financial policy and systems. Working Paper WPS 806. Washington: The World Bank.

WAHEED, A., MATHUR, I., 1995. Wealth effects of foreign expansion by US banks. Journal of Banking and Finance 19, 823-842.

WALL, L. D., GUP, B. E., 1989. Market valuation effects of bank acquisitions. In: Gup, B. (ed.): Bank mergers. Norwell: Kluwer Academic Publishers, 107-120.

WALTER, I., 1997. Universal banking: a shareholder value perspective. Financial Markets, Institutions and Instruments 6, 85-113.

WALTER, I., 2003. Financial integration across borders and across sectors: implications for regulatory structures. In: Kremers, J. J. M., Schoenmaker, D., Wierts, P. J. (eds.):Financial Supervision in Europe. Cheltenham: Edward Elgar.

WALTER, I., 2004. Mergers and acquisitions in banking and finance. What works, what fails, and why. Oxford et al.: Oxford University Press.

WANG, J. C., 1999. Do bank mergers in the 1990s create value? An event study. Working Paper, Ann Arbor: University of Michigan.

WEZEL, T., 2004. Foreign bank entry into emerging economies: an empirical assessment of the determinants and risks predicated on German FDI data. Deutsche Bundesbank Discussion Paper Series 1: Studies of the Economic Research Centre No. 01/2004. Frankfurt: Deutsche Bundesbank.

WILHELM, J., 1983. Marktwertmaximierung – Ein didaktisch einfacher Zugang zu einem Grundlagenproblem der Investitions- und Finanzierungstheorie. Zeitschrift für Betriebswirtschaft 53, 516-534.

WILHELM, J., 1985. Arbitrage theory – introductory lectures on arbitrage-based financial asset pricing. Berlin et al.: Springer.

WILLIAMS, B., 1997. Positive theories of multinational banking: eclectic theory versus internalization theory. Journal of Economic Surveys 11, 71-100.

WILLIAMS, B., 2002. The defensive expansion approach to multinational banking: evidence to date. Financial Markets, Institutions & Instruments 11, 127-203.

YAMORI, N., 1998. A note on the location choice of multinational banks: The case of Japanese financial institutions. Journal of Banking and Finance 22, 109-120.

YANNOPOLOUS, G. N., 1983. The growth of transnational banking, in: Casson, M. (ed.): The growth of international business. London: Allen and Unwin, 236-257.

YIN, R., CAMPBELL, D., 2003. Case study research: design and methods. Newbury Park: Sage Publications.

ZHANG, H., 1995. Wealth effects of US bank takeovers. Applied Financial Economics 55, 329-336.

Appendix

Figure A.1: Wealth Relatives and Mean Components in Adjusted Sample

This table shows the results for a long-term event study analyzing the mean component of the bidder/benchmark wealth relatives following the closure date of a cross-border bank merger. Wealth relatives are the ratio of bidder stock price and a regional (global) banking index as provided by Datastream and with the initial wealth level normalized to one, averaged across securities. Wealth relatives are adjusted for volatility following the procedure laid out by Jakobsen and Sørsensen (2001) leading to marginal parameter estimates of the average wealth-relative mean component. Values are given in percentages. The sample is adjusted for "noise" in the post-closure window by only including returns for bidders, that do not have other cross-border acquisitions in the selected period and acquire targets that are 10 percent of their own size or larger in terms of market value.

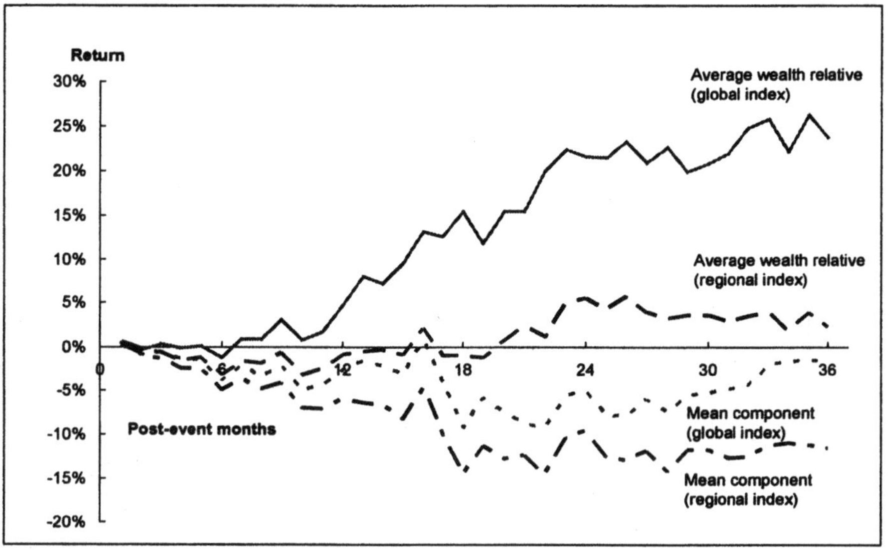

Source: Author

Table A.1: Summary Overview of Geographical Distribution of Cross-Border Bank M&A

		Continent of target																	
		Africa	Americas			Australasia			Europe										
Continent of bidder	Country/ Region	All	CDN	SA	US	JP	A	A/O	B	F	D	E	UK	NL	ROWE	ROEE	SCA	Sum	Sum Continent
Africa	All	0		0			0						0					0	0
Americas	CDN																	118	
	SA	0		165			51						273					2	489
	US																	369	
Australasia	JP																	39	
	A	0		38			19						42					2	99
	A/O																	58	
Europe	B																	67	
	F																	154	
	D																	182	
	E																	24	
	UK	0		326			95						844					306	1265
	NL																	143	
	ROWE																	300	
	ROEE																	4	
	SCA																	85	
	Sum	0	98	24	407	20	0	145	52	135	76	86	352	67	225	69	97	1853	
	Sum Continent	0		529			165						1159						

Source: Based on Berger et al. (2004)

Legend: A/O = Australia/Oceania, B = Belgium, CDN = Canada, D = Germany, E = Spain, F = France, JP = Japan, NL = Netherlands, ROA = Rest of Asia, ROEE = Rest of Eastern Europe, ROWE = Rest of Western Europe, SA = South America, SCA = Scandinavia, UK = United Kingdom, US = United States.

Table A.2: Geographical Distribution of Cross-Border Bank M&A in Amihud et al. (2002)

		Continent of target																	
		Africa	Americas			Australasia			Europe										
Continent of bidder	Country/ Region	All	CDN	SA	US	JP	A	A/O	B	F	D	E	UK	NL	ROWE	ROEE	SCA	Sum	Sum Continent
Africa	All																	1	1
Americas	CDN																	13	
	SA																	0	32
	US																	19	
Australasia	JP																	14	
	A																	13	44
	A/O																	17	
Europe	B																	6	
	F																	28	
	D																	26	
	E																	8	
	UK																	28	137
	NL																	18	
	ROWE																	17	
	ROEE																	0	
	SCA																	6	
	Sum	3	3	12	63	1	11	20	2	12	7	8	32	6	24	4	6	214	
	Sum Continent	3		78			32							101					

Source: Based on Amihud et al. (2002)

Legend: A/O = Australia/Oceania, B = Belgium, CDN = Canada, D = Germany, E = Spain, F = France, JP = Japan, NL = Netherlands, ROA = Rest of Asia, ROEE = Rest of Eastern Europe, ROWE = Rest of Western Europe, SA = South America, SCA = Scandinavia, UK = United Kingdom, US = United States.

Table A.3: Detailed Overview on Determinants of Wealth Effects in Comparison to Prior Studies

	Firm Specific Factors										Country-/Industry Specific Factors							
Study	Bidder size	Relative (target) size	Presence of existing clients in host	Relative (target) efficiency	Target efficiency	Physical distance between bidder and target	Social distance between bidder and target	Functional differences between bidder and target	Bidder M&A experience	Share of acquisition price paid in cash	Host market size	"Temperature" of equity market	Economic distance	General Economic openness of the host	Intensity of bank regulation in the host	Host country is US or UK	Bidder and target are from EU	Targets are located in Eastern Europe
Corporate Finance Literature																		
DD (1987)																		
TS (1987)		+ (b), 0 (t)																
D (1988)						- (b), 0 (t)												
HW (1989)						0 (j)												
HSw (1990)	0 (b)	- (t)		0 (b)[1]	0 (b)	- (b), 0 (t)												
AC (1991)																		
CD (1991)		0 (b)								0 (b)								
Ba (1992)		0 (b)				0 (b)				+ (b)								
CT (1992)						+ (b), - (t)												
WM (1992)			- (b)						0 (b)		0 (b)							
HS (1996)		0 (b, t)				0 (b, t)			0 (b, t)									
VV (1996)																		
A (1997)																		
B (1997)								0 (b, t)	0 (b, t)	0 (b), + (t)								
GM (1998)									- (b)		- (b)							
TT (1998)																		
P (1999)																		
TB (1999)	0 (b)					0 (b)												
CM (2000)						0 (b, t, j)		0 (b, t, j)										
SS (2000)																		
D (2001)		+ (j)			- (j)	0 (b, t, j)		- (j)		0 (j)								
A (2002)																		
BM (2002)						+ (b)												
C (2003)						- (b)		- (b)		+ (b)								
V (2003)		0 (j)		- (j)[2]	- (j)			0 (j)										
AI (2004)		+ (j)						- (j)										
Bei (2004)		0 (b, t, j)		- (b), 0 (t, j)[2]	+ (b), 0 (t), + (j)	0 (b, t, j)		0 (b, t, j)	0 (b, t), - (j)	0 (b, t, j)		- (b), 0 (t), 0 (j)						
Be (2004)																		
K (2004)	+ (b), 0 (t)	0 (b), - (t)					0 (b, t)			- (b), 0 (t)			0 (b, t)					
AP (2005)																		
CH (2005)		0 (b), + (t)				0 (b, t, j)		0 (b, t)										

Study	Firm Specific Factors										Country-/Industry Specific Factors							
	Bidder size	Relative (target) size	Presence of existing clients in host	Relative (target) efficiency	Target efficiency	Physical distance between bidder and target	Social distance between bidder and target	Functional differences between bidder and target	Bidder M&A experience	Share of acquisition price paid in cash	Host market size	"Temperature" of equity market	Economic distance	General Economic openness of the host	Intensity of bank regulation in the host	Host country is US or UK	Bidder and target are from EU	Targets are located in Eastern Europe
International Management Literature																		
GS (1980)																		
BT (1982)	0					0			+									
N (1986)			+								0			+				
S (1986)			+								+			0				
HM (1989)			+											0				
GJ (1990)			+								+			+				
B (1991)																		
GG (1991)			+			+	-											
Sa (1992)			+								0			+				
UV (1992)	+					-			+					0				
GGr (1994)			0								+			+				
BK (1996)			+								+							
FM (1996)			+			+/-	-											
MP (1998)			+								+			+				
Y (1998)			+								+							
Bu (2000)			+			0	0				+							
FP (2001)	+																	
BD (2003)						-	-				-			+			-	
G (2003)						-	-											
P (2003)	+		+						+		0							
T (2003)	+						-		0									
Be (2004)						-	-				+		-	+		+	-	+
BD (2004)						-	-				-			0	+		-	
BL (2004)	+					-	-		+		+			+	+		-	
W (2004)			+								0			+				+
B (2005)						-					+							
BD (2005)						-	-				0			+	+			
FP (2005)	+					-	0				+			-			+	
BS (2006)			+								+				+			
This Study	0 (b, t), - (j), + (ht)	- (b), 0 (t, j, ht)	0 (b), + (t), 0 (j, ht)	+ (b), 0 (t), (j), 0 (ht)	+ (b, t, j), 0 (ht)	0 (b, t, j), 0/- (ht)	- (b), + (t), - (j, ht)	0 (b), + (t), -/+ (j), 0/- (ht)	0 (b, t, j, ht)	+ (b), 0 (t, j, ht)	0 (b), + (t, j), 0 (ht)	- (b), + (t), - (j), 0 (ht)	0 (b), - (t), 0 (j, ht)	- (b), + (t), 0 (j, ht)	+ (b, t, j), 0 (ht)	0 (b), + (t, j), 0 (ht)	0 (b, t, j), - (ht)	+ (b), - (t), 0 (j, ht)

Legend (CF Literature): *DD* = *De and Duplichan (1987)*. *TS* = *Trifts and Scanlon (1987)*. *D* = *DeCossio (1988)*. *HW* = *Hannan and Wolken (1989)*. *HSw* = *Hawawini and Swary (1990)*. *AC* = *Allen and Cebenoyan (1991)*. *CD* = *Cornett and De (1991)*. *Ba* = *Baradwaj et al. (1992)*. *CT* = *Cornett and Tehranian (1992)*. *WM* = *Waheed and Mathur (1992)*. *HS* = *Hudgins and Seifert (1996)*. *V* = *Vander Vennet (1996)*. *A* = *Altunbas et al. (1997)*. *B (1997)* = *Biswas et al. (1997)*. *GM* = *Gleason and Mathur (1998)*. *TT* = *Toyne and Tripp (1998)*. *P* = *Peek et al. (1999)*. *TB* = *Tourani-Rad and van Beek (1999)*. *CM* = *Cybo-Ottone and Murgia (2000)*. *SS* = *Schiereck and Strauss (2000)*. *D* = *DeLong (2001)*. *A* = *Amihud et al. (2002)*. *BM* = *Bessler and Murtagh (2002)*. *C* = *Cornett et al. (2003)*. *V* = *Vander Vennet (2003)*. *AI* = *Altunbas and Ibañez (2004)*. *Bei* = *Beitel et al. (2004)*. *Bo* = *Bohl et al. (2004)*. *K* = *Kiymaz (2004)*. *AP* = *Ayadi and Pujals (2005)*. *CH* = *Campa and Hernando (2005)*.

Legend (IM Literature): *GS* = *Goldberg and Saunders (1980)*. *BT* = *Ball and Tschoegl (1982)*. *N* = *Nigh et al. (1986)*. *S* = *Sabi (1986)*. *HM* = *Hultmann and McGee (1989)*. *GJ* = *Goldberg and Johnson (1990)*. *B* = *Budzeika (1991)*. *GG* = *Grosse and Goldberg (1991)*. *Sa* = *Sagari (1992)*. *UV* = *Ursacki and Vertinsky (1992)*. *GGr* = *Goldberg and Grosse (1994)*. *BK* = *Brealy and Kaplanis (1996)*. *FM* = *Fisher and Molyneux (1996)*. *MP* = *Miller and Parkhe (1998)*. *Y* = *Yamori (1998)*. *Bu* = *Buch (2000)*. *FP* = *Focarelli and Pozzolo (2001)*. *BD* = *Buch and DeLong (2003)*. *G* = *Gallindo et al. (2003)*. *P* = *Piscitello (2003)*. *T* = *Tschoegl (2003)*. *Be* = *Berger et al. (2004)*. *BD* = *Buch and DeLong (2004)*. *BL* = *Buch and Lipponer (2004)*. *W* = *Wezel (2004)*. *B* = *Buch (2005)*. *BD* = *Buch and DeLong (2005)*. *FP* = *Focarelli and Pozzolo (2005)*. *BS* = *Ben Salem (2006)*.

1 + = positive impact, - = negative impact, 0 = no significant impact. b = bidder wealth, t = target wealth, j = net wealth of joint bidder-target entity (only applicable for event studies). lt = long-term wealth (only applicable to this study).
2 Only with regard to profit efficiency.
3 Only with regard to profit efficiency. No impact of cost efficiency.
4 With regard to regulatory transparency and power assigned to banking regulator.
5 Primarily with regard to cost efficiency. Profit efficiency indicators, however, mostly in line
6 With regard to cost efficiency. Target growth perspectives, however, negatively related to bidder wealth effects.
7 Negative effect on target wealth potentially driven by target leakage.

Table A.4: Detailed Overview of Identified Deals

Year	Bidder	Home	Target	Host	Year	Bidder	Home	Target	Host
1988	Royal Bank of Scotland	GB	Citizens Financial	USA	1999	Erste Bank	AUS	Ceska Sporitelna	CZ
1988	Bank of Ireland	IRL	First NH Banks	USA	1999	Banco Santander	E	Banco Totta e Acores	P
1988	Allied Irish Banks	IRL	First Maryland Bancorp.	USA	1999	Banco Santander	E	Credito Predial Portugues	P
1989	Royal Trustco.	CDN	Pacific First Financial Corp.	USA	2000	Nordea	S	Unidanmark	DK
1989	Bank of Yokohama	J	Guinness Mahon Holdings	GB	2000	Royal Bank of Canada	CDN	Prism Financial	USA
1989	Dresdner Bank	D	BIP	F	2000	Dexia	B	FSAH	USA
1989	Deutsche Bank	D	Morgan Grenfell Group	GB	2000	HSBC	GB	Credit Commercial de France	F
1990	Svenska Handelsbanken	S	Oslo Handelsbank	N	2000	Citigroup	USA	Bank Handlowy	PL
1992	Bank of Scotland	GB	Countrywide Banking Corp.	NZ	2000	Unicredito Italiano	I	Pioneer Group	USA
1993	ABN AMRO	NL	Cragin Financial Corp.	USA	2000	Fortis	B	SADE	F
1994	Bank of Montreal	CDN	Suburban Bancorp.	USA	2000	Bipop-Carire	I	Entrium Direct Bankers	D
1994	National Westminster Bank	GB	Central Jersey Bancorp.	USA	2000	UBS	CHF	PaineWebber Group	USA
1995	Commerzbank	D	Jupiter Tyndall Group	GB	2000	HVB	D	Bank Austria	A
1995	Schweizerischer Bankverein	CH	SG Warburg	GB	2000	Royal Bank of Canada	CDN	Dain Rauscher Corp.	USA
1995	Generale de Banque	B	Credit Lyonnais Bank NL	NL	2000	Banco Santander	E	Banco Caracas	YV
1995	Dresdner Bank	D	Kleinwort Benson Group	GB	2000	Deutsche Bank	D	National Discount Brokers	USA
1995	Shinan Bank	K	Marine National Bank	USA	2001	Societe Generale	F	SKB Banka	SLO
1996	LG Merchant Bank	K	Petrobank	PL	2001	Royal Bank of Canada	CDN	Centura Bank	USA
1996	Westpac Banking Corp.	AUS	Trust Bank New Zealand	NZ	2001	DBS	SGP	Dao Heng Bank Group	HKG
1996	BanPonce	PUR	Combancorp.	USA	2001	Svenska Handelsbanken	S	Midtbank	DK
1996	Banco de Santander	E	InverMexico	MEX	2001	Commerzbank	D	Bank Czestochowa	PL
1996	ABN AMRO	NL	Standard Fed Bancorp.	USA	2001	BNP Paribas	F	BancWest Corp.	USÁ
1997	Allied Irish Banks	IRL	Dauphin Deposit Corp.	USA	2001	Citigroup	USA	Banacci	MEX
1997	Den Danske Bank	DK	Ostgota Enskilda Banken	S	2001	Dexia	B	Kempen & Co.	NL
1997	Societe Generale	F	Asia Credit	T	2001	Intesa	I	Vseobcna Uvervo Banka	SK
1997	Nordbanken	S	Merita Oy	SF	2001	Societe Generale	F	Komercni Banka	CZ
1997	National Australia Bank	AUS	HomeSide	USA	2001	BNP Paribas	F	Finansbank	TR
1997	ING	NL	Banque Bruxelles Lambert	B	2001	Societe Generale	F	La Marocaine-Vie.	MA
1997	Generale de Banque	B	BGL	L	2001	HSBC	GB	DemirBank	TR
1998	Banco Bilbao Vizcaya	E	PonceBank	PUR	2001	Royal Bank of Canada	CDN	Tucker Anthony Sutro	USA
1998	ABN AMRO	NL	Bank of Asia	T	2001	KBC Bancassurance	B	Kredyt Bank PBI	PL
1998	Investec	ZA	Hambros	UK	2002	Nordea	S	LG Petrobank	PL
1998	Banco Bilbao Vizcaya	E	BHF	RCH	2002	HSBC	GB	Grupo Financiero Bital	MEX
1998	Dexia	B	BIMP	F	2002	CAH	MAL	Bank Niaga	RI
1998	Den Danske Bank	DK	Fokus Bank	N	2002	HSBC	GB	Household International	USA
1998	Deutsche Bank	D	Bankers Trust New York	USA	2003	Fubon Financial Holding	RC	International Bank of Asia	HKG
1999	Royal Bank of Scotland	GB	UST Corp.	USA	2003	Royal Bank of Scotland	GB	First Active	IRL
1999	Fortis	B	PPA Bank	PL	2003	HSBC	GB	Bank of Bermuda	BER
1999	Svenska Handelsbanken	S	Bergensbanken	N	2004	Societe Generale	F	General Hellenic Bank	GR
1999	HSBC	GB	Republic New York Corp.	USA	2004	Citigroup	USA	Koram Bank	K
1999	HSBC	GB	Safra Republic Holding	L	2004	Popular	PUR	Quaker City Bancorp	USA
1999	Banco Santander	E	Banco Santiago	RCH	2004	Royal Bank of Scotland	GB	Charter One Financial	USA
1999	Unicredito Italiano	I	Bank Pekao	PL	2004	UOB	SGP	Bank of Asia	T
1999	Bank of Nova Scotia	CDN	Banco Sud Americano	RCH	2004	Banco Santander	E	Abbey National	GB
1999	ING	NL	BHF Bank	D	2004	Toronto-Dominion Bank	CDN	Banknorth Group	USA
1999	Dexia	B	Dexia France	F	2004	Barclays	GB	ABSA Group	ZA
1999	Nordea	S	Christiana Bank	N	2005	Unicredito Italiano	I	HVB	D
1999	Deutsche Bank	D	BWR	PL	2005	Popular	PUR	E-Loan	USA

Legend: A = Austria, AUS = Australia, B = Belgium, BER = Bermuda, CDN = Canada, CH = Switzerland, CZ = Czech Republic, D = Germany, DK = Denmark, E = Spain, F = France, GB = United Kingdom, GR = Greece, HKG = Hong Kong, I = Italy, IRL = Ireland, J = Japan, K = South Korea, L = Luxembourg, MA = Morocco, MAL = Malaysia, MEX = Mexico, N = Norway, NL = Netherlands, NZ = New Zealand, P = Portugal, PL = Poland, PUR = Puerto Rico, RC = Taiwan, RCH = Chile, RI = Indonesia, S = Sweden, SF = Finland, SGP = Singapore, SK = Slovak Republic, SLO = Slovenia, T= Thailand, TR = Turkey, USA = United States, YV = Venezuela, ZA = South Africa.

Table A.5: Correlation Matrix of Determinants

	BSIZE	RELSIZE	CLIENT	RELCOEF	RELPREF	MBR	TCOEF	TPREF	MBT	DISTANCE	LANGUAGE	LAW	CULTURE	CORREL
BSIZE	1.00	-0.07	0.30	-0.26	-0.30	-0.23	-0.14	-0.04	0.05	-0.02	-0.09	-0.30	0.17	0.08
RELSIZE	-0.07	1.00	0.12	0.06	0.34	0.01	0.09	0.26	0.12	-0.09	0.05	0.04	-0.07	0.30
CLIENT	0.30	0.12	1.00	0.03	0.06	0.22	0.08	0.17	0.43	0.08	0.54	0.23	-0.42	0.36
RELCOEF	-0.26	0.06	0.03	1.00	0.05	0.14	0.92	-0.10	0.24	-0.08	-0.08	-0.04	-0.03	0.05
RELPREF	-0.30	0.34	0.06	0.05	1.00	0.17	0.01	0.06	0.16	0.18	0.26	0.28	-0.13	0.00
MBR	-0.23	0.01	0.22	0.14	0.17	1.00	0.05	0.16	0.56	-0.05	0.18	0.11	-0.14	0.23
TCOEF	-0.14	0.09	0.08	0.92	0.01	0.05	1.00	-0.18	0.21	-0.10	0.00	-0.12	-0.05	0.14
TPREF	-0.04	0.26	0.17	-0.10	0.06	0.16	-0.18	1.00	0.35	0.11	0.30	0.35	-0.11	0.02
MBT	0.05	0.12	0.43	0.24	0.16	0.56	0.21	0.35	1.00	-0.02	0.24	0.14	-0.12	0.28
DISTANCE	-0.02	-0.09	0.08	-0.08	0.18	-0.05	-0.10	0.11	-0.02	1.00	0.11	-0.06	0.00	-0.23
LANGUAGE	-0.09	0.05	0.54	-0.08	0.26	0.18	0.00	0.30	0.24	0.11	1.00	0.67	-0.36	0.08
LAW	-0.30	0.04	0.23	-0.04	0.28	0.11	-0.12	0.35	0.14	-0.06	0.67	1.00	-0.50	0.00
CULTURE	0.17	-0.07	-0.42	-0.03	-0.13	-0.14	-0.05	-0.11	-0.12	0.00	-0.36	-0.50	1.00	-0.04
CORREL	0.08	0.30	0.36	0.05	0.00	0.23	0.14	0.02	0.28	-0.23	0.08	0.00	-0.04	1.00
NONBANK	-0.13	-0.11	0.22	0.22	0.24	-0.08	0.15	0.23	0.06	0.00	0.09	0.05	-0.10	-0.02
BANKFOC	-0.10	0.14	-0.27	0.11	0.13	-0.04	0.02	0.10	0.00	-0.16	-0.15	0.06	-0.01	-0.08
PREBID	0.51	-0.09	0.07	-0.11	-0.18	-0.18	-0.05	-0.09	0.09	-0.05	-0.09	-0.03	0.09	0.06
CASH	0.00	-0.36	-0.22	-0.04	0.00	-0.01	-0.07	0.07	-0.08	0.12	-0.11	-0.13	0.15	-0.40
EFFIC	0.13	-0.02	0.12	-0.18	0.01	-0.04	-0.23	0.02	0.02	0.04	0.07	0.09	-0.03	-0.05
MARKET	-0.17	0.11	-0.08	0.16	-0.21	-0.13	0.17	-0.20	-0.06	-0.04	0.05	0.12	0.07	0.00
ASSET	-0.02	-0.02	0.23	-0.02	0.25	0.23	-0.04	0.19	0.14	0.06	-0.06	-0.17	0.04	0.08
INET	0.27	0.04	0.12	-0.08	-0.05	-0.11	-0.14	0.08	0.17	0.09	-0.09	-0.12	0.28	0.08
TELCO	0.33	0.16	0.14	-0.38	-0.12	-0.18	-0.35	0.08	0.12	-0.20	-0.15	-0.15	0.10	0.11
MSIZE	-0.03	0.24	0.71	-0.30	0.07	0.13	-0.28	0.14	0.13	-0.18	0.21	0.15	-0.34	0.23
HOTY	0.31	-0.05	0.03	-0.15	-0.17	-0.26	-0.11	-0.05	-0.04	-0.17	-0.21	-0.10	-0.09	0.11
ECSIM	-0.06	0.20	0.39	-0.09	0.19	0.07	-0.10	0.15	0.07	-0.39	0.14	0.29	-0.40	0.22
FREEDOM	0.10	-0.15	-0.52	0.31	-0.06	-0.07	0.27	-0.09	-0.10	0.07	-0.29	-0.03	0.12	-0.04
POWER	-0.15	-0.18	0.26	-0.09	0.02	0.06	0.03	-0.09	0.07	0.25	0.18	-0.15	-0.03	-0.06
MONITOR	-0.20	0.11	0.46	-0.06	0.04	0.15	-0.01	0.08	0.06	0.09	0.09	0.04	-0.22	0.19
HOSTCA	-0.15	-0.03	0.09	-0.10	0.07	0.18	0.01	0.06	0.09	0.31	0.25	-0.06	-0.18	0.05
EU	0.13	0.22	-0.02	0.03	0.09	0.17	0.00	0.08	0.03	-0.45	-0.14	0.09	-0.07	0.19
EAST	-0.01	-0.19	-0.49	-0.07	-0.27	-0.10	-0.01	-0.37	-0.14	-0.30	-0.26	-0.33	0.02	-0.11

	NONBANK	BANKFOC	PREBID	CASH	EFFIC	MARKET	ASSET	INET	TELCO
BSIZE	-0.13	-0.10	0.51	0.00	0.13	-0.17	-0.02	0.27	0.33
RELSIZE	-0.11	0.14	-0.09	-0.36	-0.02	0.11	-0.02	0.04	0.16
CLIENT	0.22	-0.27	0.07	-0.22	0.12	-0.08	0.23	0.12	0.14
RELCOEF	0.22	0.11	-0.11	-0.04	-0.18	0.16	-0.02	-0.08	-0.38
RELPREF	0.24	0.13	-0.18	0.00	0.01	-0.21	0.25	-0.05	-0.12
MBR	-0.08	-0.04	-0.18	-0.01	-0.04	-0.13	0.23	-0.11	-0.18
TCOEF	0.15	0.02	-0.05	-0.07	-0.23	0.17	-0.04	-0.14	-0.35
TPREF	0.23	0.10	-0.09	0.07	0.02	-0.20	0.19	0.08	0.08
MBT	0.06	0.00	0.09	-0.08	0.02	-0.06	0.14	0.17	0.12
DISTANCE	0.00	-0.16	-0.05	0.12	0.04	-0.04	0.06	0.09	-0.20
LANGUAGE	0.09	-0.15	-0.09	-0.11	0.07	0.05	-0.06	-0.09	-0.15
LAW	0.05	0.06	-0.03	-0.13	0.09	0.12	-0.17	-0.12	-0.15
CULTURE	-0.10	-0.01	0.09	0.15	-0.03	0.07	0.04	0.28	0.10
CORREL	-0.02	-0.08	0.06	-0.40	-0.05	0.00	0.08	0.08	0.11
NONBANK	1.00	-0.41	0.05	0.09	-0.12	-0.24	0.44	-0.02	0.00
BANKFOC	-0.41	1.00	-0.32	-0.01	0.16	0.17	-0.45	-0.04	-0.08
PREBID	0.05	-0.32	1.00	0.03	0.07	-0.12	-0.01	0.15	0.19
CASH	0.09	-0.01	0.03	1.00	-0.11	-0.19	0.13	-0.01	-0.05
EFFIC	-0.12	0.16	0.07	-0.11	1.00	-0.24	-0.06	0.13	0.10
MARKET	-0.24	0.17	-0.12	-0.19	-0.24	1.00	-0.43	0.07	-0.13
ASSET	0.44	-0.45	-0.01	0.13	-0.06	-0.43	1.00	-0.10	0.22
INET	-0.02	-0.04	0.15	-0.01	0.13	0.07	-0.10	1.00	0.41
TELCO	0.00	-0.08	0.19	-0.05	0.10	-0.13	0.22	0.41	1.00
MSIZE	0.12	-0.13	0.03	-0.24	0.11	-0.11	0.17	-0.04	0.20
HOTY	0.06	-0.08	0.26	-0.02	0.18	-0.18	-0.03	0.03	0.33
ECSIM	0.07	-0.01	-0.02	-0.35	-0.01	0.05	0.12	-0.21	0.09
FREEDOM	-0.16	0.20	0.10	0.04	-0.09	0.07	-0.24	0.08	-0.14
POWER	0.14	-0.30	-0.04	0.19	0.00	0.08	0.00	-0.07	-0.09
MONITOR	0.09	-0.26	-0.12	-0.10	-0.07	-0.18	0.27	0.00	-0.04
HOSTCA	0.20	-0.49	-0.11	-0.04	-0.03	-0.11	0.30	-0.13	-0.01
EU	-0.03	0.17	0.10	-0.33	-0.11	-0.05	0.10	-0.12	0.10
EAST	-0.06	0.05	0.00	0.16	0.01	0.00	-0.19	-0.09	-0.06

	MSIZE	HOTY	ECSIM	FREEDOM	POWER	MONITOR	HOSTCA	EU	EAST
BSIZE	-0.03	0.31	-0.06	0.10	-0.15	-0.20	-0.15	0.13	-0.01
RELSIZE	0.24	-0.05	0.20	-0.15	-0.18	0.11	-0.03	0.22	-0.19
CLIENT	0.71	0.03	0.39	-0.52	0.26	0.46	0.09	-0.02	-0.49
RELCOEF	-0.30	-0.15	-0.09	0.31	-0.09	-0.06	-0.10	0.03	-0.07
RELPREF	0.07	-0.17	0.19	-0.06	0.02	0.04	0.07	0.09	-0.27
MBR	0.13	-0.26	0.07	-0.07	0.06	0.15	0.18	0.17	-0.10
TCOEF	-0.28	-0.11	-0.10	0.27	0.03	-0.01	0.01	0.00	-0.01
TPREF	0.14	-0.05	0.15	-0.09	-0.09	0.08	0.06	0.08	-0.37
MBT	0.13	-0.04	0.07	-0.10	0.07	0.06	0.09	0.03	-0.14
DISTANCE	-0.18	-0.17	-0.39	0.07	0.25	0.09	0.31	-0.45	-0.30
LANGUAGE	0.21	-0.21	0.14	-0.29	0.18	0.09	0.25	-0.14	-0.26
LAW	0.15	-0.10	0.29	-0.03	-0.15	0.04	-0.06	0.09	-0.33
CULTURE	-0.34	-0.09	-0.40	0.12	-0.03	-0.22	-0.18	-0.07	0.02
CORREL	0.23	0.11	0.22	-0.04	-0.06	0.19	0.05	0.19	-0.11
NONBANK	0.12	0.06	0.07	-0.16	0.14	0.09	0.20	-0.03	-0.06
BANKFOC	-0.13	-0.08	-0.01	0.20	-0.30	-0.26	-0.49	0.17	0.05
PREBID	0.03	0.26	-0.02	0.10	-0.04	-0.12	-0.11	0.10	0.00
CASH	-0.24	-0.02	-0.35	0.04	0.19	-0.10	-0.04	-0.33	0.16
EFFIC	0.11	0.18	-0.01	-0.09	0.00	-0.07	-0.03	-0.11	0.01
MARKET	-0.11	-0.18	0.05	0.07	0.08	-0.18	-0.11	-0.05	0.00
ASSET	0.17	-0.03	0.12	-0.24	0.00	0.27	0.30	0.10	-0.19
INET	-0.04	0.03	-0.21	0.08	-0.07	0.00	-0.13	-0.12	-0.09
TELCO	0.20	0.33	0.09	-0.14	-0.09	-0.04	-0.01	0.10	-0.06
MSIZE	1.00	-0.03	0.56	-0.58	0.16	0.51	0.52	0.20	-0.32
HOTY	-0.03	1.00	-0.01	0.18	-0.03	-0.27	-0.22	0.02	0.27
ECSIM	0.56	-0.01	1.00	-0.29	-0.21	0.41	0.12	0.55	-0.23
FREEDOM	-0.58	0.18	-0.29	1.00	-0.28	-0.30	-0.52	0.04	0.12
POWER	0.16	-0.03	-0.21	-0.28	1.00	0.11	0.59	-0.57	0.13
MONITOR	0.51	-0.27	0.41	-0.30	0.11	1.00	0.62	0.09	-0.36
HOSTCA	0.52	-0.22	0.12	-0.52	0.59	0.62	1.00	-0.28	-0.28
EU	0.20	0.02	0.55	0.04	-0.57	0.09	-0.28	1.00	-0.22
EAST	-0.32	0.27	-0.23	0.12	0.13	-0.36	-0.28	-0.22	1.00

Table A.6: Dichotomization Analysis Results for Bidders in Leakage Adjusted Sample

The table shows the results of a dichotomization analysis of bidder abnormal returns in 96 cross-border bank mergers between 1985 and 2005. The top 30 transactions with regard to the variable analyzed are compared to the bottom 30 transactions using mean difference tests except for the dummy variables LAW, NONBANK, PREBID, EFFIC, MARKET, ASSET, HOTY, HOSTCA, EU and East, where all transactions marked "1" are compared with those marked "0". The success of a transaction is measured by the cumulated abnormal return from an event study using an OLS-market model. The sample only includes deals, were bidder-specific leakage did not occur more than 20 days before the event date.

	Results for Top-Cases				Results for Bottom-Cases				
Variable	N	Average	Std. Dev.	CAR in [-1,1] (%)	N	Average	Std.Dev.	CAR in [-1,1] (%)	Difference Top-Bottom (%)
BSIZE	20	13.31	0.32	-2.43***	20	10.57	1.07	-1.73***	-0.70
RELSIZE	20	0.87	0.08	-1.89***	20	0.52	0.14	-0.51	-1.38
CLIENT	20	11.11	0.92	-1.05	20	7.46	1.49	-1.00	-0.05
RELCOEF	20	1.21	0.18	-0.98**	20	0.80	0.14	-0.45	-0.54
RELPREF	20	1.69	0.84	-0.46	20	0.16	1.80	-1.90***	1.43*
MBR	20	1.56	0.49	-0.17	20	0.40	0.13	-1.45*	1.28
TCOEF	20	0.72	0.09	-1.51**	20	0.49	0.09	-0.36	-1.15
TPREF	20	0.21	0.09	-1.45	20	0.04	0.21	-1.43*	-0.03
MBT	20	2.09	0.31	-1.06	20	0.73	0.21	-0.46	-0.60
DISTANCE	20	2.18	0.32	0.22**	20	-1.21	1.00	-1.14*	1.36
LANGUAGE	22	1.00	0.00	-1.15**	43	0.00	0.00	-1.10	-0.05
LAW	37	1.00	0.00	-1.17***	28	0.00	0.00	-1.05	-0.13
CULTURE	20	15.81	2.86	-0.46	20	3.58	1.14	-0.81	0.35
CORREL	20	0.31	0.14	-1.87***	20	-0.02	0.06	-0.32	-1.55
NONBANK	18	1.00	0.00	0.20	47	0.00	0.00	-1.62***	1.82**
BANKFOCUS	20	0.83	0.10	-0.52	20	0.38	0.21	-2.32***	1.80**
PREBID	31	1.00	0.00	-1.19**	34	0.00	0.00	-1.06	-0.13
CASH	20	1.00	0.00	-0.36	20	0.57	0.46	-1.69**	1.33
EFFIC	30	1.00	0.00	-0.90	35	0.00	0.00	-1.30**	0.40
MARKET	31	1.00	0.00	-1.93	34	0.00	0.00	-0.38	-1.54**
ASSET	28	1.00	0.00	-0.70	37	0.00	0.00	-1.43**	0.73
INET	20	0.09	0.08	-2.02***	20	0.01	0.00	-0.20	-1.82***
TELCO	20	5.30	0.24	-1.57*	20	4.47	0.25	-2.02***	0.45
MSIZE	20	10.49	0.10	-0.97	20	9.26	0.03	-0.71	-0.26
HOTY	30	1.00	0.00	-2.24***	35	0.00	0.00	-0.16	-2.08**

Table A.6: Dichotomization Analysis Results for Bidders in Leakage Adjusted Sample (continued)

	Results for Top-Cases				Results for Bottom-Cases				
Variable	**N**	**Average**	**Std. Dev.**	**CAR in [-1,1] (%)**	**N**	**Average**	**Std.Dev.**	**CAR in [-1,1] (%)**	**Difference Top-Bottom (%)**
ECSIM	20	0.92	0.05	-2.16***	20	0.38	0.11	-1.61**	-0.54
FREEDOM	20	2.73	0.26	-0.72	20	1.53	0.30	-1.93***	1.21
POWER	20	1.14	0.00	-0.55	20	-0.91	0.83	-1.93***	1.39
MONITOR	20	1.17	0.25	-0.21	20	0.18	0.32	-1.84***	1.63*
HOSTCA	28	1.00	0.00	-0.58	37	0.00	0.00	-1.53***	0.95
EU	18	1.00	0.00	-1.83**	47	0.00	0.00	-0.84	-0.99
EAST	5	1.00	0.00	-1.05	60	0.00	0.00	-1.12**	0.07

Table A.7: Dichotomization Analysis Results for Targets in Leakage Adjusted Sample

The table shows the results of a dichotomization analysis of target abnormal returns in 96 cross-border bank mergers between 1985 and 2005. The top 30 transactions with regard to the variable analyzed are compared to the bottom 30 transactions using mean difference tests except for the dummy variables LAW, NONBANK, PREBID, EFFIC, MARKET, ASSET, HOTY, HOSTCA, EU and East, where all transactions marked "1" are compared with those marked "0". The success of a transaction is measured by the cumulated abnormal return from an event study using an OLS-market model. The sample only includes deals, were target-specific leakage did not occur more than 20 days before the event date.

	Results for Top-Cases				Results for Bottom-Cases				
Variable	N	Average	Std. Dev.	CAR in [-1,1] (%)	N	Average	Std. Dev.	CAR in [-1,1] (%)	Difference Top-Bottom (%)
BSIZE	15	13.33	0.21	33.17***	15	10.16	0.96	23.36***	9.81
RELSIZE	15	0.90	0.07	20.59***	15	0.47	0.24	30.64***	-10.05
CLIENT	15	11.40	0.60	29.43***	15	7.50	1.52	20.27***	9.15
RELCOEF	15	1.24	0.27	26.41***	15	0.76	0.14	18.03***	8.37
RELPREF	15	1.76	0.94	19.44***	15	0.50	0.47	25.36***	-5.92
MBR	15	1.60	0.50	17.85***	15	0.39	0.15	37.52***	-19.67*
TCOEF	15	0.74	0.14	12.02***	15	0.46	0.08	24.40***	-12.38*
TPREF	15	0.22	0.10	23.71***	15	0.08	0.07	25.09***	-1.39
MBT	15	2.07	0.28	17.46***	15	0.74	0.18	31.85***	-14.39*
DISTANCE	15	2.19	0.35	17.45***	15	-1.31	1.13	32.78***	-15.33
LANGUAGE	21	1.00	0.00	17.59***	32	0.00	0.00	26.89***	-9.30
LAW	33	1.00	0.00	22.70***	20	0.00	0.00	24.05***	-1.34
CULTURE	15	16.93	2.49	22.58***	15	3.26	1.09	17.17***	5.41
CORREL	15	0.31	0.13	17.48***	15	-0.03	0.07	34.61***	-17.13
NONBANK	16	1.00	0.00	26.07***	37	0.00	0.00	21.97***	4.10
BANKFOCUS	15	0.84	0.29	28.86***	15	0.38	0.23	18.39***	10.47
PREBID	23	1.00	0.00	25.83***	30	0.00	0.00	21.20***	4.63
CASH	15	1.00	0.00	32.78***	15	0.41	0.47	18.48***	14.30
EFFIC	26	1.00	0.00	27.12***	27	0.00	0.00	19.44***	7.68
MARKET	26	1.00	0.00	22.13***	27	0.00	0.00	24.25***	-2.12
ASSET	20	1.00	0.00	23.38***	33	0.00	0.00	23.11***	0.27
INET	15	0.09	0.08	30.60***	15	0.01	0.01	14.28***	16.32*
TELCO	15	5.32	0.23	34.34***	15	4.45	0.25	21.72***	12.62
MSIZE	15	10.52	0.09	29.59***	15	9.24	0.44	5.59***	24.00***
HOTY	25	1.00	0.00	28.04***	28	0.00	0.00	18.89***	9.15
ECSIM	15	0.91	0.05	29.64***	15	0.37	0.10	17.36***	12.28

Table A.7: Dichotomization Analysis Results for Targets in Leakage Adjusted Sample (continued)

	Results for Top-Cases				Results for Bottom-Cases				
Variable	N	Average	Std. Dev.	CAR in [-1,1] (%)	N	Average	Std. Dev.	CAR in [-1,1] (%)	Difference Top-Bottom (%)
FREEDOM	15	2.67	0.24	11.81***	15	1.57	0.37	34.61***	-22.80**
POWER	15	1.14	0.00	27.93***	15	-1.07	0.83	25.44***	2.49
MONITOR	15	1.07	0.20	21.94***	15	0.19	0.33	21.55***	0.39
HOSTCA	24	1.00	0.00	28.12***	29	0.00	0.00	19.15***	8.97
EU	13	1.00	0.00	30.20***	40	0.00	0.00	20.94***	9.26
EAST	2	1.00	0.00	2.48	51	0.00	0.00	24.02***	-21.54

Table A.8: Dichotomization Analysis Results for Joint Entities in Leakage adjusted Sample

The table shows the results of a dichotomization analysis of joint abnormal returns in 96 cross-border bank mergers between 1985 and 2005. The top 30 transactions with regard to the variable analyzed are compared to the bottom 30 transactions using mean difference tests except for the dummy variables LAW, NONBANK, PREBID, EFFIC, MARKET, ASSET, HOTY, HOSTCA, EU and East, where all transactions marked "1" are compared with those marked "0". The success of a transaction is measured by the cumulated abnormal return from an event study using an OLS-market model. The sample only includes deals, were joint leakage did not occur more than 20 days before the event date

	Results for Top-Cases				Results for Bottom-Cases				
Variable	N	Average	Std. Dev.	CAR in [-1,1] (%)	N	Average	Std. Dev.	CAR in [-1,1] (%)	Difference Top-Bottom (%)
BSIZE	15	13.28	0.37	-0.42	15	10.47	1.12	0.48	-0.90
RELSIZE	15	0.87	0.08	-0.20	15	0.55	0.14	1.00***	-1.20
CLIENT	15	11.25	0.81	0.14**	15	7.50	1.52	0.59	0.59
RELCOEF	15	1.17	0.18	-0.35	15	0.76	0.14	1.84***	-2.19**
RELPREF	15	1.76	0.94	1.54**	15	0.61	0.34	-0.42	1.96**
MBR	15	1.56	0.52	1.47***	15	0.43	0.13	-0.22	1.69*
TCOEF	15	0.69	0.09	-1.29	15	0.46	0.08	1.98***	-3.27***
TPREF	15	0.21	0.10	0.59	15	0.09	0.05	-0.14	0.27
MBT	15	2.02	0.28	0.44	15	0.81	0.20	0.59**	-0.15
DISTANCE	15	2.18	0.36	1.37***	15	-1.25	1.12	0.72*	0.66
LANGUAGE	17	1.00	0.00	0.62**	28	0.00	0.00	0.22**	0.41
LAW	29	1.00	0.00	0.72*	16	0.00	0.00	-0.24*	0.96
CULTURE	15	15.97	2.81	0.84**	15	3.56	1.25	0.59**	0.25
CORREL	15	0.29	0.14	0.23*	15	-0.01	0.07	0.50**	-0.27
NONBANK	14	1.00	0.00	0.76**	31	0.00	0.00	0.19**	0.57
BANKFOCUS	13	0.85	0.06	0.79*	15	0.40	0.25	-0.55	1.34
PREBID	22	1.00	0.00	0.14*	23	0.00	0.00	0.57**	-0.43
CASH	15	1.00	0.00	1.46	15	0.60	0.48	-0.73*	2.19*
EFFIC	25	1.00	0.00	0.75**	20	0.00	0.00	-0.09	0.85
MARKET	21	1.00	0.00	0.38*	24	0.00	0.00	0.35*	0.03
ASSET	19	1.00	0.00	-0.03	26	0.00	0.00	0.65**	-0.68
INET	15	0.09	0.08	-0.03	15	0.01	0.01	-0.47	0.44
TELCO	15	5.27	0.22	0.19	15	4.54	0.23	-0.45*	0.65
MSIZE	15	10.91	0.10	0.52*	15	9.31	0.48	0.22	0.30
HOTY	24	1.00	0.00	-0.85*	21	0.00	0.00	1.69**	-2.54**
ECSIM	15	0.90	0.05	-0.96	15	0.38	0.12	0.06	-1.01

	Results for Top-Cases				Results for Bottom-Cases				
Variable	**N**	**Average**	**Std. Dev.**	**CAR in [-1,1] (%)**	**N**	**Average**	**Std. Dev.**	**CAR in [-1,1] (%)**	**Difference Top-Bottom (%)**
FREEDOM	15	2.67	0.24	0.31	15	1.60	0.39	-0.48	0.79
POWER	15	1.14	0.00	0.90**	15	-1.07	0.83	-0.87*	1.77
MONITOR	16	1.03	0.16	0.09	15	0.19	0.33	-0.75*	0.84
HOSTCA	18	1.00	0.00	1.12**	28	0.00	0.00	-0.12	1.24
EU	12	1.00	0.00	-0.55	33	0.00	0.00	0.69*	-1.24
ÉAST	2	1.00	0.00	1.40	44	0.00	0.00	0.32	1.08

Table A.9: Single-Variable Regression Results for Bidders

Determinant	N	R^2 (%)	Constant	Coefficient
BSIZE	95	0.52	-0.035139 (-0.75)	0.002015 (0.53)
RELSIZE	95	3.16	0.019324 (1.25)	-0.041948 (-1.96*)
CLIENT	62	0.37	0.011142 (0.61)	-0.002374 (-1.17)
RELCOEF	63	9.82	0.010367 (1.50)	-0.020228 (-5.17***)
RELPREF	66	0.72	-0.013864 (-3.69***)	0.001708 (0.79)
MBR	86	0.01	-0.009084 (-1.34)	-0.00069 (-0.10)
TCOEF	65	8.10	0.016624 (1.59)	-0.045884 (-3.67)
TPREF	68	0.22	-0.014621 (-3.33***)	0.009888 (0.45)
MBT	89	2.30	0.001396 (0.18)	-0.008055 (1.46)
DISTANCE	96	0.00	-0.010719 (3.09***)	0.00000776 (0.00)
LANGUAGE	96	0.83	-2.952865 (0.00)	0.006492 (0.91)
LAW	96	0.02	-0.011257 (-2.04**)	0.000999 (0.14)
CULTURE	96	0.54	-0.018025 (22.63**)	0.00075 (1.35)
CORREL	96	0.65	-0.008336 (-1.81*)	-0.017932 (-0.84)
NONBANK	96	1.64	-0.013213 (-3.60***)	0.009989 (1.10)
BANKFOCUS	63	0.00	-0.013640 (-1.16)	-0.000691 (-0.04)
PREBID	96	0.00	-0.010542 (-2.09**)	-0.00038 (-0.06)
CASH	96	6.90	-0.033181 (-3.13***)	0.02649 (2.35**)
EFFIC	96	0.00	-0.010905 (-2.30**)	0.000432 (0.06)
MARKET	96	2.03	-0.005490 (-1.01)	-0.009648 (-1.38)
ASSET	96	0.22	-0.011862 (-3.00***)	0.003333 (0.43)
INET	87	0.01	-0.009440 (-2.22**)	-0.030269 (-0.69)
TELCO	92	0.00	-0.015869 (-0.29)	0.000905 (0.08)
MSIZE	96	0.41	0.027308 (0.43)	-0.003845 (-0.59)
HOTY	96	6.19	-0.003154 (-0.80)	-0.016883 (-2.42**)
ECSIM	96	0.00	-0.010612 (-1.21)	-0.000152 (-0.11)
FREEDOM	91	0.94	-0.024733 (-1.65)	0.005873 (0.84)
POWER	87	0.40	-0.012262 (-3.13***)	0.002256 (0.54)
MONITOR	87	0.12	-0.012806 (-2.75***)	0.002086 (0.38)
HOSTCA	96	0.20	-0.011887 (-2.73***)	0.003123 (0.43)
EU	66	0.93	-0.008738 (-2.17**)	-0.007305 (-0.92)
EAST	96	0.01	-0.011641 (-3.09***)	0.008069 (0.88)

* Significant at the 10 percent level.
** Significant at the 5 percent level.
*** Significant at the 1 percent level.

Table A.10: Single-Variable Regression Results for Targets

Determinant	N	R^2 (%)	Constant	Coefficient
BSIZE	95	0.20	0.047515 (0.16)	0.009228 (0.38)
RELSIZE	95	0.03	0.141999 (1.39)	0.024266 (0.18)
CLIENT	62	9.82	-0.209061 (-2.34***)	0.040533 (3.98***)
RELCOEF	63	0.01	0.152917 (2.90***)	0.004650 (0.08)
RELPREF	66	0.27	0.144449 (4.05***)	0.008630 (0.85)
MBR	86	0.73	0.201885 (3.51***)	-0.039025 (-0.87)
TCOEF	65	2.94	0.280706 (3.60***)	-0.197314 (2.02**)
TPREF	68	2.70	0.115958 (3.89***)	0.266056 (2.67***)
MBT	89	0.48	0.199869 (3.07***)	-0.026623 (-0.75)
DISTANCE	96	0.00	0.157895 (5.80***)	-0.000971 (-0.75)
LANGUAGE	96	0.58	0.171191 (4.77***)	-0.039835 (-0.87)
LAW	96	0.41	0.140306 (4.36***)	0.031737 (0.63)
CULTURE	96	1.37	0.207384 (3.75***)	-0.005119 (-1.30)
CORREL	96	1.01	0.179340 (4.12***)	-0.164555 (-0.98)
NONBANK	96	1.60	0.139359 (4.62***)	0.072554 (1.31)
BANKFOCUS	63	0.27	0.116632 (1.81*)	0.052318 (0.45)
PREBID	96	0.55	0.140503 (4.77***)	0.037079 (0.71)
CASH	96	0.00	0.156258 (4.34***)	0.001461 (0.03)
EFFIC	96	1.97	0.126759 (4.47***)	0.070259 (2.01**)
MARKET	96	0.34	0.173347 (3.88***)	-0.029261 (-0.55)
ASSET	96	0.39	0.146241 (4.34***)	0.032746 (0.65)
INET	87	0.01	0.153079 (4.85***)	0.036244 (0.11)
TELCO	84	0.00	-0.208092 (-0.85)	0.076499 (1.48)
MSIZE	96	16.83	-1.630680 (-5.02***)	0.180839 (5.37***)
HOTY	96	2.22	0.124161 (4.76***)	0.074425 (1.40)
ECSIM	96	3.82	0.012959 (0.23)	0.211882 (2.22**)
FREEDOM	91	4.64	0.378319 (4.85***)	-0.099932 (-3.23***)
POWER	87	0.30	0.158656 (4.02***)	-0.014838 (-0.31)
MONITOR	87	1.35	0.116057 (2.74***)	0.054521 (1.33)
HOSTCA	96	4.44	0.116971 (3.44***)	0.108070 (2.21**)
EU	96	0.73	0.144547 (5.69***)	0.047816 (0.69)
EAST	96	4.71	0.178863 (6.38***)	-0.186465 (-6.15***)

* Significant at the 10 percent level.
** Significant at the 5 percent level.
*** Significant at the 1 percent level.

Table A.11: Single-Variable Regression Results for Joint-Entities

Variable	N	R^2 (%)	Constant	Coefficient
BSIZE	95	0.83	0.032091 (0.67)	-0.002460 (-0.63)
RELSIZE	95	0.03	0.000297 (0.03)	0.002880 (0.19)
CLIENT	62	0.00	0.000298 (0.02)	-0.000111 (-0.05)
RELCOEF	63	13.63	0.023124 (3.34***)	-0.020651 (-4.89***)
RELPREF	66	2.67	-0.002657 (-0.75)	0.003120 (1.58)
MBR	86	0.76	-0.000478 (-0.07)	0.005173 (0.80)
TCOEF	65	14.73	0.034316 (3.48***)	-0.054575 (-4.34***)
TPREF	68	1.62	-0.004212 (-0.99)	0.025888 (1.24)
MBT	89	1.01	0.010792 (1.37)	-0.004990 (-0.97)
DISTANCE	96	0.30	0.001808 (0.55)	0.001060 (0.63)
LANGUAGE	96	1.39	-0.000535 (-0.13)	0.008079 (1.18)
LAW	96	1.90	-0.002638 (-0.49)	0.009010 (1.33)
CULTURE	96	0.02	0.001468 (0.23)	0.000079 (0.15)
CORREL	96	0.45	0.000343 (0.08)	0.014307 (0.62)
NONBANK	96	1.20	0.000183 (0.05)	0.008237 (0.92)
BANKFOCUS	63	0.21	-0.005687 (-0.39)	0.005879 (0.30)
PREBID	96	1.32	0.005679 (1.21)	-0.007498 (-1.13)
CASH	96	0.54	-0.003828 (-0.33)	0.007157 (0.58)
EFFIC	96	0.90	-0.000482 (-0.10)	0.006227 (0.94)
MARKET	96	0.18	0.003736 (0.71)	-0.002757 (-0.41)
ASSET	96	0.00	0.002326 (0.63)	-0.000243 (-0.03)
INET	87	0.90	0.002087 (0.52)	-0.035876 (-0.91)
TELCO	84	0.81	0.038172 (0.74)	-0.007370 (-0.71)
MSIZE	96	2.69	-0.091440 (-1.69*)	0.009474 (1.72*)
HOTY	96	5.62	0.009193 (2.45**)	-0.015518 (-2.30**)
ECSIM	96	1.31	-0.008836 (-1.03)	0.016240 (1.26)
FREEDOM	91	0.18	0.006883 (0.52)	-0.002511 (-0.40)
POWER	87	0.66	-0.000532 (-0.14)	0.002839 (0.74)
MONITOR	87	3.11	-0.006691 (-1.60)	0.010715 (2.21**)
HOSTCA	96	3.58	-0.002527 (-0.62)	0.012718 (1.83*)
EU	96	0.33	0.003376 (0.86)	-0.004184 (-0.55)
EAST	96	0.49	0.003059 (0.85)	-0.007123 (-0.75)

* Significant at the 10 percent level.
** Significant at the 5 percent level.
*** Significant at the 1 percent level.

Table A.12: Detailed Results from Analysis of Determinants of Wealth Effects

Determinant	Proxy	Expec-ted sign of proxy	Short-term evidence from dichotomization analysis			Short-term evidence from regression analysis			Long-term evidence	Hypothesis...
			bidder	target	joint	bidder	target	joint		
Bidder size	BSIZE	(0) +	0	0	-	0	0	0	+	partly supported
Relative (target) size	RELSIZE	(0) +	-	0	0	0	0	0	0	not supported
Presence of existing clients in the host	CLIENT	+	0	+	0	0	+	0	0	supported
Relative (target) efficiency	RELCOEF	(0) +	0	0	-	-	0	-	0	not supported
	RELPREF	- (0)	0	0	+	0	0	0	0	
	MBR	- (0)	0	0	0	0	0	0	0	
Target efficiency	TCOEF	-/+	0	-	-	-	0	-	0	strongly supported
	TPREF	-/+	0	0	0	0	0	0	0	
	MBT	-/+	0	0	0	-	0	0	0	
Physical distance between bidder and target	DISTANCE	- (0)	0	0	0	0	0	0	-/0	partly supported
Social distance between bidder and target	LAN-GUAGE	+	0	0	0	+	-	0	0/+	supported
	LAW	+	0	0	+	0	0	0	0	
	CULTURE	-	0	0	0	0	0	0	0	
Functional differences between bidder and target	CORREL	(0) +	0	0	0	0	-	0	0/+	partly supported
	NONBANK	- (0)	0	0	+	0	0	0	0	
	BANK-FOCUS	(0) +	0	0	+	0	0	0	0	
Bidder M&A experience	PREBID	(0) +	0	0	0	0	0	0	0	not supported
Share of acquisition price paid in cash	CASH	(0) +	+	0	0	0	0	0	0	supported
Bidder intent to create operational synergies	EFFIC	(0) +	0	+	0	0	0	0	+	supported
Bidder intent to diversify geo-graphically	MARKET	(0) -	-	0	0	-	0	0	+	supported
Bidder intent to diversify functionally	ASSET	(0) -	0	0	0	0	0	0	0	not supported
Bidder IT sophistication	INET	+	-	+	0	0	0	-	0	not supported
	TELCO	+	0	0	0	0	0	0	0	not supported
Host market size	MSIZE	+	0	+	+	0	+	0	0	strongly supported
"Temperature" of equity market	HOTY	-	-	+	-	-	+	-	0	strongly supported
Economic distance between home and host country	ECSIM	+	0	+	0	0	0	0	0	supported
General economic openness of the host	FREEDOM	-	+	-	0	+	0	0	0	partly supported
Intensity of regulation in the host country	POWER	+	0	+	+	0	0	0	0	supported
	MONITOR	+	0	0	+	0	0	0	0	
Host country is the US or UK	HOSTCA	+	0	+	+	0	0	0	0	supported
Bidder and target are from the EU	EU	(0) +	0	0	0	0	0	0	-	not supported
Targets are located in Eastern Europe	EAST	+	0	(-/0)[1]	0	+	(-/0)[1]	0	0	supported

1 Biased results due to leakage issues. Since leakage adjustment decreases sample size strongly target effects could not be thoroughly analyzed.

Christine Häcker

Information Asymmetries and Investment Banking in Mergers & Acquisitions

Frankfurt am Main, Berlin, Bern, Bruxelles, New York, Oxford, Wien, 2007.
XIII, 195 pp., num. tab. and graph.
European University Studies: Series 5, Economics and Management. Vol. 3255
ISBN 978-3-631-56310-6 · pb. € 41.10*

This book examines information asymmetries in mergers and acquisitions, specifically focusing on the role of the investment banker. When capital markets are imperfect, the investment banker may add value as an intermediary by reducing transaction costs and mitigating information asymmetries. Here, a theoretical model is developed, which shows that the investment banker is able to reduce the degree of hidden information between seller and buyer. The model indicates that the investment banker will recommend a specific buyer, taking the nature of the buyer, expected synergy benefits, and the acquisition probability into account. Based on that recommendation, the selling company can obtain maximum value by selling to the highest bidder.

Contents: Mergers & Acquisition Principles · Transaction Types · The Mergers & Acquisitions Process · Intermediaries · Capital Market Imperfections · Intermediaries and Perfect Capital Markets · Intermediaries and Imperfect Capital Markets · Information Asymmetry between Buyer and Seller · Reporting Regulations · Information Categories · Buyer Types · Confidentiality Agreements · Information Disclosure Dilemma for the Seller · Information Disclosure Model · Offering Price per Buyer Type · Disclosure of Private Information · Investment Banker's Recommendation to the Seller